JUST WAR AND HUMAN RIGHTS

JUST WAR AND HUMAN RIGHTS
FIGHTING WITH RIGHT INTENTION

Todd Burkhardt

Published by State University of New York Press, Albany

© 2017 State University of New York

All rights reserved

Printed in the United States of America

No part of this book may be used or reproduced in any manner whatsoever without written permission. No part of this book may be stored in a retrieval system or transmitted in any form or by any means including electronic, electrostatic, magnetic tape, mechanical, photocopying, recording, or otherwise without the prior permission in writing of the publisher.

For information, contact State University of New York Press, Albany, NY
www.sunypress.edu

Production, Eileen Nizer
Marketing, Fran Keneston

Library of Congress Cataloging-in-Publication Data

Names: Burkhardt, Todd, 1969– author.
Title: Just war and human rights : fighting with right intention / Todd Burkhardt.
Description: Albany : State University of New York Press, [2017] | Includes bibliographical references and index.
Identifiers: LCCN 2016031449 (print) | LCCN 2016049368 (ebook) | ISBN 9781438464039 (hardcover : alk. paper) | ISBN 9781438464022 (pbk. : alk. paper) | ISBN 9781438464046 (e-book)
Subjects: LCSH: Just war doctrine. | Responsibility to protect (International law) | War—Protection of civilians. | Human rights.
Classification: LCC U22 .B88 2017 (print) | LCC U22 (ebook) | DDC 172/.42—dc23
LC record available at https://lccn.loc.gov/2016031449

10 9 8 7 6 5 4 3 2 1

For Eileen, Missy, Abigail, and Ellie

*A special thank you to
David Reidy for his support, guidance, and mentorship*

Contents

Preface		ix
Acknowledgments		xi
Introduction		1
Chapter 1.	Right Intention and a Just and Lasting Peace	9
Chapter 2.	Reasonable Chance of Success: Analyzing Postwar Requirements in the *Ad Bellum* Phase	41
Chapter 3.	*Post Bellum* Obligations of Noncombatant Immunity	59
Chapter 4.	Negative and Positive Corresponding Duties of the Responsibility to Protect	85
Chapter 5.	Justified Drone Strikes are Predicated on Responsibility to Protect Norms	127
Chapter 6.	Updating the Fourth Geneva Convention	145
Conclusion		165
Notes		169
Bibliography		195
Index		205
Vita		209

Preface

Over the last twenty-five years, I have served the citizens and the government of the United States. I have been a soldier (a private, a noncommissioned officer, and an officer) in the U.S. Army. My assignments have been unique, enriching, and demanding. As a teenager, I enlisted for three years as an M1 tank crewman (loader and gunner). After my enlistment, I returned to college and enrolled in ROTC. Upon graduation, I was commission as an infantry officer.

As an infantry officer, I have served in mechanized and light infantry assignments (as a rifle platoon leader, support platoon leader, headquarters and headquarters company executive officer, company commander, and division G3 assistant planning and operations officer). I also have had the opportunity to train both U.S. and foreign soldiers. As an active component/reserve component observer controller, I trained and evaluated U.S. Army Reserve and National Guard units. As an infantry battalion executive officer I assisted, planned, and resourced training for a fourteen-week infantry soldier course. In addition, I have conducted security forces assistance for the Kingdom of Saudi Arabia and for the government of the Islamic Republic of Afghanistan.

In Saudi Arabia, I spent a year as an advisor to two Saudi motorized infantry battalions. I assisted these units in becoming more efficient, effective, and lethal. My first two months in Afghanistan were focused on garrison life support activity and sustainment (food, security, potable water, electricity, and sewage treatment and removal) for a 2,500 Afghan soldier base. The remaining ten months of my deployment, as the G3 operations officer and then later as the deputy commander of a special operations advisory group, I oversaw the planning, resourcing, and execution of operations and intelligence, human capital, and logistics and sustainment of the Afghan National Army Special Operations Command. This is a ten thousand-plus force of Afghan Commando and Special Forces that work all across Afghanistan from its cities to its hinterlands in order to defeat nonstate actors (Taliban, al-Qaeda, ISIL, etc.) in order to secure and protect its citizens and the legitimate governance of Afghanistan. While in Afghanistan for a year, I worked with U.S. Army, Navy, and Marine special operations forces as well as Canadian and Slovakian special operation forces.

In addition to the assignments listed above, I have also had the opportunity to earn my masters and doctorate in philosophy. With this undertaking came the opportunity to teach political and just war philosophy to cadets—our Army's future leaders—attending the United States Military Academy, West Point. In addition, to the robust ethics of war class that I had the opportunity to teach to almost six hundred cadets over the course of five years, I had the opportunity to engage with and learn from other distinguished military and civilian professors (who teach at the academy, who visit the academy in order to present their ideas, or from conferences that I attended across the country), and they are just as deeply passionate and even more insightful about the ethics of war than I. West Point has been an incredibly enriching assignment. Nonetheless, I am currently the Professor of Military Science at Indiana University—Bloomington, which will continually afford me the opportunity to train, educate, and (hopefully) inspire young men and women cadets who will become Army officers and future leaders. To say the least, I am incredibly thankful for the experiences and opportunities that I have had and to my future as a Hoosier.

The book that you are about to read is not autobiographical. It is philosophical. However, I do feel the need to explain my background. Although I have spent many years in college as a student learning philosophy and a few years teaching philosophy, being in the military for more than twenty-five years informs my perspective and worldview. Although academically trained as a philosopher, my experiences (stateside and abroad) as a soldier—pure joy, thrill, accomplishment, brotherhood, camaraderie, love, humility, disappointment, fear, anger, pain, sorrow, and extreme grief—inform (whether for good, bad, or indifferent) my views, my beliefs, and what I trust is worth arguing for. That being said, if the goal of just war theory "is to restrain both the incidence and destructiveness of warfare,"[1] then it is the synthesis of my military and academic backgrounds that enlightens and compels me—which I attempt to pursue and articulate in the following chapters—to argue for necessary changes in just war theory so that civilians can, as they should, be better protected from the harmful effects of war.

Acknowledgments

Chapter 2 ("Reasonable Chance of Success: Analyzing the Postwar Requirements of *Jus Ad Bellum*") was originally published in *Routledge Handbook of Ethics and War (Just War Theory in the 21st Century)*, edited by Fritz Allhoff, Nicholas Evans, and Adam Henschke, (Routledge: London), 2014.

Chapter 3 ("*Post Bellum* Obligations of Noncombatant Immunity") is derived in part from an article published in the *Journal of Military Ethics* (JME), June 2016, copyright Taylor & Francis, available online: www.tandfonline.com/doi/full/10.1080/15027570.2016.1178471.

Chapter 5 ("Justified Drone Strikes are Predicated on Responsibility to Protect Norms") was originally published in the *International Journal of Applied Philosophy* (IJAP), February 2016, available on line: www.pdcnet.org//pdc/bvdb.nsf/purchase?openform&fp=ijap&id=ijap_2015_0029_0002_0167_0176&onlyautologin=true. It was also published in *The Army Press*, March 2016, available on line: armypress.dodlive.mil/2016/03/01/dealing-with-drone-ethics/.

The views and ideas expressed within this book are the author's and do not necessarily reflect the views or policy of the U.S. Government, the U.S. Department of Defense, or the U.S. Army.

Introduction

The nonideal conditions we face often involve conditions or circumstances of unjust international attacks and/or unjust domestic institutions that might seem to call for war as a just response. While war might be permissible as a response to severe injustice, there are limits on the conduct of war even when it is permissible (or even required) as such. A state pursuing a just war must do so with "right intention." The idea of right intention is the overarching constraint on war; a right intention aims at a just and lasting peace. A lasting peace is not possible unless certain standards of basic justice are secure. Although this concept has been around since at least St. Augustine's work in the fourth century AD, it has lost momentum over the years, but has resurfaced over the last century.

The aim of this book is to explore certain key elements of the claim that a just war is one fought with the right intention of not only vindicating a just cause and doing so in a just manner but also reliably serving as a means to a just and lasting peace. Fighting with right intention and establishing conditions for a just and lasting peace demand certain reforms to just war theory. Establishing a lasting peace is predicated on safeguarding basic human rights, fidelity to the principle of noncombatant immunity, political self-determination and international toleration, and the recognition of the international responsibilities to protect. I argue further that these norms governing right intention should be realized as international legal norms.

Just war theory has been a part of Western political philosophy for the past two thousand years. Theologians such as St. Ambrose, St. Augustine of Hippo, St. Thomas Aquinas, and Francisco de Vitoria as well as the jurist Hugo Grotius and the philosopher Emmerich de Vattel have been the frontrunners in advancing moral arguments (regarding obligations, restrictions, and proscriptions) that states and their armies should abide by in the three phases of war: before, during, and after. More specifically, just war theory establishes a moral framework regarding when the use of force is not only morally justified (such as in self-defense) but also sets limits to the destructive acts of war by appealing to standards of conduct that incorporate discrimination, proportionality, and necessity. Just war theory also frames what is morally required of the victor and vanquished regarding rebuilding, reparations, and reconciliation during the postwar period.

Contemporary just war philosophers such as Michael Walzer, Brian Orend, Jeff McMahan, and Larry May have made considerable contributions to the just war tradition. Contemporary human rights philosophers such as Henry Shue, Allen Buchanan, Charles Beitz, and David Reidy have made considerable contributions to political philosophy. This book is an amalgamation of their work. More than any other philosopher, John Rawls has significantly influenced my view. Rawls's perspective in *The Laws of Peoples* relating to human rights and just war is the template for my work, and I believe that in order to improve upon the just war tradition, honoring basic human rights has to be a central theme, because human rights are a class of rights that play a special role in foreign policy: "They restrict the justifying reasons for war and its conduct, and they specify limits to a regime's internal autonomy."[1] I take Rawls's articulation of traditional principles of justice (in particular the right to self-defense and observing certain restrictions in war and the honoring of human rights) that can reasonably be accepted by states that are neither internally aggressive toward their own citizens nor externally aggressive toward other states as my guide.

The human rights movement has marked the latter half of the last century and shows little sign of losing its history-shaping force. Political control of a territory and population no longer guarantees the moral right to nonintervention. Although this was thought sufficient to underwrite political sovereignty and so a right to nonintervention, it is now thought merely necessary. The additional requirement of meeting basic human rights is also necessary. The idea of sovereignty is still tied to the right to nonintervention. However, we have come to recognize/accept that sovereignty is something that depends on certain moral conditions being met, to include basic human rights being reasonably safeguarded. In addition, resorting to war for reasons of self-defense does not just entail fighting until a state's rights have been vindicated.

Rather, "the aim of a just war waged by a just well-ordered people is a just and lasting peace."[2]

Aligning the just war tradition with the norm of right intention is essential in order to set conditions for a just and lasting peace. There can be no lasting peace without justice, and justice is predicated on the fulfillment of human rights, which constitute the core of international justice. Unjust war, oppression, and genocide arise from unjust state institutions. Hopefully, by engaging in discourse about right intention we can determine what "policies and courses of action are morally permissible and politically possible as well as likely to be effective"[3] in our long-term goal of reaching a stable and peaceful international global order. A just war tradition that places significant emphasis on human rights can be squarely made part of a state's foreign policy.

Although the nonideal conditions that we face present some demanding challenges, I cannot take up all just war issues; but I want to address key issues. These issues are pressing now and can all be argued for from the root idea that if force is to be governed by a right intention oriented toward peace with justice, various reforms are required.

I will focus on six main issues: that just war is governed by an overarching principle of right intention; that having right intention compels states to proactively analyze postwar obligations before they arise; that the residual effects of war continue to kill civilians after the fighting is over, so there are obligations to mitigate these harms; that states are morally required to intervene when a state has failed in its responsibility to protect its own citizens' physical security, subsistence, and basic liberty rights; that justified drone strikes can be predicated on responsibility to protect norms; and that the Fourth Geneva Convention needs to be updated in order to reflect right intention and the human rights movement.

First, right intention is what unifies *ad bellum*, *in bello*, and *post bellum* (of, in, and after phases of war). A state with right intention establishes conditions for a just and lasting peace by respecting human rights, taking due care to insulate civilians from the harms of war, allowing for political self-determination, and by educating its military and political culture. Furthermore, a state's public acts are evidence of its intention. There is no way to determine if a state actually fights with right intention without looking at the totality of its conduct.

Second, most refer to the *jus ad bellum* tenet of a reasonable chance of success as the probability of winning the conflict, but this viewpoint is too limited and undercuts the significant analysis that should be taken into account. As the victor, it is very possible to resort to war for just reasons and fight the war justly, but then completely fail in the postwar phase to fulfill just expectations to the vanquished. Analyzing the likelihood of successful military operations as the only consideration for the *jus ad bellum* reasonable chance of success tenet is inherently shortsighted and problematic, because a state can win the war but still make a moral mess of the aftermath. The benefit of incorporating *jus post bellum* obligations into a state's reasonable chance of success calculation is twofold: (1) a state could possibly curtail specific types of military operations thereby lending to that state's ability to more effectively and efficiently fulfilling is postwar obligations, and (2) a state would engage in preliminary postwar scenario planning at the forefront instead of waiting until the war is over (or nearly over), which is way too late to deal with such a huge undertaking.

Third, we need to address what we owe to the civilians of a state with which we are militarily engaged. The old notion of noncombatant immunity needs to be rethought within the context of both human rights and into the postwar phase. For instance, although the laws of war declare the utmost protection of civilians, in modern war more civilians have died than soldiers. This has been the case in World War II (not even including the Holocaust), the Vietnam conflict, the Persian Gulf War, the Second Iraq War, and in the current conflict in Afghanistan. Over the past century, tens of millions of civilians have been killed in warfare.

Although military technological advances have grown by leaps and bounds in the last thirty years with the development and use of precision strike weapons (smart munitions, laser guided bombs, and unmanned aerial vehicles [drones]), even in the twenty-first century, conservative estimates suggest that civilian deaths in war are at least fivefold to that of soldiers killed. Overwhelmingly, these high death rates (in the wars over the past ten years) are not from civilians being intentionally targeted by military forces but from the residual effects of war, many of which stem from the targeting of dual purpose facilities.

No doubt, civilians will be killed in war. However, much more can be done during and after the fighting to protect civilians' basic human rights from the ills of war. I argue for making belligerents accountable *ex post* by requiring them to repair destroyed dual purpose facilities that are essential for securing basic human rights of the civilian populace. I argue also that a belligerent's targeting decisions should be reviewed *ex post* by an impartial commission.

Fourth, the Responsibility to Protect (R2P) is the doctrine that supports intervention into a state that has failed (whether deliberately or not) to reasonably protect a group of its citizens' physical security rights. However, civilians—whatever their religious, national, ethnic, or racial group—have the basic human right to not only physical security but also subsistence and basic liberty. The idea is that rights entail duties, and that the duties must be assigned to determinate parties but that they may be assigned to parties in a kind of order. For example, the duty falls first to X, but if X fails, then the duty falls to Y (as a backup obligor), and so on. States have the initial duty to protect the human rights of persons within their borders and then backup duties to protect the human rights of persons outside of their borders. When there is a systematic and widespread manifest failure to protect citizens from grievous harms, other states are required as backup obligors to protect and aid those people.

Although a state loses its moral right to nonintervention because it has committed acts that violate its citizens' physical security, subsistence, or basic liberty human rights, only physical security violations (i.e., genocide, war crimes, crimes against humanity, or ethnic cleansing) entail possible military intervention. My view is that to have a right to nonintervention a state must secure basic human rights, but that it does not follow from its lack of a right to nonintervention that any particular intervention is morally permissible or required. It only follows that an intervention would not violate the state's right to nonintervention since it does not have one. When states violate basic liberty rights and/or subsistence rights but not basic physical security rights other states might permissibly intervene but only through less intrusive measures (public condemnation, economic sanctions, etc.). A state losing its moral right to nonintervention because it committed acts of genocide does not entail that this is a sufficient condition for required military intervention. Rather, military intervention is required and so permissible only if a number of further necessary conditions are fulfilled. The only sufficient condition is the fulfillment of all the necessary conditions.

Fifth, the United States, although not under imminent threat, routinely conducts drone strikes into nonconsenting states. According to just war theory, this constitutes a violation of traditional *jus ad bellum* principles (just cause and last resort). As it currently stands, attempting to use *jus ad bellum* criteria to discern a state's moral justification for implementing force short of war (drone strikes) is not only unhelpful but fails to provide a reasonable framework. The use of armed drones is a recent phenomenon that will continue to evolve, and with this comes a need for establishing a set of moral guidelines on a state's implementation of them. In an attempt to remedy this shortcoming, we need to look at drone strikes not as an act of war but as an act or force short of war. I want to make the case that drone strikes can be morally justified using the Responsibility to Protect norms. That is, the R2P norms should be the guiding norms with regard to *jus ad vim* (the just use of force short of war). Incorporating the R2P norms into a *jus ad vim* account provides a much-needed framework of when states can morally resort to the use of force.

Lastly, the Fourth Geneva Convention (which is the convention that specifically deals with the treatment of civilians during and after war) needs to be updated and revised. It can be argued for from the root idea that if force is to be governed by right intention oriented toward peace with justice, then the Fourth Geneva Convention is currently inadequate, because it does not reflect current human rights practices and standards which are essential if our goal is establishing conditions for a just and lasting peace. Just as human rights should be realized not only as moral but also as (international) legal rights, so too the norms of just war that follow from right intention should be realized. Just war norms should not only be realized as moral norms but as (international) legal norms to point parties more squarely toward justice, because without legal embodiment justice becomes more difficult to secure or maintain.

Additionally, the UN is the appropriate institution not only to facilitate this process but also to play a role in institutionally expressing and adjudicating the relevant treaty. First, the UN is the global structure that specifically deals with fostering the cooperation of states regarding issues of peace and security. Second, the UN should monitor and report compliance failures, much as the UN already does when it comes to grave human rights violations.

To some considerable degree, my just war perspective is inevitably tied to and has been shaped by being a U.S. soldier over the last twenty years. Although I take up some just war issues that might have some reference to the point of view of a U.S. soldier, what I propose is my own view and not representative of all U.S. soldiers or even the U.S. government. I do, though, reference key examples from U.S. history as a way to help substantiate certain claims that I make. These empirical facts are important because they provide real-world situations that allow us to realize moral obligations that might otherwise go unnoticed.

Although there are plenty of other examples, I lean on mostly U.S.-based examples predominately because those examples are not only applicable but also I am most familiar with U.S. and U.S.-led operations based on my background. In addition, being a member of the U.S. Army I am better qualified to critique, criticize, and commend the organization that I am a part of than a foreign military in which I have never served. However, just because most of my examples are U.S.-based does not suggest that right intention and the philosophical advancements that I propose do not apply to other states and other wars.

I recognize that a complete account of proposing to reorient just war theory around a particular idea of what it means to fight with right intention would need to address examples outside U.S. history and issues (e.g., nuclear weapons, supreme emergency, outlaw regimes at war with one another, etc.) and beyond those that I currently address. For now, I have limited aspirations but hope in the future to pursue these other areas that fighting with right intention would also regulate.

The aim of this book is not that this be the last word about fighting with right intention but rather the starting point from which I hope further discussion will follow; my hope is that the exploration of what fighting with right intention entails leads to improvements in the ethics of war.

1

Right Intention and a Just and Lasting Peace

Historically, the norm of *right intention* has been a constitutive part of the *ad bellum* phase of just war theory, and "aims to overcome the possibility that a state may have a just cause, but still act from a wrong intention."[1] Wrong intentions aim or intend acts or effects (e.g., punishing the state one is at war with, using the resources of that state, causing more destruction than is needed, or pursuing a war longer than is necessary) that are not warranted by and do not serve to vindicate a state's just cause. "Having the right reason for launching a war is not enough: the actual motivation behind the resort to war must also be morally appropriate; the only right intention allowed is to see the just cause for resorting to war secured and consolidated"[2] Without the condition of right intention, "the connection between one's action and the reason that justifies it remains contingent, and this allows for the possibility that just cause could be only a pretext or excuse for bellicose action aimed at some further goal beyond that which one's justifying reason supports, or at some completely independent goal that can be pursued using the justifying reasons as a rationalization only."[3]

Having a just cause does not necessarily entail that the state's leaders and citizens will not have ulterior motives. However, as Joseph Boyle posits, "This does not mean that one cannot engage in war in anticipation of benefits that go beyond one's justified war aims. Those aims are goals that instantiate, often in a minimal way, the good of peace."[4] Moreover, "further goals that instantiate that good and that can be seen as possibilities if one's war aims are realized are thus justified if the war aims are."[5] A state can have a just cause and yet (its leaders and/or citizens) still hope for, perhaps might even be moved by a desire for, many other results (improving political and economic ties and/or securing of other national interests: maintaining open sea lanes, stabilizing the world's oil supply distribution, and having more influence in regional or global politics) in addition to vindicating its just cause. Achieving these other types of ends does not seem particularly problematic as long as these results and the means to achieve them are not inconsistent with the norm of right intention. If vindicating a just cause with right intention can possibly be expected to bring other goods, then those are acceptable. In a sense, "[t]hat intention was for actions and benefits that became real prospects once the normal international relationships were restored by the successful achievements of the war aims."[6]

Although right intention has habitually been tied to just cause as a way to ensure that the fighting is only conducted long enough to vindicate the rights that were originally violated, this cannot be all that "right intention" entails. Fighting with right intention is not merely a matter of having a just cause and fighting with the intention to vindicate one's just cause. On my view, right intention is a separate requirement from just cause, with its own content. In order permissibly to go to war, a state must not only have a just cause and limit its war-making activity to that necessary to vindicate the just cause, but it must also seek to vindicate its just cause in a manner likely to yield a "just and lasting peace," which is the overarching result at which acts of war must be directed.

In this book, I try to articulate when states may resort to force justly and that those states must have a right intention. Before attempting to discuss right intention, I would first like to elaborate on what the concept of *Just Cause* entails because just cause undergirds right intention. That is, right intention doesn't follow if there isn't a just cause in the first place.

Just Cause is a foundational principle regarding the morality of war (*jus ad bellum*) and is a familiar and traditional principle of justice. It is a principal tenet that at least dates back to St. Augustine (a fourth-century theologian and philosopher). Just cause is what gives a political community the moral warrant or justification to use armed force. The reason a political community or state (I use the term *state* to refer to the governance of a country) has a just cause to resort to armed conflict is because the rights that a state possesses has been unjustly or wrongly violated.

St. Thomas Aquinas (a thirteenth-century theologian and philosopher) in his work *Summa Theologica* posits, "Namely that those who are attacked, should be attacked because they deserve it on account of some fault."[7] Aquinas's point is that a state is just in responding to a wrong—the aggression—it has suffered. Acts of force that are unwarranted constitute aggression, and, "Aggression is the name we give to the crime of war."[8] Michael Walzer asserts that "[w]e know the crime because of our knowledge of the peace it interrupts—not the mere absence of fighting, but peace-with-rights, a condition of liberty and security that can exist only in the absence of aggression itself."[9] Acts of aggression "involve the infliction of serious and direct physical force,"[10] which violates not only a state's rights to political sovereignty, self-determination, and territorial integrity but also the basic human rights of that state's citizens.

Acts or wars of aggression not only interrupt the victim state's autonomy and governance but also wrongly jeopardize if not completely infringe upon the victim state's citizens' basic human right to physical security (as well as possibly the human right to subsistence and basic liberties). The wrongness of aggression is that it "forces men and women to risk their lives for the sake of their rights,"[11] which men and women should not have to fight for because, fundamentally, men and women are entitled to these rights. However, aggression confronts these men and women "with a choice: your rights or (some of) your lives!"[12]

And so, men and women unduly forced into such a position of confronting an act of aggression have to respond. "Groups of citizens respond in different ways to that choice, sometimes surrendering, sometimes fighting, depending on the moral and material condition of their state and army, but they are always justified in fighting."[13] States have both legal and moral rights to resort to actual, intentional, and widespread acts of self-defense (physical resistance/force) or collective self-defense (come to the defense of an ally or coalition partner who is being attacked) when the victim of aggression.[14] St. Augustine declared: "A just war is wont to be described as one that avenges wrongs, when a nation or state has to be punished [stopped], for refusing to make amends for the wrongs inflicted by its subjects, or restore what it has seized unjustly."[15] Now, granted, punitive wars (or wars of punishment) are no longer seen as just, but St. Augustine's words remain prevalent because we still recognize today that a state that makes no amends for its violations or does not restore what it has seized unjustly needs to be stopped. And using force to stop those acts of aggression is justified.

Although "[w]ar should be understood as an actual, intentional, and widespread armed conflict between political communities,"[16] there may be acts of aggression that are actual and intentional but are not actually widespread. These can constitute a just cause of allowing military armed response but based on other *jus ad bellum* factors (proportionality, reasonable chance of success, last resort, etc.), it is determined that full-blown war is not the best option and so limited force or *jus ad vim* (justified force short of war) such as incorporating special forces units, drone strikes, security forces assistance, or a combination thereof is a reasonable and justifiable course of action in a given circumstance.

In order permissibly to go to war, a state (no matter how large or small it is) must not only have a just cause and limit its war-making activity to that which is necessary to vindicate the just cause. This suggests that war as an act of self-defense or collective defense should only be waged until the rights that were violated by the aggression are secured and no longer threatened. So the proper aim of a just war "is the vindication of those rights whose violation grounded the resort to war in the first place"[17] This does not necessary mean that State A successfully defends itself against an offensive operation from aggressor State B and then must stop fighting. In a sense, it depends on the magnitude, scope, and intention of the aggressor state. In one particular instance that might be enough, but in another, extensive offensive operations into State B might be warranted in order to actually secure State A's political sovereignty and its right to exercise its self-determination, to maintain its territorial integrity, and to protect the human rights of its citizens. However, "The principle of rights vindication forbids the continuation of the war after the relevant rights has, in fact, been vindicated. To go beyond that limit would itself become aggression: men and women die for no just cause."[18] That is, that men and women—both soldiers and civilians from both sides—would continually be subjected to the harms of war, even though the state that resorted to war justly as an act of self-defense no longer is warranted to continue the fight because the victim state's rights are no longer violated, threatened, or in jeopardy of being threatened.

I attempt to articulate and illuminate the *jus ad bellum* tenet of Right Intention throughout this book. However, I do recognize that the in-depth analysis of what right intention entails might not always fit a given scenario. Although all just wars should be waged with right intention, the level of commitment might be less than others, which doesn't mean that right intention is not present or that its absence is somehow excusable. Although every state has the moral responsibility to vindicate its just cause in a manner likely to yield a just and lasting peace, there is a comparable difference, for example, between actions such as the 2003 U.S. invasion in Iraq and the 1944 uprising against the Nazi occupation army in Warsaw, Poland. The former example and ones similar to it will be my focus, whereas the latter example of attempting to repel an unjust occupation force will not. Understandably, Poland's sole focus was on expelling the Nazis from their country in order to restore its boundaries, its state's right to governance, and its citizens' basic human rights, without worrying about developing a just and lasting peace per se. It seems unreasonable to suggest that Poland—whose existence was in serious jeopardy due to Nazi brutality, subjugation, and extermination—should have had to worry about setting the conditions for developing a just and lasting peace when it teetered on the verge of annihilation. That being said, the Polish home army and its partisan forces still were subject to the moral responsibility to engage only legitimate enemy combatants, offer quarter to those that surrendered, and limit collateral damage. Doing so would have been consistent with Poland vindicating its just cause in a manner that would have been likely to yield a just and lasting peace. That is, Poland did not conduct acts of aggression, but rather defended itself justly. Poland acting in this way set the conditions for a *possible* just peace once the Nazi regime was removed from power. I am aware, though, that other particular states (in a given situation) might only attempt to defeat the aggressor state's offensive strike force as it rolls across its border because, given the strength of such an aggressor, the goal of achieving a just and lasting peace might be unrealizable. Yet a defensive war is just, even though the victim state only attempts to secure or vindicate its own rights, which have been violated, instead of trying to achieve a just peace but rather only a cessation of hostilities (its state has stopped the attack and expelled aggressor forces from its state). Although the war is over, the regime of the aggressor state still remains in power because the victim, or a coalition of states, is/are too weak or is/are currently unable to remove the outlaw state's regime.

Although these are possible scenarios—among many types of scenarios—I do not plan on covering them all. Rather, my focus throughout this book remains in the vein of first world powers or other states that are not on the verge of destruction or capitulation but rather have the means (political, military, informational, and economic resources) to realize and actualize what right intention entails, as opposed to the example cited above of Poland in 1944, in which the main concern—quite legitimately—was the nation's own existence.

In order permissibly to go to war, a state must not only have a just cause and limit its war-making activity to that which is necessary to vindicate the just cause, but it must also seek to vindicate its just cause in a manner likely to yield a just and lasting peace, which is the overarching result at which acts of war should be directed. In order to establish conditions for a just and lasting peace, two elements must be addressed: peace and justice.

That is to say, the intended goals of waging war are (1) those that derive from the requirement that a state aim to achieve *peace* (by fighting with restraint, immunizing civilians from the harms of war, and educating its military); and (2) those that derive from the requirement that a state aim to achieve *justice* (by fighting only until the rights that were violated have been vindicated, respecting human rights, leaving the enemy in a position to secure human rights, allowing for political self-determination, tolerating regimes that honor basic human rights, and supporting a public political culture that adheres to just war).

Before moving farther, I think some historical context is not only necessary in order to illuminate but to also gain an appreciation for the concept of right intention, which has been a part of the just war tradition since at least the fourth century. Although right intention has been a guiding principle in just war, it has lost some traction throughout the centuries. With this in mind, my aim is to give the concept of right intention the prominence it deserves.

St. Augustine (AD 354–430) is commonly referred to as the father of the just war tradition because of his works, as found in his sermons, writings, pastoral letters, and in particular his book *De Civitate Dei* (*The City of God*). It is not that Augustine wrote solely on war; rather, he wrote about war while discussing other critical ideas in society: politics, governance, Christianity, peace, etc. Augustine, through his writings, attempted to set parameters that allowed for only just reasons to resort to war. He also declared that military acts should only be pursued out of necessity, and that the harms of war should be restricted as best as possible. Augustine's work privileges the concept of right intention as a fundamental principle of just war that spans *all* phases of war. However, through the centuries, Augustine's perspective and influence regarding right intention, though it still has momentum, has been reduced to that of addressing merely one phase of war, as a principle that can only be consistent with a state's reason of when to resort to war.

Yet, there is much more to St. Augustine's concept of right intention. This being the case, right intention as an underlying principle to the just war tradition needs to be given full articulation. In a sense, we need to "go back to the future." That is, we need to look at the past—the works of St. Augustine—in order to rediscover the importance of the Right Intention principle/axiom, which should inform our present and future developments regarding war. Especially since nowadays, probably because of international law, so much emphasis is simply on the external action and there is agnosticism about internal actions. However, intention, right intention, is an essential part of war and needs to be further explored and resurfaced as not only a mainstay in the just war tradition but in fact the only principle that unites all three phases of war.

St. Augustine of Hippo (modern-day Annaba, Algeria), a Catholic bishop and theologian, significantly influenced Christian, political, and military thought regarding war. Living in North Africa, he experienced war firsthand as a civilian and felt its effects "having lived through the period of Alaric's sack of Rome in 410 AD and seeing the spread of the Vandal armies across North Africa."[19] Both civilians and soldiers feel the grave effects of war. However, the civilian population is much more helpless. Furthermore, civilians have no control over where war will be fought, where operations will be conducted, or where bombing runs will take place. War promises death, and civilians are killed just the same as combatants. In addition, war causes deterioration of the life-supporting services that a state's infrastructure provides to its civilian population. As if trying to survive in deleterious conditions were not hard enough, civilians are also at the mercy of an enemy military force. "Augustine's own experiences and the age of plundering and slaughter in which he lived left him with a deep hatred of war and a great scorn for those who thought that conquest and military victories were glorious and noble accomplishments."[20] He believed that war will always be a part of the human condition and will be "inevitable as long as men and their societies are moved by avarice, greed, and lust for power, the permanent drives of sinful men. It is, therefore, self-delusion and folly to expect that a time will ever come in this world when wars will cease."[21] Thus, St. Augustine thought it was necessary to write about war. He realized that peace might be an aftereffect of war but that security is never guaranteed and acts of greed and aggression will never cease. "For in the great mutability of human affairs such great security is never given to any people, that it should not dread invasions hostile to this life."[22] Although war is a central characteristic of human civilization, Augustine's goal was to try to limit its occasion and its destructiveness. And he did this by articulating that both Christians and non-Christians fundamentally wanted the same thing as they inhabited the earth.

As a theologian, Augustine wrote about two cities, the earthly city and the city of God, and believed that these two cities were inextricably linked. Although, as a Christians, both men and women should strive to be accepted into the city of God upon their death, in order to achieve eternal salvation, these Christians should also seek peace and the advantages associated with doing so will "aid them to endure wither greater ease, and to keep down the number of those burdens of the corruptible body which weigh upon the soul."[23] In addition, Augustine did not believe that peaceful disposition pertained to only Christians but to all men. All people should seek peace in the earthly city (living on earth), which is the natural order of things. St. Augustine states: "The earthly city, which does not live by faith, seeks an earthly peace, and the ends it proposes, in the well-ordered concord of civic obedience and rule, is the combination of men's wills to attain the things which are helpful to this life."[24] Helpful to life on earth is peace: "The things which this city desires cannot justly be said to be wrong, for it in itself, in its own kind, better than all other human good, for it desires earthly peace for the sake of enjoying earthly goods, and it makes [just] war in order to attain this peace."[25] The attainment of peace sets the condition for harmony: "The peace of the body and soul is the well-ordered and harmonious life and health of the living creature."[26]

Although peace is desired, sometimes war must be fought, but, "It is therefore with the desire for peace that wars are waged."[27] Augustine proclaims that "[h]e, then, who prefers what is right to what is wrong, and what is well-ordered to what is perverted, sees that the peace of unjust men is not worthy to be called peace in comparison with the peace of the just."[28] Surely, we can have peace that is not just (coercion, subjugation, etc.), but what we should seek is a peace that is just. A just and lasting peace assures a harmonious community of human beings: "The peace of all things is the tranquility of order, and order is the distribution which allots things equal and unequal, each to its own place."²⁹ Moreover, a just peace is "the fulfillment which is realized most fully in the active neighborliness of willing cooperation in purposes which are both good in themselves and harmonious with the good purposes, and enterprises of others."³⁰

Critical to the Augustinian claim that "we fight so we can live in peace"³¹ is achieving a just peace. And the way in which this is accomplished is by fulfilling the tenet/principle of *right intention*. According to St. Augustine, a just war can only be fought with a right intention. The idea of right intention is the overarching constraint on war. A state must only fight out of necessity as well as limit death, destruction, and harm, with a true and lasting peace as the actual aim of such a war. Right intention is not only the motivation behind the resort to war but must also influence and guide both a state's fighting as well as the reconstruction and reconciliation after the war ends. Right intention is what unifies *ad bellum*, *in bello*, and *post bellum* (of, during, and after phases of war). A just war is one fought with the right intention of not only vindicating a just cause and doing so in a just manner but also reliably serving as a means to a just and lasting peace.

St. Augustine's advice given to Roman general Boniface in *On the Presence of God: Letter 187* (dated AD 418) captures his perspective on such matters: "If peace is such a delightful dimension of man's temporal happiness, how much sweeter is the divine peace that belongs to the eternal happiness of angels. And so, let it be because of the necessity rather than your own desire that you kill the enemy fighting against you."³² Augustine posits that a just army fights similarly to a loving father who must discipline his son for wrongdoing. The father only disciplines his son to the point that is absolutely necessary, and there is no ill-will or bitterness between the father and son. After the incident, the father and son return to their harmonious relationship founded on a just peace. Using this analogy, Augustine tells General Boniface, "Even in the act of waging war be careful to maintain a peaceful disposition so that by defeating your foes you can bring them the benefits of peace."³³

Fast forward thirteen hundred years, and we encounter Immanuel Kant's perspective regarding right intention. It is hard not to believe that St. Augustine influenced Kant's work regarding war. Kant discusses a state's rights before, during, and after war. In particular, he articulates that states need to restrict the destructiveness of war. "No nation at war with another shall permit such acts of war as shall make mutual trust impossible during some future time of peace."³⁴ This is similar to Augustine's father/son analogy. Additionally, Kant suggests that states must refrain from the use of force, and that force should only be used as a means "in accordance with the principles of external freedom, that is to say, it permits the use of force only to maintain and preserve what belongs to one [state rather than another]."³⁵ That is, justified force is sometimes necessary because it is used to defend and protect the inherent rights of a state and its people. This use of justified force in no way, then, allows for the degradation or the continuation of harm to the people of the other state once that war is over. Rather, civil freedom should remain and is a necessary component of a just and lasting peace. "It can be said that the establishment of a universal and enduring peace is not just a part, but rather constitutes the whole, of the ultimate purpose of justice and law."³⁶ Kant further illustrates that not only formulating but actually implementing a universally just and enduring peace is integral to harmonious living among states and people. "Only in this way is it possible to approach continually closer to the highest political good—perpetual peace."³⁷

As many would agree, there is a Kantian influence in John Rawls's work, and I would suggest that there is also an Augustinian influence as well. In *The Law of Peoples*, Rawls discusses and elucidates familiar and traditional principles of justice among free and democratic peoples, which include honoring human rights, observing certain restrictions in war, and assisting other people living under unfavorable conditions.³⁸ Here, I have only briefly laid out Rawls's concept which I will further elaborate on in due course. But for now, with this in mind, I set out to discuss the overarching principle of right intention which—I believe—has been greatly influenced by St. Augustine, Immanuel Kant, and John Rawls.

This chapter aims to accomplish the following: (1) to establish that a state with right intention fights only when it is necessary to vindicate a just cause in a manner likely to yield a just and lasting peace; (2) to show that public acts are evidence of right intention; (3) to specify that a state with right intention establishes conditions for a just and lasting peace by respecting human rights, taking due care to insulate civilians from the harms of war, allowing for political self-determination, and educating its own military and political culture; and (4) to demonstrate that there is no way to assess whether a state fights with right intention without looking at the totality of its conduct.³⁹

GENERAL CONDUCT REQUIRED FOR A JUST AND LASTING PEACE

In addition to having a just cause and limiting its fighting to the vindication of that just cause, a state must fight with right intention, and this means that it must, generally speaking, fight only as necessary and with constraint and with an eye toward peace. A belligerent must think about a wide range of longer-term impacts of the conflict undertaken, because any acts that "unnecessarily increase the destruction and bitterness of war endanger the prospects for true peace."[40] The main point, as John Rawls notes, is that since "[t]he way a war is fought and the deeds done in ending it live on in the historical memory of societies,"[41] overly aggressive and indiscriminate attacks will undermine peace and future relations with the state one is currently at war with. States must not fight in a way likely to poison future relations, but rather their actions must be aimed at peace. Future justice requires peace and trust and a shared commitment to the priority of certain norms and human rights.

A state abides by right intention by vindicating its rights that have been wrongly infringed upon, which means requiring "that it behave in a certain way, specifically, that it do no more in the war than what would be consistent with that goal."[42] Moreover, Steven Lee remarks, "The state's actions should not go beyond those necessary to achieve that intention."[43] This perspective is also echoed in the U.S. Catholic Bishops' letter: *The Harvest of Justice Is Sown in Peace*. "Even in the midst of conflict, the aim of political and military leaders must be peace with justice, so that acts of vengeance and indiscriminate violence, whether by individuals, military units or governments, are forbidden."[44]

Although violent acts are pursued, each state should attempt to maintain a peaceful disposition that will facilitate a continuation of negotiations between the engaged states. Fighting must be conducted in a way that allows for a conclusion other than unconditional surrender. Acts of war that continue beyond what is necessary, or continue even though the rights that were originally violated have been vindicated, violate right intention.

Unconditional surrender by the Nazi regime was a necessary and morally justified undertaking. In addition to blatant acts of military aggression, the Nazi regime propagated the persecution of non-Aryans and not only was responsible for the widespread murder of members of certain groups within its own borders (including physically and mentally disabled persons, homosexuals, Jews, and Catholic clerics) but also instituted a systematic genocide campaign that killed millions of Jews and Slavs from all European countries. Some historians see Germany's aims as global, ultimately. However, others believe that Germany never intended to take over the world. Its actual goals were to conquer Europe, North Africa, and western Russia. For example, Germany's objectives in the East were "first, the destruction of the Russian armies in western Russia; and then an advance into Russia deep enough to secure Germany against the risk of air attack from the east, carried as far as a line from Archangel to the Volga."[45]

It is hard to imagine in retrospect that Germany had any desire to push the bounds of its empire farther east than the Volga River or that it would have attempted a cross-Atlantic invasion of the United States. Although its aims might have been more limited than was accepted at the time, Nazi Germany's sovereignty was not acknowledged during the war by the Allies as legitimate for the purposes of negotiation. This was a consequence both of its proven and repeated acts of aggression toward other sovereign states and its extreme brutality toward civilians and prisoners of war (particularly on the Eastern front). The Allies regarded unconditional surrender as the only acceptable option for concluding the war, because the National Socialist Party's ideology could not be rehabilitated; to attempt any lesser resolution would have been futile. The German state would, in a sense, have to be captured and its political and social institutions completely reconstructed. Unconditional surrender is a punitive policy whereby the moral right to political self-determination is denied. Nazi Germany was a case where the denial of political self-determination was morally justified.

However, Imperial Japan was a different matter. It can be argued that forcing unconditional surrender on Japan was neither necessary nor morally justified. Japan's aggression had been based on imperial aims of territorial and resource expansion, rather than genocide and domination. By late 1945, Japan's navy and air force had been decimated. The Japanese army had been beaten back to its mainland. Japan's aspirations of expanding its empire had been crushed. According to some historical interpretations, there was potential for negotiations to be carried out and for Japan to surrender with some dignity, instead of the United States coercing it into unconditional surrender by not only firebombing Tokyo but then striking Hiroshima and Nagasaki with atomic munitions. Although all three cities had military targets located in them, the blast radii of the atomic explosions were so widespread and the devastation wrought by the firebombing so overwhelmingly extensive that to consider those bombings as either necessary or proportionate would be farcical. There is, though, some evidence to suggest that, without the examples of destruction provided by the American bombing raids on Japanese cities, Emperor Hirohito might have been prevented from negotiating with the Allies for a conditional surrender, and that if he had attempted to do, it might have inspired a military coup, with even more catastrophic results for the Japanese people, for example, the Japanese military might have forced civilians and soldiers to continue to fight even after the death and destruction that unfolded at Nagasaki and Hiroshima. Although this could have been the case, it does not change the fact that the United States decided to continue the fight in order to press for unconditional surrender, even though Japan was clearly beaten and the United States' threatened or violated rights had been secured, the Americans decided to continue the fight in order to press for unconditional surrender. This seems unjust. "People have a right not to be forced to continue fighting beyond the point when the war might be justly concluded."[46] To press the war further until there is unconditional surrender violates right intention, and also kills many more people (both civilians and soldiers) than is in fact truly necessary.

Any excessive and wanton violence increases the harshness of war, and has the real potential to not only encourage further violent acts but also significantly degrade any communication between belligerents. Restraint in combat does not require that the state have in mind the specific intention of securing a just and lasting peace, but it does govern how a state fights.

PUBLIC ACTS

"It is not clear what it means for a state to have an intention, since it has no mind, and the mind is normally thought to be where intentions reside."[47] However, we do know—to some degree—the intention of the state through observing the state's actions. "An act, a deed, is essentially what the person who chooses to do it intends it to be. Intention looks always to the point, the end, rather than to means precisely as such."[48] But, "any complex activity," explains John Finnis, "is a nested order of ends which are also means to further ends, so though intention is of ends, it is also of all the actions which are means."⁴⁹ Overall, then, regarding war, we presume that "the just cause is the reason for action and the benefit it promises is what one intends."⁵⁰

Underlying motives and mental states can be hard or even impossible to discern, but actions can be observed and through the observation of this communal, public act is how intention is determined.⁵¹ This is one way in which we can understand a state's intention, that is, conceived of in terms of its actions, which are the best (maybe even the only) evidence of right intention by states. We look to those public acts because we are keen to determine whether a state has right intention, and right intention is what matters.

The way a belligerent fights has special importance because "their actions and proclamations, when feasible, foreshadow during a war both the kind of peace they aim for and the kind of relation they seek."⁵² Having right intention, a nation shows a commitment to a just international society of states oriented around ideals of human rights and peaceful, respectful international relations, etc.

SPECIFIC CONDUCT REQUIRED FOR A JUST AND LASTING PEACE

A state that espouses justice will respect human rights, leave its enemy in a position to secure human rights, exercise due care to further insulate civilians from war, fight only until the rights that were violated have been restored, allow for political self-determination, tolerate regimes that honor basic human rights, and educate its own public political culture.

Thus, a state going to war with just cause and right intention must conduct itself in a way that manifests its aim to secure a just and lasting peace in all of these regards. In doing so, a state meets the particular substantive account of what qualifies as setting conditions for a lasting peace with justice.

Human Rights

In order to be a member in good standing in the international community, a state must provide a political environment that fulfills human rights obligations. "Political entities are legitimate only if they achieve a reasonable approximation of minimal standards of justice, again understood as the protection of basic human rights."⁵³ Not only do states have to protect the human rights of their own citizens but they must also respect the human rights of persons in other states as well.

The relevant definition of human rights is Rawlsian. Basic human rights are those rights that are owed to all people and are the minimum reasonable demands upon all people to respect and satisfy. They are universal in scope but are not prepolitical. Human rights are a practical political creation based on common ground and shared principles and provide a practical function within contemporary international relations. Rawls mentions that all groups of people would adopt as a first principle that "all persons have equal basic rights and liberties," and "proceeding this way would straightaway ground human rights in a political (moral) conception of liberal cosmopolitan justice."⁵⁴ That is, we recognize that people have certain rights and that the instantiation of human rights is really derivative of the political process. Within the international context or as a matter of international public reason, human rights need not be bound up with any particular conception of the person or any comprehensive doctrine. They can be, and on Rawls's view are, affirmed simply as conditions, affirmed by liberal democracies and other reasonably well-ordered polities, that any nation must fulfill inside its borders and respect beyond its borders in order to enjoy a right to nonintervention. The Rawlsian idea of human rights tries to avoid giving human rights any particular "grounds" beyond their key role in a reasonable Law of Peoples or in reasonable principles of international relations. Instead, they are constituted as a fundamental basis of foreign policy.

If a state has the responsibility to protect the human rights of its own citizens and to respect the human rights of persons in other states in order to be considered legitimate, then these responsibilities do not change or diminish just because states are involved in war. States must continue their commitment to basic human rights as best as possible even during war.

Although a just state's immediate objective is to defend itself against unjust aggression, "The aim of a just war by a just, liberal democracy is a just and lasting peace among peoples, and especially with the people's present enemy."⁵⁵ A just and lasting peace is one within which all states are in full compliance with basic human rights. In order to achieve a just and lasting peace, states must take some special responsibility for ensuring that the human rights of the civilian population of their enemy are secured (during and) after the war. A state going to war with just cause should conduct itself in a way that manifests its aim to respect the human rights of its enemy's civilian population (and soldiers).

States and their armies need to set/establish certain conditions in order to actually meet or attempt to meet this long-run aim, because as, Larry May indicates, "[i]f the object of war is a just and lasting peace, then all of Just War considerations should be aimed at this goal."[56] The goal is not any old peace (achieved by power, impotence, *modus vivendi*, or *status quo ante bellum*) but peace with justice, and it is the realization of that state of affairs that constitutes the right intention for how belligerents should interact during and after war.

A state should fight in a way that not only respects human rights but also leaves its enemy in a position to secure human rights. A decimated, war-torn state will not have the ability to reasonably safeguard its population from standard threats to basic human rights. Lack of potable water, food, sewage removal, shelter, physical protection, and medical attention are standard threats to basic human rights that leave civilians vulnerable to significant harm and even death as well as at the mercy of others. Although civilians are not intentionally targeted, they inevitably suffer consequences just as serious as if they were. It is reasonable to believe that even the legitimate destruction of military targets (necessary and proportionate to the military advantage to be gained) can still gravely affect civilians. Even more so, the destruction of dual purpose facilities (those that have both a military and civilian purpose, such as bridges, electrical grids, rail and road networks, etc.) leaves the civilian populace exposed to residual harm and standard threats. The harm that this situation presents to civilians should require a commitment from a state to repair its enemy's dual use facilities (those dual use facilities that contribute to securing basic human rights) in order to protect those civilians.

Lack of potable water, food, shelter, medical treatment, sewage and trash removal, and physical security is detrimental to any authentic process of developing a just and lasting peace. The basic human rights of the people of a war-torn state need to be met before any realistic attempt at reconciliation and transitional justice is implemented. Doing so will also assuage hostility of the enemy's civilian populace toward its own government and possibly the occupation force.

A state that fights with right intention would commit *ex ante* to *ex post* obligations such as ensuring that the duration of the war does not extend longer than is actually necessary (fight only to the point where actually its own government's and people's rights have been secured), not demanding the unconditional surrender of their enemy when not warranted, repairing destroyed dual use facilities that are essential for securing core human rights, and treating and safeguarding noncombatants in a way that insulates them from the effects of war as best as possible during and after the cessation of hostilities. In addition to observing the principle of noncombatant immunity because it is right, Rawls states, it should also be followed "to teach enemy soldiers and civilians the content of those rights by the example set in the treatment they receive; in this way the meaning and significance of human rights are best brought home to them"[57]

Some might say that all of this follows simply from the idea that a state should fight only to vindicate its just cause. However, it does not. My claim is that fighting with right intention requires more than fighting only to vindicate one's just cause. Of course, abiding by the principles of discrimination, proportionality, and necessity fit within the context of fighting only to vindicate one's just cause. However, fighting for the sake of peace with justice requires more than just fighting solely to vindicate one's just cause. Fighting with right intention requires positive efforts such as exercising due care to provide greater protection for civilians than proportionality calculations require. Fighting for the sake of peace with justice also requires a state to repair the enemy's infrastructure, which is essential to securing core human rights of the enemy's civilian populace. Furthermore, having right intention allows for self-determination (instead of believing that a coercive regime change can be justified within the bounds of vindicating a state's just cause). And lastly, that the state educate its own military and political culture about fundamental just war principles is a necessary requirement of right intention. Fulfilling these obligations entails an easier transition toward reconciliation and facilitates the development of a more harmonious relationship between states.[58]

Due Care

Right intention not only requires fidelity to the war convention but a positive commitment to insulating civilians from the harms of war, and this will require that a state go out its way to avoid civilian casualties even if this means that its own soldiers face additional risks.

Going out of its way means that a state exercises due care. Michael Walzer describes due care as "a positive commitment to save civilian lives."⁵⁹ Due care is "not merely to apply the proportionality rule and kill no more civilians than is militarily necessary,"⁶⁰ but a positive effort to reduce further harm even if the dangers imposed are proportionate to the military advantage expected to be gained. "Whenever there is likely to be a second effect [e.g., foreseen but unintended civilian deaths caused by a legitimate and proportionate military attack], a second intention is morally required."⁶¹ The second intention is implemented in order to reduce harm to noncombatants (even if the target attacked is considered necessary and proportionate and the tactical bomber pilot can be considered a justified threat to the civilians who are at or in close proximity to the military target).

Just because noncombatant's rights are straightforwardly overridden by countervailing considerations does not suggest that belligerents cannot implement a second intention (due care) of reducing even "acceptable" collateral damage. Reducing harm to civilians will inevitably place soldiers at greater risk while they conduct military operations. Although there is a limit to the additional risks we can ask soldiers to undergo in order to further protect civilians, there are clearly some risks that might be acceptable. "The degree of risk that is permissible is going to vary with the nature of the target, the urgency of the moment, the available technology, and so on."⁶² I am not discounting the rights of soldiers. There are inherent risks associated with the role of a soldier. I am merely suggesting that when soldiers can reasonably accept more risk in order to protect or even immunize civilians from the harms of war, they should do so. I am not suggesting that soldiers have to accept a level of risk that has the potential to undermine the success of their mission or their lives. In the following paragraph, I provide some examples in order to further develop this concept.

The urgency of the situation at hand (e.g., bombing a bridge before the enemy can cross it) might impinge on a belligerent's ability to take due care. However, taking due care can be applied in other situations, such as bombing a munitions factory. In such a scenario, due care is exercised when soldiers take positive action in order to reduce the harm to noncombatants by plausibly accepting more risks. For example, a bomber pilot flying at a lower altitude than usual or in daylight may expose himself to more risk, but this could very well be reasonable to accept, especially if the enemy's anti-aircraft defense systems (weapons designed to destroy incoming aircraft) have been previously neutralized. Flying in daylight at a lower altitude would improve accuracy of the bombing strike, because the pilot would not only be able to visually observe the target but the lower altitude mitigates the effect on munitions of wind, drift, and barometric pressure.

Using only the amount of force necessary (economy of force) and low-yielding collateral damage munitions are other viable options. The plan for bombing a specific facility should determine the required amount of ordinance that is necessary to make the target inoperable. In addition, certain targets, especially those in center city locations, should be targeted with appropriately sized munitions that are sufficient to do the job but are not liable to cause overkill—more collateral damage than necessary.

In addition, intelligence and target acquisition officers need the proper training in order to be able to analyze the significance and contribution of particular dual use facilities to the civilian population by incorporating residual (second and third order) effects into the proportionality calculation. For example, French, Italian, and British target acquisition officers that determined and planned the target array during the 2011 NATO air campaign against Libya lacked essential training. NATO's after action report concluded that "allies struggled to share crucial target information, lacked specialized planners and analysts, and overly relied on the United States for reconnaissance and refueling aircraft."[63] But also those officers need to be held accountable for their decisions. This will, hopefully, further facilitate thorough target planning instead of permitting the urgency of the situation to dictate the decisions.

Implementing control measures that notify civilians of an impending attack (e.g., leaflets or radio broadcasts that announce when a facility such as a munitions factory is going to be bombed, so that civilians can evacuate the area or not show up for work at the factory) is another way that exercising due care can save innocent people from unnecessarily being killed. Of course, this can only be reasonably implemented when doing so does not adversely affect the likelihood of the bombing mission's being successful from a military standpoint.

Implementing these measures (in most cases) will not place unreasonable risks on soldiers while it exposes civilians to fewer risks. Trying to implement measures that further immunize and protect civilians from the harms of war is acting in a way that serves the cause of a just and lasting peace, where such a peace is one which human rights are secured and respected.

Saint Thomas Aquinas's work regarding murder is applicable for this discussion. Aquinas states:

> Nevertheless it happens that what is not actually and directly voluntary and intended, is voluntary and intended accidentally, according as that which removes an obstacle is called an accidental cause. Wherefore, he who does not remove something whence homicide results whereas he ought to remove it, is in a sense guilty of voluntary homicide. [This happens], when he does not take sufficient care. Hence, according to jurists, if a man pursue a lawful occupation and take due care, the result being that a person loses his life, he is not guilty of that person's death: whereas if he be occupied with something unlawful, or even with something lawful, but without due care, he does not escape being guilty of murder, if his action results in someone's death.[64]

Aquinas's point regarding killing someone as a result of negligence also pertains to bombing in war. If soldiers pursuing their lawful occupation take due care, having made a positive effort (a second intention) to reduce the unintended but foreseeable harms they might impose, then those soldiers should not be held guilty of those civilians' deaths. Exercising due care when possible (as in the case of a munitions factory) is necessary. When belligerents have a duty to implement reasonable due care but fail to do so, those belligerents are guilty of negligent homicide or harm, because, as Rawls states, "Strategies and tactics that lead to avoidable casualties are inconsistent with the underlying intention of the just-war tradition of limiting the destructiveness of armed conflict."[65] States manifest right intention by securing human rights and exercising due care, as evidenced through public acts.

Self-determination

Pursuing a just cause with right intention means vindicating it in a way that brings about a lasting peace with justice, and the only way to set a lasting peace with justice is to allow for a significant degree of political self-determination for peaceful peoples that respect human rights. There are two sets of considerations in favor of prohibiting liberalization or democratization as intended aims of war: (1) those that derive from the requirement that states aim at peace by not fighting longer than necessary; and (2) those that derive from the requirement that states aim at justice by allowing for self-determination.

First, many theorists believe that democratization is the only way to guarantee peace, and that a just and lasting peace is a peace between states that are already just, and thus so liberal and democratic. For example, Darrell Cole states, "Thus, when one begins the business of regime change with the goal of a just and lasting peace, that regime must be transformed into a democratic one."[66] And James Turner Johnson posits, "Americans would insist that a rightly ordered and just society—thus one at peace within itself and open to peace with other societies as well—is one whose people have personal freedom and whose government is democratic."[67] Many will argue that there cannot be a just and lasting peace until all states are liberal democracies, either because only such states are just or because peace is likely to obtain only between such states, or both.

Rawls, aware of the benefits of liberal democracies, recognizes the fact and states, "The absence of war between major established democracies is as close as anything we know to a simple empirical regularity in relations among societies."[68] Rawls's democratic peace thesis is rooted in the empirical claim that war is much less likely to occur between two democracies (because of their democratic social and political institutions) than between two nondemocratic states or between a democratic and a nondemocratic state. An instrumental value of democracies is that they do not go to war with other democracies. "Historical records show that a society of Democratic peoples, all of whose basic institutions are well-ordered by liberal conceptions of right and justice is stable for the right reasons."[69] Democracies are neither internally nor externally aggressive and citizens of democracies reasonably respect and honor the rights of other free and equal citizens of not only their own state but of other states as well. These citizens do not desire war and can usually get what they want through treaties, relations, and commerce and trade.

However, even if empirical evidence suggests that democracies can be relied upon not to go to war with one another, it is an open question whether or not we can create stable, enduring democracies by coercive force. It might be argued that democracy can in fact be achieved by military coercion; both Germany and Japan have become stable enduring democratic states that were implemented through coercion. Nazi Germany and Imperial Japan were forced to accept the Allies' stipulations for unconditional surrender, which included democratization. The Allies refused to negotiate with the German government, having stated in their terms of surrender that "there is no central Government or authority in Germany capable of accepting responsibility for the maintenance of order, the administration of the country and compliance with the requirements of the victorious Powers."[70] Nazi Germany had committed acts of genocide against millions of civilians, committed war crimes against millions of Russian prisoners of war, committed crimes against humanity against millions of Slavs, and committed acts of aggression against no fewer than fifteen sovereign states. It can be argued that Nazi Germany had clearly lost its moral right to self-determination and that any action short of subjecting the German government to democratic reform would have been irresponsible on the Allies' part. The discredited Nazi political and social institutions had to be completely overhauled and developed anew. The Allies were justified and their coercive efforts were warranted in transforming Nazi Germany into a democratic state.

The proclamation defining the terms for Japan's unconditional surrender stated, "The might that now converges on Japan is immeasurably greater than that which, when applied to the resisting Nazis, necessarily laid waste to the lands, the industry and the method of life of the whole German people; the full application of our military power, backed by our resolve, WILL mean the inevitable and complete destruction of the Japanese armed forces and just as inevitably the utter destruction of the Japanese homeland."[71] Japan initially refused these terms, but realized that it could no longer resist the Allies' demands after atomic bombs were dropped on Hiroshima and Nagasaki. Although the democratization of Japan has also become a success story, it does not mean that coercing the Japanese government into a establishing democratic state was morally justified. Coercing the Japanese government into democratic reform was a calculation in utility.

Even though history suggests that international peace is most likely when the states involved are democratic, it is still not obvious that coercive military force is a just or effective means to produce stable, enduring democratic states. In any case, it is an open question whether decent peoples may be relied upon to remain peaceful with one another or even with well-ordered, liberal democracies, but I believe that they in fact may, because decent societies have institutional constitutions that honor basic human rights.

I agree with Walter Riker's perspective on the matter. Much like Rawls, Riker believes that the conditions that secure peace between democracies can be found in decent societies. As constitutional republics, decent societies not only "meet minimal conditions of justice and legitimacy,"[72] but also have "well-entrenched norms restricting the use of political power and regulating and defining the transfer of political power; any society committed to basic human rights and the equality of peoples must have constitutional restrictions on the ability of leaders to violate these commitments"[73] to constrain aggressive state behavior.

It is still an open question whether decent peoples will remain peaceful, since we have not seen many decent illiberal constitutional republics in history yet. However, a decent society's political institutions encompass both justice and legitimacy. "Justice refers, in the broadest sense, to some appropriate distribution of benefits and burdens (however defined) among the morally significant entities (e.g., individuals, associations, peoples) in a society (domestic or global); and political legitimacy refers to a state's right or authority to use coercive force against its citizens to compel obedience to its laws"[74] Decent societies deserve full recognition and should be considered to be in good standing in the international community because they "have genuine law, i.e., law that is legitimately enforceable because they are genuine structures of political authority which is consistent with reciprocity and shared reason."[75] That is, the law involves public discourse and serves the common good (it respects its citizens' interests to some acceptable extent) and the ends of justice.

Riker goes on to say that because "decent societies are constitutionally committed to fundamental norms that explicitly restrict aggressive behavior, e.g., rules defining *jus ad bellum* and *jus in bello,* and others that implicitly restrict such conduct, e.g., norms regarding basic human rights and the equality of peoples, these commitments bind members to certain political institutions, practices, and procedures, all of which reduce the chance of war."[76] Furthermore, such commitments support "a willingness to seek non-lethal remedies to disputes."[77] Decent societies respect traditional principles of justice (safeguarding human rights, honoring a state's right to nonintervention, and conducting war in only self-defense) and see all peoples as equal and free. "They are non-aggressive and non-expansionist, and respect the duties of non-intervention and aid; thus, the interests of decent societies are compatible with those of democratic and other decent societies.[78] In any case, "If decent societies pose no special threat to global peace, then the democratic peace thesis does not justify efforts to democratize them."[79]

Implementing a liberal democratic regime by coercive force runs counter to the just war tradition. If right intention is supposed to guide a state against pursuing a war longer than necessary and fighting only until the rights that were violated have been secured, and it also includes aiming at a just and lasting peace, then instituting a type of government by coercive force against the will of its people seems at odds with the requirement that states aim at peace by not fighting longer than necessary.

I am not suggesting that an aggressive nondemocratic state does not require rehabilitation. Suppose that, for one reason or another, an aggressive nondemocratic state did unjustly attack a liberal democracy. Maybe, in the imagined scenario, the resort to armed conflict was the result of a border dispute or an attempt to obtain more natural resources and territory. However, any subsequent rehabilitation imposed by the victors should eventuate reform that is decent, although not necessarily democratic if the people of that state do not want democratic reform. Coercively transforming a nondemocratic state into a democracy is not necessarily consistent with an enduring peace with justice. Democracy might be viewed "in some way distinctive of western political tradition and prejudicial to other cultures"[80] which has the potential to undermine a state's comprehensive (religious) doctrine that fundamentally guides and "influences the government's main decisions and policies."[81]

Furthermore, it would seem that if coercive implementation of a more liberal government is just, then this might set a precedent by which democratic states would initiate war not on account of individual or collective defense but as a new just cause—one designed to transform all decent, well-ordered nondemocratic regimes based on the perception that they cannot be trusted to maintain the peace. Even if a decent, well-ordered regime had always respected human rights and was nonaggressive in its relations with other states, this would not guarantee its safety, because evidence has suggested that only democracies may be tolerated by other democracies, because democracies can be relied upon not to go to war with each other. This suggestion cannot be a just cause to initiate a war. Neither were the democratic state's rights violated nor did the decent nondemocratic state forfeit its moral right not to be invaded (since it had not been either internally or externally aggressive).

Rather, such an armed conflict would constitute a preventative (preventive) war: liberal State A attacks nonliberal State B because of the possibility that sometime in the near or distant future nonliberal State B *might* attack liberal State A. Engaging in preventative war disregards the moral requirement of using force only when absolutely necessary and is not in alignment with the just war tradition. If preventative war is wrong and coercive liberalization/democratization is essentially preventative war, then coercive liberalization/democratization is wrong as well.

In principle, the question of whether a state can adopt liberalization or democratization as its goal in pursuing war arises only when there is also, independently, a just cause for war. However, if liberalization or democratization is believed to be a just aim of war, then this notion has the possibility to gain momentum where practical means-ends reasoning take over. Using such practical means-ends reasoning, it would be permissible to attack nonliberal State B, because doing so would facilitate its being transformed into a democratic state. The ends justify the means. However, given the complexities of our world, it would be impossible to make headway toward a realistic utopia if we as liberal democratic people excluded nondemocratic and nonliberal polities from recognition as equal members in the international community of states and instead targeted them for a regime change. Instead, liberal democracies should focus their finite ability, time, and resources toward the significant nonideal conditions that aggressive outlaw regimes and burdened societies present.

Second, fidelity to right intention requires that states aim at justice by allowing for self-determination. A key feature of right intention is affirming a liberal commitment to tolerating self-determination of nondemocratic, even nonliberal polities. Denying a state's right to political self-determination by forcing another society, which is already well-ordered and liberal, to become more just—i.e., more democratic or more liberal—is not a legitimate aim of coercive international force or war. A state that goes to war without allowing for self-determination (of polities that respect basic human rights) among its "intentions" lacks right intention.[82]

States have a moral right to self-determination, which includes the possibility of democratic institutions, but the moral right to self-determination does not presuppose that democratic institutions and practices are the only form of permissible governance. States have the moral right to self-determination provided it is a reasonable political conception that is "understood as an irreducibly collective right held by groups that are willing and able to perform requisite functions."[83] Even democratic governance "is itself an exercise in collective, not individual, self-determination."[84] Individuals in a democracy rule themselves through elected officials and a representative government, which possess the power to determine the outcome of political decisions. Therefore, "it is simply false to say that an individual who participates in a democratic decision-making process is self-governing; he or she is governed by the majority."[85] It is possible that some citizens want democracy but are in themselves insufficiently powerful to bring about an internal regime change because they are governed by the majority. Through an exercise in collective self-determination, the form of governance remains nondemocratic. As long as "a nonliberal society's basic institutions meet certain specified conditions of political right and justice and lead its people to honor a reasonable and just law,"[86] this is a sufficient reason for democratic liberal regimes not to attempt to force something more liberal or more just.

The right to political self-determination does not depend on the question of which form of government is more reliable at bringing about just political outcomes but rather with the question of legitimacy. Legitimacy refers to a state's being able to perform the requisite political functions that safeguard its members from standard threats (internally, protecting human rights) as well as its respecting the human rights of citizens in other states (externally, nonaggressive). As long as a state has a legitimate form of government—and as long as it behaves decently—then "due to the moral right to self-determination, it is impermissible for an external agent to interfere with a group's exercise of its self-determination, even if the external agent could do a better job of protecting human rights."[87]

It is likely that, once the war is over, the defeated, war-torn state will need assistance from the victor (the just, liberal democracy) in restoring the essential services that secure the core human rights of its populace, but this does not imply that the vanquished nation loses its moral right to self-determination.

Of course, it is permissible to gradually shape and encourage progressive reform of a decent regime, but this should not be done by coercive means (military force, economic sanctions, etc.). Rather, a liberal democratic regime should be cooperative and provide assistance. Rawls states, "A liberal constitutional democracy should have the confidence in their convictions and suppose that a decent society, when offered due respect by liberal peoples, may be more likely, overtime, to recognize the advantages of liberal institutions and take steps toward becoming more liberal on its own."[88] I think it is quite possible that Rawls would agree that a just and lasting peace is one in which all states are just but have become so as a consequence of their own free development under conditions of peace. That is, decent and nonliberal states have become just and democratic by their own efforts and progression. Only then can we conclude that a just and lasting peace is one in which all states are just. All states have become internally just through political self-determination, "the mutual agreement of men acting in choice of their government, and forms of government,"[89] and not as a result of coercion.

If we are trying to establish a lasting peace with justice, then allowing a state to decide for itself what type of reasonable political conception it wishes to pursue seems plausible. It should be allowed to find its own way to justice under conditions of peace. Forcing a state to become more liberal when it has already met the minimum necessary conditions of decency would most likely occasion the hostility and animosity of the people as well as "frustrate their vitality."[90] In addition, it could hamper any authentic reconciliation after the war between the two states.

Right intention places some restrictions on a state. Its aim in or through war to move a state to undertake liberalism or democracy against the will of its people is unjust. It is legitimate to aspire to assure that human rights are met, but once they are, a people's right to political self-determination must be respected. States must refrain from pursuing such ends as democratization or liberalization; they should aim to end the war in a way that allows for respectful toleration, self-determination, etc., of well-ordered states. A just and lasting peace is one within which liberal democracies tolerate (in the sense of granting recognition and respect to) other nonliberal and/or nondemocratic states provided that those states honor basic human rights and are well ordered and externally nonaggressive.

Education

Right intention involves actions taken long before war breaks out, namely, educating the military and supporting a public political culture committed to conducting war subject to constraints. That is, a state should be cognizant of what is morally required of it in regard to adhering to restrictions in warfare as well as what is morally necessary in establishing conditions for reconciliation and peace with justice before war begins.

Long before politicians and generals commit to strategic operations and soldiers map out tactical decisions to meet those aims—just war— the moral framework for armed violence must be incorporated into the consciousness of the state. Without sufficient grasp of the moral norms and principles governing war and its applications, it becomes much easier to acquiesce or resort to practical means-ends reasoning. "Means-ends reasoning justifies too much, too quickly, and provides a way for the dominant forces in government to quiet any bothersome moral scruples."[91]

Rawls suggests that "[t]hese principles [regarding specific restrictions in the conduct of war] must be in place well in advance of war and widely understood by citizens generally."[92] Not only does a state need institutions that provide a moral education to its citizens, but incorporated into that education needs to be basic just war understanding along with the norms and principles that apply. "These matters need to be part of the political culture; they should not dominate the day-to-day contents of ordinary politics, but must be predisposed and operating in the background."[93]

For example, regardless of the fact that, in 1945 when the Allies were clearly going to win the war against Nazi Germany and Imperial Japan, the United States nonetheless decided to firebomb Dresden (killing an estimated 20,000-plus civilians) and Tokyo (killing an estimated 100,000 civilians) even though both targets offered little military value. At the time that these cities were chosen as targets, "there was not sufficient prior grasp of the great importance of the principles of just war for the expression of them to have blocked the handy appeal to practical means-end reasoning,"[94] so the murder that unfolded at Dresden and Tokyo was generally accepted as merely part of war.

It is too late to discuss conflicting principles or the issue of subordinating proportionality to military necessity when the situation is already at hand and when the general public and even the military lack the basic education and awareness of such moral issues. It is difficult to respect the principles of just war when people are not even aware of such moral principles. Winston Churchill was a dynamic and charismatic leader, but his own expressed views show that there was no awareness or recognition of just war principles in the public political culture during World War II. In a 1941 London radio broadcast regarding the Royal Air Force's strategy of carpet bombing German cities, Churchill stated that the Allies were making "the German people taste and gulp each month a sharper dose of the miseries they have showered upon mankind."[95] It is very hard to argue for the rights of others as well as obligations and restrictions in war when the political leaders of a country lack that perspective, which continues to thrive as evidenced by some United States political figures that have expressed the will to carpet bomb cities in the current fight against ISIS, as well as to waterboard detainees and enemy combatants. These beliefs are the antithesis of my moral philosophy and my profession as a United States Army officer. These ignorant comments continue to degrade our society's understanding and awareness of not only humanitarian law but also moral constraint on the battlefield.

In the United States public consciousness regarding just war is being enhanced through cable news, the Internet, and social media. However, discussion of it has been intermittent at best; most citizens have never even heard of it. In addition, U.S. military culture lacks education regarding just war and the awareness and recognition of its principles. Of course, soldiers are given legal briefings concerning the law of armed conflict, but they are not taught just war.

Officers are responsible for planning military operations and leading soldiers into combat. However, there is not a uniformed and standardized curriculum regarding the teaching of just war doctrine. This can possibly lead to potential issues. All cadets at the United States Military Academy (West Point), prior to becoming commissioned officers, are enrolled in a semester-long just war class where they engage with foundational material from Plato, St. Augustine, St. Aquinas, Locke, Kant, Walzer, Orend, and other philosophers regarding the ethics of war. These cadets look at historical and modern day examples and apply theories, tenets, and concepts that they have learned in order to argue verbally and through written prose cogent, coherent arguments of why something is or is not moral. This course, not only exposes these future Army officers to Western-thought philosophy regarding war, but also helps shape their analytical problem solving capabilities. Additionally, it provides these future military leaders with a philosophical understanding and construct regarding war. In order to further enhance an officer's ability to recognize and deal with complex issues in war, just war theory should be an essential and abiding component of an officer's education. This is probably why West Point makes this course a mandatory graduation requirement. However, trying to mirror such a course for ROTC (Reserve Officers' Training Corps) cadets at over 250+ universities and colleges across the U.S. is just not feasible or realistic. This is done easily at West Point, because West Point owns its entire academic curriculum and its whole cadet population is on one campus. However, ROTC does not own the academic curriculum outside of its own military science curriculum (which is a 4-year academic program which constitutes all the necessary subjects that need to be taught in order for a student to graduate from the ROTC program in order to be commissioned). In addition, most college and university philosophy departments do not even offer just war/ethics of war courses which—personally—strikes me as odd.

ROTC develops and creates over 60% of the commissioned officers in the U.S. Army every year. ROTC has done a tremendous job training, educating, and inspiring young men and women for the rigor of the Army profession. And like any good organization, it self-evaluates in order to ensure what it produces meets the demand of what is required. That being said, the ROTC curriculum is consistently refined and a lot of the curriculum is focused on leadership development and case studies, the code of conduct, law of war case studies, the ethics of military service, and Army values. These are all essential building blocks to developing future Army officers, but ROTC does not have the capacity to formally educate its cadets through a semester long course that is built around the ethics of war (*jus ad bellum*, *jus in bello*, and *jus post bellum*). I think that there is a gap in the current system, and I believe that college and university philosophy departments could offer such a course, if those philosophy departments do not already do so. College and university philosophy departments can take part in the formal academic develop of future Army leaders. Some of the larger universities, have over 100+ cadets in their ROTC detachment, so there are more than enough cadets on many campuses to enroll in a just war course. I surmised that developing a partnership between Philosophy and ROTC departments is the way forward, and my intent is to be a part of this at Indiana University.

Additionally, I would think many non-ROTC students would be interested in such a course. Understanding and awareness of the ethics of war is critical to situational awareness, citizenry, and to many professions outside of the military. There are incidents by recent or current political figures that use terms such as 'carpet bomb' as a viable and acceptable military strategy even though it clearly violates the laws of armed conflict, international humanitarian law, the Geneva Convention, and the morality of war. Rawls states, "The grounds of constitutional democracy and the basis of its rights and duties need to be continually discussed in all the many associations of civil society as part of citizens' understanding and education prior to taking part in political life."[96] A constitutive part of citizens' understanding and education prior to taking part in political life must be that of just war: understanding that states "have the right of self-defense but no right to instigate war for reasons other than self-defense and to observe certain specified restrictions in the conduct of war."[97]

In order to abide by the norm of right intention, these principles must be instilled into the consciousness of politicians, citizens, and military officers before war even surfaces. Otherwise, the obligations and restrictions that the norm of right intention demands will be undermined.

"Political leaders and military commanders have the chief responsibility to see that war is waged justly, but citizens have a responsibility to hold leaders and commanders accountable for the justice of their nation's war conduct."[98] In order for citizens to take this obligation seriously they need to be reasonably informed and educated so it becomes a part of the public consciousness.

TOTALITY OF CONDUCT

Although right intention is a constitutive part of *jus ad bellum* (justice of war), a state cannot suggest that it has met the conditions of right intention before the war has even begun, which is the case for other *jus ad bellum* tenets. Legitimate authority, just cause, last resort, and proportionate response can all be reasonably addressed and answered prior to the ensuing conflict. However, right intention is different. Political leaders may believe that they have right intention, but the only real way to evaluate right intention is by observing a state's action throughout all phases of war, because right intention is evidenced by observable acts that serve the cause of a just and lasting peace. There is no way to assess whether a state fights with right intention without looking at the totality of its conduct, beginning before the war, to the start of the war, through the war itself, and into the postwar context—the implications of the *ad bellum* "right intention" requirement are, then, significant.

All *jus ad bellum* judgments regarding right intention are provisional until the entire process is concluded. Only then can we compare the actual prosecution and termination of the war (the observable evidence available to the parties to the conflict and the international community) to see if they square with each other. This would require the creation of an external, impartial commission (comprised, for instance, of the permanent and nonpermanent members of the United Nations Security Council [UNSC] as well as representatives from the parties to the conflict), which would be tasked with substantial *ex post* review and assessment of the conflict, the acts of war, and the rebuilding and reconciliation effort between the warring parties. The findings and evaluation would then be made public and disseminated among the international community.

This procedure would be the only way that we could, in fact, be confident that, after reviewing all four phases of war (pre, of, in, and after), an impartial decision could be made as to whether the conflict was just. Just because a belligerent might have a just cause to resort to war does not necessarily suggest that conducting the war and its aftermath will be just. If anything, an impartial commission reviewing belligerents' actions might instigate further incentives for states to do what is morally required.

CONCLUSION

St. Augustine's perspective—that we fight so that we may live in peace[99]—may be true; however, there is no peace—morally desirable—without justice. Having right intention, a state not only limits its war-making activity to what is necessary to vindicate its just cause but also publicly conducts its activity in a manner favorable to a just and lasting peace.

The content of "right intention" is given by the idea of a "just and lasting peace," and the idea of a just and lasting peace is best understood by reference to that which is required by peace and justice. A state must meet both aims: peace and justice. Aiming at both peace and justice will facilitate an enduring respectful relationship between both parties. A state whose goal is peace fights with restraint, immunizes civilians from the harms of war, and educates its military. And a state whose goal is justice respects human rights, leaves its enemy in a position to secure human rights, exercises due care in order to further insulate civilians from war, fights only until the rights that were violated have been secured, allows for political self-determination, tolerates regimes that honor basic human rights, and supports a public political culture that adheres to just war. In doing so, a just, liberal democracy lives up to the particular, substantive account of what qualifies to set conditions for a just and lasting peace that can be assessed by looking at the totality of its conduct.

2

Reasonable Chance of Success

Analyzing Postwar Requirements in the *Ad Bellum* Phase

Just because a war ends, it does not necessarily mean that the death and dying are over. Repeatedly, civilians are harmed during the postwar phase by foreseeable but unintended consequences, the residual effects of war, and poorly planned postwar occupation. Not only is it important that states realize that postwar obligations pertain to all parties, but even more so, states should be cognizant of these demanding obligations even before the fighting begins. This is consistent with the idea of right intention.

Moreover, *jus post bellum* (justice after war) obligations must be considered not in isolation, but alongside and integrated with *jus ad bellum* (justice of war) and *jus in bello* (justice in war) considerations. Analyzing the likelihood of successful military operations as the only consideration for the *jus ad bellum* reasonable chance of success tenet is inherently shortsighted and problematic, because a state can win the war but still make a moral mess of the aftermath. The benefits of incorporating *jus post bellum* obligations into a state's reasonable chance of success calculation are twofold: (1) a state could limit or curtail specific types of military operations, thereby lending that state the ability to more effectively and efficiently fulfill its postwar obligations, and (2) the state would engage in postwar scenario planning in advance instead of waiting until the war is over (or nearly over), which is way too late to deal with the huge *post bellum* undertaking.

War encompasses three distinct phases: prewar, war, and postwar. However, the importance of the postwar phase has waned over the last two centuries. Only recently (over the last decade or so) have postwar concerns taken center stage, and still there is much to be done. Larry May, Brian Orend, and many other scholars have done considerable work in this area. However, as of yet, there is not any agreed-upon systematic set of principles governing *jus post bellum* roles and responsibilities, as there is for the prewar and war phases. According to the UN Charter, states have the legal and moral right to self-defense. Additionally, armed conflict is governed by international laws (the 1949 Geneva Conventions). However, currently there is not any set of universally recognized or instituted *post bellum* norms.

Michael Walzer concludes that there are three legitimate wartime ends: to resist aggression, to restore the peaceful *status quo ante*, and to reasonably prevent future aggression.[1] However, Walzer does not expound upon any specific framework governing how states might actually attempt a legitimate restoration of the peaceful *status quo*. It is possible to enter a war for just reasons and fight it justly but then be morally unjustified in postwar conduct.

With this in mind, the aim of this chapter is to discuss what is morally required of a state after major conventional combat operations have ended. To avoid giving thought and articulation to postwar considerations until the war has ended can have disastrous results. The residual effects of warfare continue to harm civilians long after the fighting stops. Larry May captures an important truth about the postwar period's importance by stating, "If the object of war is a just and lasting peace, then all of Just War considerations should be aimed at this goal, and the branch of the Just War tradition that specifically governs the end of war, *jus post bellum*, should be given more attention, if not pride of place."[2] Therefore, before a war begins we need to come to some resolution of what is required of the victor in regard to the vanquished. A state that resorts to war without a plan for postwar occupation and reconstruction ends up causing not only large amounts of suffering and loss of life among its enemies, but mention unnecessary sacrifice of its own lives and money.

May, Orend, and Gary Bass believe that rebuilding, rehabilitating, and reconstructing (respectively) is morally required. I also agree that repairing essential infrastructure and reforming degraded political institutions is seminal. However, something is missing in the just war literature, which seems to suggest that postwar concerns only manifest themselves after the war is over or while it is coming to an end. That is, it is a sequential process—now that the fighting is over we should rebuild. For example, I am not sure if Orend's rights vindication tenet or Bass's restraining conquest tenet do as much work as envisioned. Orend mentions that "[t]he principle of rights vindication forbids the continuation of the war after the relevant rights has, in fact, been vindicated."[3] This seems intuitive, and it does not really express any substantial depth or account for what is actually needed. Similarly, Bass states that warring parties must restrain their conquest: "They should use the minimum violence necessary to achieve just ends," and, "once a state has surrendered, its sovereignty must be respected again."[4] However, Bass does not really explicate his point beyond suggesting that states should fight limited and not total war, although, again, this seems intuitive.

I believe that May does a great job of capturing an essential element of *jus post bellum* by incorporating the notion of proportionality into it. May states that "this involves the conditions necessary for achieving a just peace: they cannot impose more harm on a population than the harm that is alleviated by these postwar plans."[5] May suggests that whatever harm is done during the fighting phase should be rectified (so that it fits within the proportionality algorithm) in the postwar phase. However, May does not suggest that planning postwar obligations should be done concurrently with planning combat operations. Although many have discussed *post bellum* considerations, they have dealt with each phase separately. However, I want to make the case that all three phases of war need to be integrated and evaluated collectively instead of planning and dealing with postwar concerns in isolation and only after major combat operations have ended.

This chapter attempts to remedy a portion of that oversight by presenting the claim that a state should not only be cognizant of its postwar obligations but moreso should factor those obligations into its calculation of "a reasonable chance of success," in order to bring to light the significant and challenging issues that will arise in the postwar phase. By incorporating postwar considerations into its reasonable chance of success calculation, the state is forced to be mindful of such demands before it finds itself in the postwar phase with no sense of direction. And by understanding what it will be responsible for in the postwar phase, even before the fighting begins, the state is best prepared to undertake those demanding obligations and make better choices that facilitate obligation fulfillment.

Most of the writers who examine just war refer to the *jus ad bellum* principle of reasonable chance of success as a calculation of a state's chances of militarily winning the conflict, but this calculation of success is too limited and undercuts the significant analysis that should be taken into account. The case should be made that the *jus ad bellum* tenet of reasonable chance of success requires more than simply estimating the likelihood of military success alone during the war. It is possible for a liberal democracy to resort to war for just reasons and fight the war justly, but then completely fail—make a moral mess of the postwar phase—by not fulfilling necessary requirements (life-support necessities) to the vanquished. To rectify this, a state needs to analyze *jus post bellum* requirements as part of the reasonable chance of success tenet of *jus ad bellum*. That is, a state should recognize that it has *ex post* responsibilities that should factor into the *ex ante* calculation of determining its reasonable chance of success, because responsibility does not end just because major combat operations are over. Additionally, a two-tier approach as part of a solution to effectively fulfill postwar obligations should be implemented. I mention the example of a liberal democracy, because I assume that a peaceful liberal democracy is just, and that its action will be guided by what is right and reasonable, and furthermore, that it has resorted to war as a response to acts of aggression by an outlaw regime.

Responsibility for postwar rebuilding can be broken into two areas: (1) the just victor should be responsible for providing security to the citizens of the defeated country, and (2) the international community should be responsible for the reformation of the outlaw regime's political and social institutions. This two-tier model represents the best way to mitigate harm to civilians while also effectively reforming the vanquished state's institutions. Fulfilling both tiers of responsibility simultaneously is the best way to achieve, restore, or redevelop peace with justice.

Before explaining the two-tier model in more detail, I want to make it clear that I am in no way suggesting that a state must wait to defend itself against attacks by an aggressor state until it can calculate its probability of success. In this kind of example, postwar planning must be part of the concurrent planning. Of course, a state is morally and legally (UN Charter, art. 51) justified in stopping these attacks by using defensive and offensive operations. But even if a state is defending itself against such attacks, it should be cognizant that it still faces postwar responsibilities, which might range from removing the outlaw regime, rebuilding infrastructure, and reestablishing the rule of law to pursuing negotiations and resolving issues diplomatically. In certain cases, a regime change, although warranted, might not actually be possible.

I tried to elaborate on this earlier by citing the example of Poland during World War II. Poland's goal was to push the Nazi forces out of the country in order to reclaim its boundaries, its autonomy, and its citizens' human rights. Poland was not focused on postwar responsibilities nor should it have been; it was fighting for its sheer existence. There have been other cases, though, such as the 1991 Desert Storm incursion into Iraq and Kuwait, wherein a coalition of states more powerful than the aggressor state, Iraq, did not pursue a regime change as one of its postwar goals. The goal of the coalition forces was to reclaim and protect the rights of those who had been unjustly harmed by the Iraqi regime. Coalition forces pushed Iraqi forces out of Kuwait, thereby enabling Kuwait to regain its territorial integrity, political sovereignty, and human rights security. Coalition forces believed that Iraq's aggressive nature could be contained without a regime change, and so decided that a full invasion of Baghdad was not proportionate, since Kuwait's rights could be vindicated without the invasion of Baghdad. That is, the additional loss of hundreds if not thousands of coalition soldiers and the loss of thousands of Iraqi civilians and soldiers would not have been morally justified as being necessary for Kuwait's subsequent self-defense. In addition, the loss of military equipment and the cost of the resources necessary to invade Iraq and overthrow Saddam Hussein in 1991 were not proportionate to the objectives of the invasion, which had been morally justified as defending Kuwait from acts of aggression.

However, when a just state decides to preemptively (as a form of self-defense) attack another, that state should have been planning postwar operations even before the hostilities began, as opposed to initiating the planning of postwar responsibilities at the tail end of the war.

Now, of course, the extent of postwar responsibilities must be consistent with the degree of complexity of the war itself. If the strategic goal is to only defeat the aggressor state's offensive strike force as it rolls across the border, there is not really any significant postwar obligation required of the responding nation if it is victorious, because the outlaw regime's civilian infrastructure was, presumably, not affected. That is, only military assets (military headquarters, tanks, planes, combatants, etc.) were targeted and neutralized, defeated, or destroyed. In such a scenario, postwar considerations are still important but much less demanding. They might only include the institution of no fly zones or a demilitarized zone, limits placed on weapons stockpiles, etc., which can be implemented and orchestrated by some combination of the just victor and international community. These operations are limited in scope and require relatively few resources to accomplish. However, pursuing unconditional surrender (which in extreme cases can be considered morally justified) or a regime change requires an exorbitant amount of resources.

Operations that require unconditional surrender or a regime change are quite demanding, especially during the postwar phase, so it should not come as a surprise that the victor has a morally demanding role in such a scenario. When a state's goal is to change the government of an outlaw regime, it should take steps to plan such an endeavor instead of thrusting itself into only the military part of the operation without a plan for follow-on activities of the postwar phase. The inherent complexity of trying to plan wartime and postwar operations simultaneously might seem overwhelming, so that planners only focus on one phase at a time. With this in mind, planning is relegated to focusing on only how to force the enemy to capitulate, and this is usually done by incorporating a destructive strategy without much thought about anything else.

The inherent military strategy of operations such as regime change or unconditional surrender is to undermine the enemy state's war-making capability (its physical ability as well as its resolve) by attacking its physical infrastructure. "Any act of force that contributes in a significant way to winning the war is likely to be called permissible," as long as it is consistent with the notions of military necessity and proportionality.[6] Attacking the enemy's infrastructure is considered permissible because this type of operation still targets military assets. However, these targets are classified as dual purpose targets since they have dual purposes. They serve a purpose not only to a state's military but also to the civilian population. Electrical grids, power plants, bridges, railroads, and major highway interchanges are considered legal targets and are targeted in order to significantly degrade a state's ability to wage war and undercut its center of gravity and will to fight.

Armies do not have to adopt a dual purpose target bombing strategy, but they elect to do so for two reasons: (1) it brings war to the whole state, thereby crippling that state's overall ability to function; and (2) this type of campaign will cause a state to sue for peace much quicker than just striking military assets. The implication of such a strategy is that civilians will be killed. Although not intentionally attacked, they suffer death as a residual effect of these operations, notwithstanding that "noncombatants, whatever their political affiliation, have the right not to have war waged on them."[7]

EMPIRICAL CASE

Although moral obligations may be based on rational reflection rather than empirical examples, empirically achieved facts are important because, presumably, they derive from real-world situations that one can apply to the realm of practical reason. Iraq in 2003 is a case of what can happen when postwar considerations are not entertained until major combat operations are winding down. The United States was so short-sighted in its articulation of a regime change in Iraq that it failed altogether to develop a plan that would facilitate even the perfunctory operation of an Iraqi government after its leadership had been removed. Richard Haas, U.S. State Department Director of Policy Planning, 2001–03, has stated in regard to the 2003 Iraq invasion that "[t]he initial phase of planning for the aftermath [postwar operations] took place just before and during the war itself."[8] This was far too late to develop an effective plan, especially inasmuch as major combat operations lasted only six weeks.

If the State Department had initiated a thorough mission analysis regarding reconstruction, humanitarian assistance, and political governance, the plan that resulted would presumably have been much different from what unfolded as a consequence of inadequate interagency coordination, nonexistent preliminary planning, and a lack of clear strategic guidance. Instead of a solid plan addressing postwar requirements, the lack of adequate preplanning and postwar engagement led to poor decisions that exacerbated undesirable conditions in Iraq.

For example, the removal of Ba'ath party members from government positions, the disbanding of the civil service, as well as the dissolution of the remnants of the Iraqi Army were absolutely detrimental to any normalcy or rebuilding efforts. By denying Ba'ath party members any employment in government positions, the United States created a power vacuum in Iraq. "The disqualification of so many Iraqis denied the country the experience and skills it desperately needed at the same time as it alienated many of the Sunnis who, without access to the new Iraq, supported or at least tolerated the insurgency."[9] The lack of any guideline or framework for postwar responsibilities led to uninformed and superficial analyses: the U.S. secretary of defense during the George W. Bush administration, Donald Rumsfeld, believed that there was not going to be any need for a large occupation force since the Iraqis would welcome the overthrow of the Saddam Hussein regime.[10] In addition, "Civilians in the Defense Department seemed determined to demonstrate that they could improve upon the previous Iraq war and in doing so render obsolete the Powell Doctrine and its call for large number of troops."[11] But this analysis by Department of Defense (DoD) civilians never took into account postwar needs—because combat strength was analyzed only for the fight and not for the occupation. U.S. civilian officials' belief that the Iraqis would see the Americans as liberators might have had some merit before the fact, but it disintegrated in the face of the alienation, animosity, and fear triggered among Iraqi citizens by the power vacuum the U.S. occupation engendered.

Furthermore, the United States failed to follow its own guidelines (in particular, numbers five and six) found in the Powell Doctrine:[12] A military force needs a coherent exit strategy with clearly defined and tenable objectives as part of a strategic end state that the president and secretary of defense formulate. Termination is critical in planning because, "it [termination] is discussed first among the elements of operational design because effective planning cannot occur without a clear understanding of the end state and the condition that must exist to end military operations."[13] Another important objective of developing postwar parameters and responsibilities is to benefit the defense and state departments' planning cells. Before preliminary operations even take place, political leaders, military advisors, and planning cells should be cognizant of the robust normative requirements obligated of the victor after the war is over. Imposed postwar stipulations facilitate and enhance the planning process since certain tenets must be satisfied and planning committees, leaders, and advisors should be familiar with these before any planning is initiated.

The existence of recognized postwar guidelines provides for unified action, synchronization, and integration of intergovernmental, nongovernmental, and federal organizations, which is essential to taking advantage of the military disposition of forces—on the ground—in order to implement the postwar plan to achieve political aims and postwar stipulations. Otherwise, the plan becomes reactive, and military occupation forces attempt to compensate for its shortcomings. Iraq was a case of failure to unify and synchronize action. Because planning for combat operations was never integrated with planning for postwar operations in

Iraq, Haas concludes that "[t]actical and strategic decisions that made sense in one context (for example, having US units move with great speed and largely avoid cities) had large and adverse consequences for the other [postwar operations] as security vacuums emerged in urban areas that were quickly filled by hostile irregular forces."[14]

The postwar stipulations are specified tasks that need to be planned, resourced, and implemented. This has multiple benefits: more emphasis on negotiations by diplomats and world leaders, because postwar stipulations drain countries of men, material, and money; limitations on the scope and ambitions of military operations, because of the imposed postwar stipulations (the *jus in bello* tenet of proportionality in particular);[15] and the concurrent pursuit of political and civil planning along with military planning, in order to develop an effective transition plan for postwar stability and reconstruction operations. For example, in Iraq, the United States would have had to keep units positioned near cities that had been bypassed, along with some units held back in order to retain ground they had previously seized, instead of moving all forces at breakneck speed toward enemy forces. This type of operation would have taken more than six weeks to complete but it might have prevented or at least mitigated the serious security vacuums that took place. Such an implementation would not only have achieved the militarily desired end state but also set better conditions to achieve what is morally required of the postwar parameters.

It is absolutely seminal that leaders and planners critically analyze not only *jus ad bellum* and *jus in bello* requirements but also *jus post bellum* requirements before any disembarkation of troops. The main takeaway from not analyzing postwar considerations as part of the *ad bellum* phase of the Iraq invasion is that civilians continued, and still continue, to die even though the war is nominally over, and the degraded and chaotic conditions created as a result of implementing a dual purpose target strategy became the perfect breeding ground for an insurgency.

THE VICTOR'S RESPONSIBILITY

I invoke a two-tier model of responsibilities because some obligations are not the victor's responsibility whereas others are, just as some obligations are not the international community's responsibility whereas others are. The victor should be cognizant of the restoration owed to the vanquished as a consequence of having destroyed dual purpose targets. Once the opposing force surrenders, the war might be over but civilians continue to die because of the lack of basic necessities. Andrew Altman and Christopher Wellman state that, "the risks to the safety and security of noncombatants that arise from an intervention should not be disproportionate to the rights violations that the intervention helps avert."[16] Although they are discussing military intervention, Altman and Wellman raise a good point about the use of force in general: even if the victor is able to force the outlaw regime to capitulate, the very use of force could be considered disproportionate to the rights violations that the use of military force helps avert. If tens of thousands of noncombatants continue to die in a postwar situation because its state—overwhelmed and underresourced—is unable to quickly restore essential services, and the victor does nothing to alleviate the harmful situation, this might be classified as a disproportionate use of force.

Rather than suggest that a state should not bomb dual purpose targets, after the war the victor should acknowledge a responsibility to assist in repairing infrastructure that provides essential services to noncombatants. If the victor does nothing to alleviate the deleterious situation that civilians face in the postwar phase, then we can say that the victor is morally blameworthy for its failure to protect civilians. The victor is, therefore, morally required to assist in the repairing of infrastructure that provides essential services such as electricity, potable water, trash removal, sewage disposal, shelter, and medical attention to help the civilian population and secure their basic human rights. Doing so is the first step toward bringing normalcy to a war-torn people. Without an effective postwar plan, civilians continue to die as a result of a lack of necessities. For example, "by the end of 1992 [after Operation Desert Storm], more than a hundred thousand Iraqi civilians died from the lack of clean water and sewage disposal, and the breakdown of electrical service to hospitals,"[17] and estimates for "the loss of civilian life from the [2003] Iraqi war has concluded that at least 100,000 Iraqi civilians may have died because of the U.S. invasion."[18]

In his 1758 *Law of Nations*, Emmerich de Vattel mentions that women, children, and the infirmed (of the state that one is warring with) can be classified as enemies, "but it doesn't hence follow that we are justifiable in treating them like men who bear arms, so we don't have the same rights against all classes of enemies."[19] Vattel goes on to say, "These are enemies who make no resistance; and consequently we have no right to maltreat their persons, or use any violence against them, much less to take away their lives."[20] It is this foundation and underlying value that is the drive behind international positive law that dictates that civilians are not to be harmed during war. However, honoring the concept of right intention would also require this line of thought be carried over into the postwar phase, because the postwar phase can be just as devastating to noncombatants as war itself when it is in full swing. In the postwar phase, bombs no longer kill civilians but the residual effects of bombing campaigns do.

In *The Doctrine of Right*, Immanuel Kant discusses the rights of states regarding war and how states have rights specific to each phase (prewar, war, and postwar). Kant states that these rights after war specify that "neither the vanquished state nor its citizens [should] lose their civil freedom."[21] By this, Kant is referring to the point that citizens of the vanquished state have the right to be free from subjugation or enslavement, but history shows us that this is exactly what happens when a war-torn state is left to fend for itself. Maybe those citizens are not technically being subjugated as if they were colonized; however, "the suspension of hostilities does not provide the security of peace."[22] Although the cannons might have been muzzled, civilians still live in fear.

This fear is intensified by their lack of access to basic necessities. To be denied adequate access to basic necessities is a form of enslavement, under which citizens of a defeated nation are deprived of freedom and are forced to focus solely on mere survival. Innocent civilians—regardless of their political affiliation—should never lose the civic freedom entailed by the right to life and liberty, and the absence or denial of basic necessities undermines a person's reasonable freedom and threatens his or her ability to live. Kant states: "Every action is just [right] that in itself or in its maxim is such that the freedom of the will of each can coexist together with the freedom of everyone in accordance with a universal law."[23]

Kant further declares that "[i]f, therefore, my actions or my condition in general can coexist with the freedom of everyone in accordance with a universal law, then anyone who hinders me in performing the action or in maintaining the condition does me an injustice, inasmuch as this hindrance (this opposition) cannot coexist with freedom in accordance with universal laws."[24] What Kant is saying is that after a war is over, civilians should not lose their civic freedom, either. That is, civilians should be free from subjugation of an environment that does not afford basic life-support necessities. Trying to exist in deleterious conditions hinders the freedom and autonomy of civilians. A lasting peace is not possible unless certain standards of justice are assured. Therefore, every attempt must be made to mitigate the harms that affect civilians during the aftermath of war. In order to set the conditions for a just and lasting peace, a state needs to allocate planners and resources as well as develop a reasonable plan of action.

In order to achieve meaningful reconciliation and develop a just peace, civilians must be not only protected against physical threats but afforded reasonable expectations for postwar life, such as the ability to return to work and to send their children to school. Firing and removing all government employees is inconsistent with this process and can often exacerbate a difficult or dangerous situation. It is essential that postwar obligations are recognized and reviewed before the fighting starts, in order to adequately plan and synchronize assets in the postwar phase. If a state recognizes that it has such obligations then it could very well lead to a postwar phase that is less chaotic. By doing some preliminary estimates, planning cells could (hopefully) conclude that a state cannot function without its government employees.

Disbanding the civil service completely shuts down all levels of government. In such a case, citizens cannot even apply for a driver's license since there are not any employees working at the department of motor vehicles. Trying to hire and train new employees for all positions and at all levels of government would take months if not years. Additionally, disbanding the army (instead of using them in some type of security role and enforcing the rule of law) further exacerbates the problem. Disbanding the losing state's army creates a significant challenge since tens of thousands of young men are now unemployed, alienated, and have nothing but idle hands. "The United Nations has even expressed concern that rising numbers of Iraqi youths have been recruited into militias and insurgent groups."[25] Young men with no employment, living in decimated housing with garbage, standing sewage, and infestations, provide a terrific recruitment base for insurgents and jihadists. Someone living in these conditions has nothing to lose. After all, it is very easy to understand how someone living in abject, squalid conditions could enlist as an insurgent or turn to a life of crime in order to acquire scarce resources. Tactics such as young men quickly throwing grenades at occupation forces then fading back into a crowd of civilians "has been used in fighting before but takes on added significance as the

Americans have been trying to improve relations with the Iraqi public in a bid to stem support for the insurgency."[26] But it is quite impossible to improve relations when civilians live in squalid conditions and suffer due to a lack of resources.

If a legitimate war time end is to return to a peaceful *status quo* as Walzer mentioned,[27] but even more so to set the conditions for a just and lasting peace then steps need to be taken by the victor to ensure this. This belief of establishing a true and lasting peace as the only reason to fight is clear in Saint Augustine's letter *De Praesentia Dei Ep.* 187 (On the Presence of God: Letter 187) to General Boniface, which states that "[p]eace should be your aim; one does not pursue peace in order to wage war; he wages war to achieve peace."[28] What St. Augustine was referring to was not necessarily returning to the *status quo ante bellum* (because that situation actually led to war), but a true and lasting peace as the actual aim or end of war. That is, certain conditions need to be addressed and remedied in the postwar phase as a sincere attempt to instigate a peaceful relationship that is governed by what is reasonable and right.

Winning the hearts and minds of the civilians of the war-torn state is the best way to formulate meaningful reconciliation and establish peace, and the best way to accomplish such a task is by restoring basic services, providing physical security, preventing alienation of a group or groups, and expediting employment opportunities, which not only help the country return to a state of normalcy but also, by fulfilling such obligations, is a panacea by significantly reducing the insurgent recruitment base. Just as the victor has certain obligations (such as mitigating the harmful effects of war during the postwar phase because these harmful effects continue to kill noncombatants even though noncombatants are not supposed to have war waged against them), so does the international community.

THE INTERNATIONAL COMMUNITY'S RESPONSIBILITY

The international community should be responsible for the reformation of an outlaw political regime and its social institutions, as well as for monitoring the victor's behavior during the postwar occupation period. The political organization/government of an outlaw state must change, given evidence of its aggressiveness toward other states and/or its illegitimacy given its failings to its own citizens. If such a regime is permitted to survive following its military defeat, peace with other states may not be possible; rather, a multilateral organization such as the United Nations or other regional organizations or coalitions of states, representing the international community, should be the ultimate authority and oversee postwar implementation to ensure a transition of institutions as well as ensure that the victor fulfills its obligations to the civilians of the war-torn state.[29]

First, with no oversight except by the victor how can justice in the postwar phase be guaranteed, and if it becomes unjust what is the recourse? Regardless, if a state attacks another state without approval from the United Nations, the UN or other another multinational union may usurp control of the aftermath. By overseeing such an endeavor, a multinational partnership could ensure that the occupation is legitimate and not self-serving in that the vanquished state is not used for the victor's gains. To guarantee future legitimate occupations, the UN has to convince all countries, whether directly involved in the fighting or not, that it is inherently the responsibility of all independent states as members of the international community to oversee the postwar phase through the use of the United Nations or other multinational partnerships.

However, this is easier said than done. For example in the case of Iraq, neither did the UN demand that authority be relinquished to it, nor did U.S. officials want to relinquish authority. The U.S. State Department had mentioned that the UN had had a lot of experienced in postconflict situations and should be given a lead role in postwar Iraq, but this suggestion "was roundly rebuffed" by the U.S. National Security Council.[30]

The concern is that a hegemonic country having all the power and no oversight during the occupation could resist repairing essential infrastructure or force the vanquished into unfair contracts which provide kickbacks and favors to the victor's corporations, lobbying groups, government officials, or even misappropriation of funds because the victor cannot properly handle the sheer scope of the operation by itself. For example, the Special Inspector General for Iraq Reconstruction (SIGIR), Stuart Bowen, "has found serious weaknesses in the government's controls over Iraq reconstruction funds that put billions of American taxpayer dollars at risk of waste and misappropriation."[31] Additionally, SIGIR's "audit of a Department of State contract for Iraqi police training program found that more than $2.5 billion in US funds was vulnerable to fraud and waste as a result of poor Department of State oversight."[32] These large-scale financial endeavors seem quite problematic and overwhelming to a state that attempts to do everything itself, not to mention trying to coordinate contracts with new, underqualified, and inexperienced Iraqi government officials, since the former government officials were removed from their position of employment by the United States, which only compounded the problems. Additionally, a single country should not have the authority to take ownership of the complete overhaul of another state. The victor should not be involved in nation building. With this type of unilateral and unchecked power coupled with the removal of government employees, the victor not only has undue influence on the vanquished state but also compounds the difficulty of trying to alleviate the chaos that the war created.

Brian Orend suggests that the UN should be "both watchdog and junior partner."[33] I agree with Orend that the UN should not only be a watchdog, but even more so it or some other multinational partnership should be the supervening authority (not a junior partner) for all postwar situations. Just as the UN has defined the circumstances under which a country has the legitimate right to resort to armed conflict and how armies should fight according to the law of armed conflict, the UN should also define postwar obligations and responsibilities, which might then be measured and regulated by the UN or another multinational body operating with, hopefully, an unbiased approach in order to prevent the victor from implementing unfair contracts, imposing undue political influence, or wielding victor's justice.

Further, this should keep the postwar focus on the desired end state. A multilateral approach is also more beneficial because the outlaw regime will be assisted in reforming its political and social institutions in the way that the international community thinks is best instead of from the victor's unilateral perspective (allowing for self-determination and illiberal decent regimes versus coercive democratization). Additionally, a multilateral approach should lessen animosity toward the victor and occupation force on the part of not only the vanquished state but also the international community since the victor's role would be restricted to repair and security and not the institutional changes of the defeated state. After all, "[M]ultilateralism is more and more essential, not simply as a way to get others to share burdens, but also as a way to forge global arrangements that are essential to address global challenges such as the spread of nuclear weapons, terrorism, protectionism, disease, and climate change,"[34] and reconstruction of a war-torn state is not any different.

CONCLUSION

During his Nobel Peace Prize address, President Obama noted, "No matter how justified the cause, war promises human tragedy."[35] It may be true that war promises death, or as George Santayana states, "Only the dead have seen the end of war,"[36] but at least we can prevent the needless deaths of many innocent civilians by declaring that sates should be responsible for restoring essential services and providing physical security during the postwar phase. A step in the right direction is for states to be aware of the obligations even before any fighting starts. A significant reason for analyzing postwar requirements in the *jus ad bellum* phase is that this will, hopefully, shed light on what a state is responsible for even before a state invades or plans to invade another country. This is a huge endeavor, and it needs to be thought through and critically analyzed before any combat operations ever begin. It is way too late to think about *jus post bellum* requirements once the enemy has capitulated. I believe that by incorporating postwar considerations into a state's reasonable chance of success calculation, it forces the state to be mindful of such demands before it finds itself in the postwar phase with no sense of direction or that it somehow believed that it is not accountable for postwar civilian deaths.

The tenet of reasonable chance of success is more demanding than just war gaming military strategies to see what might be successful. Rather, it should include the obligations that the victor has during the postwar phase. Success not only includes the fighting phase but the postwar phase as well. A state can only say that it has a reasonable chance of success by first identifying all demands then leveraging assets against them in order to determine if it can be successful. Doing so forces a state to explore preliminary considerations for postwar operations before shots are even fired.

It could be the case that the country resorting to war determines that they cannot achieve all that is morally required to do. Maybe this is a good thing. This might send those leaders back to the drawing board—so to speak. Maybe then politicians and statesmen can determine that there are other viable elements of national power regarding flexible deterrent courses of action (diplomatic, economic, and/or informational or a combination of these) besides a military solution that ultimately can achieve what is needed. Or at least the scale of military operations might be more limited in order to accomplish what is absolutely essential and nothing more. "To say that force may sometimes be necessary is not a call to cynicism—it is a recognition of history: the imperfections of man and the limits of reason."[37]

Further recognition of history is the fact that the postwar phase can be just as debilitating for the civilians of a beleaguered nation. In order to mitigate these inherent harms and residual effects of war, the scale, duration, and intensity of the conflict should be limited to the minimum necessary in that "[t]he means have to be commensurate with the ends, and in line with the original provocation"[38] in order not to produce more harm than not going to war would have. Sensible steps must be taken during the postwar phase to ensure that the postwar phase does not become a moral mess. Furthermore, a truly multilateral force like the UN or maybe another type of international partnership must have ultimate authority in postwar operations. First, in order to ensure the victor complies with its obligations, and second that a multilateral approach to reforming decrepit political and social institutions is the best way to foster any type of peaceful *status quo* as a legitimate wartime end.

3

Post Bellum Obligations of Noncombatant Immunity

War has three distinct phases: prewar, war, and postwar. Within the just war tradition the postwar period has received the least amount of attention. However, over the past decade a groundswell of discussion of the postwar phase has occurred. But, as of yet, no set of moral principles about how previously warring parties should conduct themselves has been agreed upon.

However, the legitimate wartime ends of resisting unjust aggression, reasonably preventing future aggression, and establishing a just and lasting peace[1] will inform any plausible account of the principles of justice after war (*jus post bellum*). But before moving solely into the *post bellum* phase and looking at norms that are relevant to only the postwar phase, we need to look at the norm of right intention. The aforementioned legitimate wartime ends specify not only going to war with right intention but also fighting with right intention, as well as rebuilding relationships with right intention. The norm of right intention runs through all three phases of war. By having right intention, a state must not only have a just cause and limit its war-making activity to that necessary to vindicate the just cause, but it must also seek to vindicate its just cause in a manner likely to yield a just and lasting peace. That is, there are constraints that follow from aiming at a just and lasting peace that entails a commitment to civilian immunity to the idea that civilian immunity has, for dual purpose targeting, some *post bellum* implications. Therefore, we should explore the *post bellum* (postwar) implications of the *ad bellum* (of war) and *in bello* (in war) commitments before we move too far with *post bellum* thinking to distinctly *post bellum* norms, which are germane to only the postwar phase.[2]

I will argue that a just state unjustly attacked and justly defending itself, acting with right intention, has an obligation to restore infrastructure destroyed as part of targeting dual purpose facilities if the damage done threatens core human rights. This obligation has not been adequately addressed and so needs full articulation. A liberal democracy victorious in a war justly fought against an unjust aggressor state has an obligation to the citizens of the unjust aggressor, even if the liberal democracy tried reasonably to honor necessity and proportionality targeting requirements, *ex ante*. The impact on civilians in a war zone—given the empirical facts of modern warfare—extends well beyond the cessation of hostilities even if the just war is fought justly.

Granted, some wars end inconclusively, with neither adversary occupying the other—a paradigm case is the Korean War. Other wars end with one adversary winning but not occupying the other adversary—a paradigm case is the first Gulf war. There are many that don't involve occupation and regime change. I believe that it can be suggested in both of these paradigm cases that the rights that were violated by the aggressor state had been vindicated to an extent but for other compounding reasons there wasn't an occupation and regime change. In the former paradigm case, UN Forces responded to North Korean forces' acts of aggression against South Korean forces. The Korean War raged for two years followed by a stalemate, and an armistice was signed between the two states in 1953. And in the later paradigm case, coalition forces pushed Iraqi forces out of its unjust occupation of Kuwait as well as destroyed Iraq's military offensive capability as it was attempting to withdraw into Iraq.

The 1950 Korean case and the 1991 Iraqi case are important to discuss. However, my focus for this chapter is different. In the imagined case that I will discuss, the unjust aggressor state has surrendered and the just victor has an occupation force. The occupation force will be used to enforce the rule of law, to assist with restabilizing basic necessities, and to help implement a regime change or with the rehabilitation of decrepit institutions. I recognize that many conflicts and wars do not have an occupation force. However, the United States had an occupation force in its two most recent conflicts, in Iraq and Afghanistan. Iraq surrendered after only six weeks of major combat operations, but the postwar phase, which included a U.S. occupation force, lasted more than eight years.

The shortcomings of how the United States initially planned and the executed its postwar plan is what caused the groundswell of discussion regarding the postwar phase and its resurgence in just war theory. Prior to the 2003 Iraq war, contemporary just war theory focused primarily on the *ad bellum* and *in bello* phase that is evidenced by Michael Walzer's *Just and Unjust Wars* (one of the most influential contemporary just war theory books), which does not even address the postwar phase except to note that there are three legitimate wartime ends: resist aggression, restore the peaceful *status quo*, and reasonably prevent future aggression.[3] Although an occupation force will not be the case in every war, it is important to discuss situations like these, since conflicts like those in Iraq and Afghanistan are occurring, hopefully by shedding light on such cases, states will not only recognize their *post bellum* obligations but also better plan and implement in order to meet their moral obligations.

Adhering to the *jus in bello* principle of noncombatant immunity, which is part of fighting with right intention, imposes significant *jus post bellum* obligations. Belligerents must fulfill certain reconstruction obligations *ex post* even though those obligations arise really as a matter of *jus in bello* civilian immunity norms. Fighting with right intention would entail a more robust account of securing human rights, and provides some of the impetus for the idea that a victor should repair necessary infrastructure. I am not arguing for any new norms, but rather for a new requirement imposed in order to respect the core human rights of civilians, which the principle of noncombatant immunity already recognizes.

Immunizing civilians from harms that threaten human rights fits into any plausible account of what the principle of noncombatant immunity requires. More specifically, belligerents are required to restore damaged dual use facilities to a level adequate to secure human rights even if the *ex ante* targeting was necessary and proportionate, etc. Not only does the new requirement render compliance with the existing norm much more likely than it would otherwise be (or has been), but also abiding by this requirement shows a commitment to a just society of peoples oriented around human rights and peaceful, respectful international relations, etc.

The following is a seven-section analysis of noncombatant immunity and its *post bellum* implications. The first two sections detail the distinction between combatants and noncombatants and the link between noncombatant immunity and human rights. The third section demonstrates that destroying dual purpose facilities is detrimental to the civilian populace, and, therefore, requires special treatment. The fourth section shows that the destruction of purely military targets may also kill civilians, but these types of targets do not cause residual effects on civilians and so do not require special treatment. The two sections that follow advance the point that belligerents have an obligation to ensure that the human rights of their enemy's civilian populations are not compromised after hostilities are over because of damage it inflicted on dual use facilities, and that routine *ex post* independent review of all decisions to target dual use facilities needs to be instituted with followup to assure that facilities have been restored. The final section distinguishes between a belligerent's primary obligations regarding noncombatant immunity and other states' backup obligations regarding human rights.

THE DISTINCTION BETWEEN COMBATANTS AND NONCOMBATANTS

From both an international law and just war standpoint, there are two distinct classes of persons during war: combatants and noncombatants.[4] Soldiers are authorized to kill and liable to be killed by enemy combatants. Soldiers have a collective identity and represent the political entity for which they fight. As Michael Walzer states, "War itself isn't a relation between persons but between political entities and their human instruments."[5] Soldiers acting on behalf of their state attempt to impose the will of their country upon the enemy. Whether actively shooting at the enemy, sleeping on their cots, or driving trucks, soldiers are viable targets, and an enemy soldier is morally and legally permitted to kill them.[6] "The claim is that if a soldier is morally justified in killing a person in war, that is usually because the other person has acted in a way that has made him liable to be killed."[7] Although combatants are allowed to be killed, refusing quarter to those that wish to surrender, causing injury to soldiers who have surrendered, and causing unnecessary suffering (e.g., by using weapons such as lances with barbed heads, irregular-shaped bullets, projectiles filled with glass, and poisons) are strictly forbidden.

Soldiers are authorized to kill because they are given power rights that enable them "to act in a way that makes them morally liable to defensive violence."[8] Although combatants have power rights to kill enemy combatants, this authorization to kill is not extended to the point that it allows civilians to be intentionally killed. Rather, civilians do not occupy a recognized combatant role within the war convention because they neither pose a direct or current threat to others, nor have they been officially designated as an official organ of the state.[9] Because they are "non-combatants and do not themselves pose a direct threat to others, they are never legitimate targets of force."[10] Civilians have immunity rights and are not only exempt from being intentionally targeted, but should also be immune from the effects of war as best as possible.[11]

Noncombatant immunity (the right to life and liberty) is a necessary feature of just war and a norm binding on belligerents. Regardless whether a state enters justly or unjustly into armed conflict, it does not forgo the noncombatant immunity of its citizens.[12] Article 27 (Part III: Status and Treatment of Protected Persons) of the Fourth Geneva Convention states, "Protected persons [noncombatants/civilians] are entitled, in all circumstances, to respect for their persons, their honor, their family rights, their religious conviction and practices, and their manner and customs; they shall at all times be humanely treated, and shall be protected especially against all acts of violence or threats thereof and against insults and public curiosity."[13]

Noncombatant immunity entitles civilians to a level of protection of more than just their basic human rights (e.g., respecting religious conviction and practices, honoring manners and customs, and barring threats and insults). Belligerents acting in accord with what the principle of noncombatant immunity demands would not only have to protect civilians from the harms of war but also make special efforts to avoid harming their places of worship, museums, hospitals, schools, buildings that house charities, and monuments.

HUMAN RIGHTS

Although the perspective that all persons have the right to a social minimum (the realization of basic human rights) is not universally recognized, it is widely recognized. There is widespread agreement over basic human rights to subsistence, physical security, and certain basic liberties. Human rights consist of a combination of both positive and negative dimensions of rights that necessarily entail each other. Human rights can be given any number of deep philosophical, moral, or religious justifications. For example, a naturalistic account of humanity "as such" approach; James Griffin's autonomy, minimum provisions, and liberty approach; Immanuel Kant's unconditional dignity and respect of persons approach; etc. I wish to remain agnostic to these particular groundings. The Rawlsian position does not aspire to give any deep grounding for human rights.

Rather, they are part of global/international public reason and as such enjoy the support of an overlapping consensus between well-ordered peoples, liberal democratic or otherwise. That is, basic human rights are so foundational to a person's existence (food, water, shelter, security, and bodily autonomy) that regardless of what religion, philosophy, or doctrine a person subscribes to, there is a lot of consensus and recognition of the necessity of these basic human rights regardless of whether the belief for this being the case is constituted through inalienable privileges, God-given rights, beliefs of dignity and worth, or by a practical political creation. Human rights just are valid claims to social guarantees against standard threats to certain goods, so the absence of the social guarantee just is the violation/failure to secure the human right in question. The fulfillment of these rights is necessary in order to reasonably safeguard persons from standard threats that would otherwise impinge upon the necessary conditions needed for any attempt at an adequate life. Without a social guarantee (a government-implemented base requirement of necessary infrastructure, e.g., police, medical, food and water access, rule of law) against standard threats, one's enjoyment of basic human rights will be significantly jeopardized. These valid claims to social guarantees against standard threats to certain goods (not only adequate food, water, shelter, and clothing but protection from harm and access to medical care) do not change when states are at war. That is, the circumstances of war do not negate civilians' entitlement to this social minimum.[14]

The principle of civilian immunity is interpreted through the standard of basic human rights. That noncombatants should be immunized from the activity of war can be taken for granted. While civilians are to be held immune from war and its effects, not all effects are equal: those that threaten or violate basic human rights are especially problematic because they undercut the social guarantees that protect civilians against standard threats. So while civilians are to be immune from many effects of war, the most important effects they are to be immune from are those effects that threaten their basic human rights.

All civilians need to be able to make free decisions and choices under conditions that are free of fear, insecurity, strife, hopelessness, and hunger. But in a war-torn state where food, drinking water, medical attention, and physical security are luxuries, it is not possible to live in any state of normalcy. In these deleterious conditions, persons are dominated or controlled by external factors that violate their core human rights. It is obvious that war threatens the basic human rights of those civilians who are located in the state where the war is being fought. Civilians subjected to the devastation of war cannot adequately develop, express, or follow any rational plan for survival until physical infrastructure and social services are restored to a threshold level that secures basic human rights (physical security, subsistence, basic liberties) and enables civilians to live instead of merely exist.

Although noncombatant immunity entitles civilians to protection of more than just their basic human rights (e.g., respecting religious conviction and practices, honoring manners and customs, and barring threats and insults), civilians need to be immunized from costs that compromise their basic human rights, and that means that they must be left not only with potable water, food, shelter, access to medical attention, sewage and trash removal, etc., but also with a state that can effectively secure those rights for them. Without securing core human rights first, nothing else can reasonably follow.

Before any other rights can be secured, core human rights need to be safeguarded, first in order to protect civilians from standard threats and harms. However, conventional military strategies—ones that focus on destroying dual purpose facilities as a way to undermine the enemy state and its army—affect the basic human rights of noncombatants. My main underlying concern is that if civilians are supposed to be immune from the harmful effects of war, then they should be immune from the harmful effects of war as best as possible. However, this does not happen when dual purpose facilities are targeted.

DUAL PURPOSE TARGETS

Although the laws of war declare the utmost protection of civilians, in modern wars more civilians have died than soldiers. This has been the case in World War II (not even including the Holocaust), the Vietnam conflict, the Persian Gulf war, the second Iraq war, and the current conflict in Afghanistan. Over the past century, tens of millions of civilians have been killed in warfare. Even in the twenty-first century, conservative estimates suggest that civilian deaths in war are at least five time those of soldiers. Overwhelmingly, these high death rates (in the wars over the past ten years) are not from civilians being intentionally targeted by military forces but from the residual effects of which many stem from the targeting of dual purpose facilities. Civilians die as an effect of otherwise permissible conduct in war. That is, many die because of indirect effects of conduct that does not obviously violate civilian immunity.

Civilians die as a consequence of military necessity and legitimate acts of war. Legitimate acts of war, although not directed at civilians, kill them just the same. "A legitimate act of war is one that doesn't violate the rights of the people against whom it is directed."[15] An intentional attack against an enemy combatant is allowed because it does not violate the rights of that soldier, because he or she is liable to be killed. However, civilians are killed as side effects to legitimate acts of war. Specifically, what I am referring to are dual purpose (dual use) targets. According to the international law of armed conflict, "combatants, and those objects which by their nature, location, purpose, or use make an effective contribution to military action and whose total or partial destruction, capture or neutralization, in circumstances ruling at the time, offers a definite military advantage—are permissible objects to attack (including bombardment)."[16] For example, a bridge could be deemed a dual purpose legitimate military objective that belligerents are legally allowed to destroy because its *location* is pivotal in resupplying enemy troops or by its very *nature* (bridge qua bridge) it is designed to enable movement of (military) traffic from one location to another, so it can legally be destroyed. On a side note, museums, places of worship, and hospitals are protected buildings. It is not legally permissible to target protected buildings. Even if soldiers are being treated and triaged at a particular hospital, it is still not a permissible target because those soldiers have been incapacitated. By being incapacitated, they have lost their combatant status and are no longer liable to be killed. On another note, although a building can lose its protected status if a belligerent uses it for a military purpose, it is still best (if possible) not to attack such a building because of the enemy's propaganda and media exploitation that will follow from it.

Just as the name suggests, dual purpose targets serve dual purposes: generating plants provide electricity for residential use, but they also provide electricity for an army's command and control centers and barracks. Destroying a belligerent nation's infrastructure (oil and fuel depots, communication centers, electric grids, transportation networks, and factories that contribute to the war effort) is, in theory, supposed to induce the enemy to capitulate faster because its center of gravity has been crushed since its communication network, infrastructure, and resupply capacity have been crippled.

Although it seems reasonable to suggest that hostility should be focused directly at the object that is actually causing the harm (such as enemy soldiers and their tanks, planes, and cannons), this is not always the case in modern warfare.[17] Modern war takes place in and around cities, and populated areas provide essential features/facilities (power grids, road and rail networks, radio towers, etc.) that enable a state's war fighting abilities. These facilities are permissible targets since they contribute to military activity. However, it does seem as if attacking dual purpose facilities is not directing "one's hostility or aggression at its proper object, but at a peripheral target which may be more vulnerable, and through which the proper object can be attacked indirectly."[18] Bombing dual use facilities is seen as an opportunity or as an easier path to one's goal. A belligerent is, obviously, not required to bomb dual purpose facilities yet chooses to do so for the expected military advantage to be gained by it. Along with the usual considerable advantage to be gained by destroying dual purpose facilities, belligerents risk taking too permissive a stance toward the targeting of these facilities.

Belligerents bomb dual purpose facilities as a way to bring about certain results and can do so as long as they abide by the war convention and apply the concepts of necessity and proportionality. There has to be a military necessity—a need, not a desire (that is, these facilities must have a clear military use even if they also have civilian uses)—in order to engage specific targets; for example, radio stations and radio cell site/base station towers could qualify as military necessity because (if destroyed) it cripples internal military communication between forces. Attacks on these structures are supposed to meet the requirements of proportionality in order to mitigate harm and collateral damage.[19] "Loss of life and damage to property incidental to attacks must not be excessive in relation to the concrete and direct military advantage expected to be gained."[20] But shock and awe campaigns, although legal, invoke serious moral issues. The side effects of attacking the belligerent's infrastructure only become exacerbated over time.

The end of major combat operations does not necessarily entail that the death and dying for noncombatants is over. The devastation from the war phase carries over to the postwar phase. The residual effects of warfare continue to harm the civilians long after the fighting stops, and months later civilians continue to die as a result of inadequate living conditions. For example, "by the end of 1992 [after Operation Desert Storm], more than a hundred thousand Iraqi civilians died from the lack of clean water and sewage disposal, and the breakdown of electrical service to hospitals."[21]

A frayed or nonexistent defeated government coupled with inadequate, decimated city services will neither be able to enforce the rule of law nor prevent residual deaths, because it cannot reasonably safeguard its citizens from standard threats to basic human rights. However, noncombatants are supposed to be insulated against the ills of war because, "Noncombatants, whatever their political affiliation, have the right not to have war waged on them,"[22] but this seems farthest from the reality of the situation in a war-torn state.

The just war concepts of proportionality and necessity are essential in modern warfare because modern war is fought in and around cities; the battles of yore—where standing armies met in an open, unpopulated area—are gone. The concepts of military necessity and proportionality are used in order to reconcile conducting legitimate acts of war with the absolute proscription against intentionally targeting civilians.

However, in the context of war, it may not be enough just to have a moral and legal principle of civilian immunity and a moral and legal principle allowing for the targeting of dual use facilities when proportionality and necessity criteria are met. The empirical evidence suggests a need for institutional restrictions, because the costs to civilian immunity and the incentives to abuse the permission to target dual use facilities may be too high if we do not frame the legal permission to target dual use facilities with something like demanding more accountability from belligerents. The current way of thinking allows states to target many civilian facilities provided that they can point to some military use or justifying connection to military use.[24]

The reasons to single out dual use facilities for special treatment are twofold: (1) targeting them presents a special risk of allowing war activities to slip beyond the range of conventional military targets, to spill over to the civilian sector. States might willingly aim at key civilian installations, citing a theoretical military use as a cover to legitimize their shock and awe campaign. If such targeting is to be allowed to continue, we need to place specific heavy restrictions (*ex post* stipulations) in order to justify making them targets. After all, we need to restrict the activities of war to recognized role players and recognized sites of conflict if we hope to avoid a descent into some sort of no-holds-barred chaos. (2) Dual use targeting presents a special risk of miscalculation when it comes to the proportionality criterion, for the long term (residual) effects on civilians will almost always be more substantial than is expected. These miscalculations enable too permissive a stance regarding the bombing of dual purpose facilities as if they were nearly purely military in nature. That is, the importance of their civilian use is often sidelined and downgraded in order to conclude that the dual purpose facilities should be targeted and destroyed.

PURELY MILITARY VERSUS DUAL PURPOSE TARGETS

Jeff McMahan states, "Sometimes an agent acts with objective moral justification but nevertheless threatens to inflict wrongful harm on an innocent person—that is, harm that would wrong the victim, or contravene his or her rights."[24] A tactical bomber that drops a bomb on an important enemy military facility (e.g., an army headquarters, military vehicle motor pool, munitions factory, etc.) and in the process kills civilians (although unintentionally) is an example of what McMahan refers to as a *justified threat*. In such a case, McMahan argues that legitimate acts of war (that meet the criteria of military necessity and proportionality) override those civilians' noncombatant immunity rights. The tactical bomber pilot is a justified threat to civilians and is "morally justified in acting in a way that infringes the rights of an innocent person as a foreseen but unintended effect."[25]

Suppose that the military planners and pilot of the aircraft know that by bombing a military facility they will inevitably kill some innocent civilians who live nearby. However, they also know that the number of noncombatant deaths is proportionate "in relation to the importance of destroying the facility."[26] In this case, the planners and pilot are objectively morally justified (they are considered to be a justified threat to those civilians) although they kill civilians who have done nothing to forfeit their right not to be killed. The tactical bomber pilot justifiably threatens noncombatants because the important military facility was permissible to attack, and there was no other plausible way to successfully neutralize this facility except to bomb it. McMahan notes that this is a familiar example in "debates about the doctrine of double effect."[27] In deciding to bomb it, the military advantage realized is sufficiently large to justify the foreseeable (but unintended) death of a small number of innocent civilians. The collateral damage (causing foreseen but unintended damage) will be proportionate to the overall good of destroying the military target.

Although discussing these types of examples is important, it does not adequately get to the heart of the matter. McMahan discusses the bombing of important military facilities but does not deliberate about the bombing of dual purpose, facilities although he notes that "it is important to identify the considerations that would be relevant in war."[28] One of the considerations that is absolutely important to identify as relevant in war is dual purpose targeting and destruction. Because the destruction of dual purpose facilities presents special problems, our discussion on bombing must evolve and incorporate the significant issues surrounding dual purpose targeting instead of lumping all bombing together and pointing to the doctrine of double effect as a way to alleviate any culpability regarding legitimate military targets.

Bombing a target that only has a military purpose (such as a munitions plant) will inevitably (depending on what the target is) have foreseeable harms. A munitions plant does not provide any purpose to the civilian sector such as a rail network or electrical grid does. Sure, it employs civilians, but the facility itself is not needed by the civilian population. Therefore, I refer to such a facility as only having a military purpose. The factory makes bullets and bombs in order to arm its country's military so that they can shoot at the enemy.

Bombing a munitions factory would probably kill civilian factory workers and possibly those civilians who happened to be in close proximity to the blast radius. However, bombing a target that served *both* military and civilian purposes, has not only foreseeable but also residual and even unforeseen harms. The destruction of a dual use facility is liable to kill civilians who are in the neighborhood of the intended target, as well as the civilians who actually work at the facility, but beyond that will cause residual effects to civilians long after the dual use facility was bombed. Plenty of empirical evidence suggests that destroying dual use facilities (specifically those facilities that contribute to and or secure core human rights) continues to cause harm and kill civilians long after the bombing and even the war is over. Second and third order (residual) effects will plague the civilian population until the facility is repaired. When the long-term effects of targeting a dual use facility involve a threat to the human rights of civilians, then special requirements apply.

Dual use target strategies are a mainstay in the bombing campaigns of the twenty-first century, because this strategy destabilizes a state's ability to wage war by destroying or impairing transportation networks, electrical grids, radio towers, oil refineries, fuel depots, industry, etc. But we must also recognize a way to most effectively try to compensate for dual purpose facility destruction, since it has lingering effects on civilians more so than the enemy military force for which the target was deemed legitimate to destroy in the first place.

It is one thing to suggest that civilians' rights during war can be overridden if certain conditions are met (legitimate act of war, proportionate, military necessity, urgency of the situation, military advantage to be gained, justified threat, etc.). However, it is quite another thing to suggest that civilians can be continually harmed even after the war is over. For example, a tactical bomber pilot can be a justified threat to civilians working at a munitions plant because at the moment when the pilot attempts to destroy the factory those civilians who will be threatened and most likely harmed and even killed is proportionate and, therefore, acceptable collateral damage to the military advantage that will be gained by destroying the munitions factory. That is, those civilians are allowed to be threatened, even killed, because there is a military advantage to destroying the factory and denying bullets to one's enemy.

However, in the case of bombing a dual purpose facility, it *cannot* be the case that a tactical bomber pilot is not only a justified threat to civilians when he attacks the facility but that those civilians are then continually justifiably threatened not only throughout the war but after the war is over as well. It seems odd and immoral to suggest that civilians can continually be justifiably threatened by an act even after the war is over because at one point during the war the tactical bomber pilot was a justified threat to the civilians in or around the facility at the moment of the bombing.

Once the enemy capitulates, soldiers no longer have the right to kill enemy soldiers. That is, soldiers can longer be considered a *just threat*. I am using Jeff McMahan's terminology here. A just threat is one in which a person is "objectively morally justified in posing a threat of harm to which the potential victim is morally liable."[29] In other words, the just threat is the threat justly posed, that is, a soldier poses a just threat to an enemy soldier. "The harm that a just threat would inflict would neither wrong the victim nor infringe his or her rights."[30] If there is no longer a just threat, then there is no longer an objective moral justification, which means that a tactical bomber pilot can no longer be a justified threat to civilians, either. However, it seems as if he still is, because his actions during the war still continue to harm and kill civilians long after the dual purpose facility was destroyed.

After the war ends, it is no longer permissible to inflict harm on civilians as an unintended side effect, but decisions that were made during the war continue to effect civilians just the same. Destroying dual use facilities (ones that are essential to safeguarding basic human rights) continues to harm civilians during the postwar phase when there is not any permissibility to override the rights of noncombatants. Failing to repair destroyed dual purpose facilities *ex post* denies civilians their rights to life and liberty, which are the two main entitlements bestowed upon civilians and commonly referred to as noncombatant immunity.

My point is that when the destruction of dual use facilities threatens or violates noncombatants' basic human rights, two special obligations to correct that situation arise: (1) recognition of a state's obligation to ensure that the human rights of its enemy's civilian population will not be compromised after hostilities have ceased, and (2) routine *ex post* independent review of all decisions to target dual use facilities. The first obligation (when fulfilled) insulates civilians from the harms of war, and the second obligation (when fulfilled) holds belligerents accountable if they unreasonably subordinated proportionality to military necessity, and assures that repairs will be accomplished.[31]

EX POST OBLIGATION: BELLIGERENTS SHOULD IMMUNIZE CIVILIANS FROM RESIDUAL EFFECTS

Although military necessity and proportionality are obligatory criteria that need to be met before bombing of a facility is conducted, these two criteria allow for latitude and interpretation. Attacking dual purpose targets is a contested matter from a moral perspective, but it can also be contested from a legal perspective. There is a lot of gray area in the law when determining if a dual purpose target has met the *nature, use, location, or purpose* conditions and if, in fact, the military advantage to be gained actually outweighed the incidental harm to noncombatants.

Given these difficulties in making and monitoring proportionality judgments at the front end, there are good reasons to not only affirm an *ex post* obligation to cover certain costs of targeting dual use facilities but also to hold belligerents accountable for their proportionality determinations.[32]

Buchanan and Keohane believe that because unilateral actions can be problematic under international law in the absence of *ex post* accountability, the key to authorizing force is that "accountability operates both *ex ante* and *ex post*."[33] In similar fashion, the key to bombing dual purpose facilities is accountability that also operates both *ex ante* and *ex post*. There is a standing need for *ex post* accountability given the undesirability of *ex ante* authorization (which is usually determined while trying to account for incomplete data, the fog of war, etc.). The only way we can say that attacking a dual purpose target is morally permissible is if in addition to the criteria of proportionality and necessity, belligerents must protect civilians from the residual effects of war.

In order to allow the targeting of dual use facilities, specific restrictions (*ex post* stipulations) need to be placed on the belligerents that destroy dual purpose facilities. Imposing *ex post* stipulations helps contain the activities of war instead of allowing it to spill over unnecessarily into the civilian sector. Once hostilities are over, belligerents should be held accountable for repairing the destroyed dual purpose facilities (electrical generating plants, railroad junctions, bridges) that enable the protection of civilians from standard threats such as a lack of or access to food, water, and shelter, which violate basic human rights.[34] These obligations on the part of a victor are fully consistent with *jus post bellum* considerations rooted in right intention aimed at a just and lasting peace. Surely, a victor will be committed to a lasting and just peace rooted in respect for human rights, etc., and acting in a way that (by restoring damaged dual purpose facilities if the damage threatens the human rights of civilians) will advance this end. If anything, fulfilling this obligation makes the occupation force more palatable to the defeated state. Repairing dual purpose facilities would help set the conditions toward reconciliation.

The victor should repair such facilities not to the level that is consistent with restitution (restoring what has been lost back to the *status quo ante*) but to the level that is consistent with reparations (not restoring it to the original condition, but to the good enough condition).

Dual purpose targets (those that help secure core human rights) should be repaired (to a level that is good enough) although not necessarily to the *status quo ante* level, but just to meet the minimum necessary standard to secure the physical security, subsistence, and basic liberty rights of civilians.

For example, if a bridge (located along a major highway) had been targeted and destroyed, that bridge would either be repaired or a new one erected, if that bridge was necessary to sustain the basic human rights of some of the civilian populace, for instance, if it provided the only access to a hospital or to a well. The requirements for the repaired bridge would only have to meet the "good enough standard," that is, it would have to support traffic, but not at the maximum tonnage allowances are necessary for military capabilities (the moving of tanks), even though the original bridge had met those standards. If a power grid were destroyed, the whole grid would not have to be built anew, but simply repaired or rebuilt sufficiently that it might adequately provide electricity to hospitals, shelters, kitchens, government buildings, etc. Beyond this point, it would be up to the host state to do more. That is, the belligerent who destroyed these facilities would just assist the defeated state to get back on its feet (by repairing destroyed dual use facilities in order to prevent more unnecessary deaths to civilians) as the defeated state starts to rebuild.

Civilians should be protected against threats to their basic human rights, which means that they should not only have access to potable water, food, shelter, physical security, sewage and trash removal, and medical attention, but a government apparatus that can effectively secure those rights for them and assure that courts, police precincts (which enable the rule of law), markets, etc. will be operational. Disbanding the civil service of a state will be detrimental to any attempt to secure core human rights of the people of that state, because civil service employees run city, state, and federal levels of government. Without them a vacuum is created in which government systems cannot function. A victor committed to ensuring the rights of civilians within the state it has defeated, as well as a just and lasting peace, must not leave them without these institutional prerequisites. That is, noncombatant immunity entails immunity from residual effects, and aiming at a just and lasting peace entails ensuring that civilians have the institutions and resources necessary to guarantee basic human rights. That means more than just repairing government buildings, bridges, electrical grids, etc. Upon the cessation of hostilities, a defeated state will not be able to accomplish this restoration rapidly or effectively without the assistance of the victor.

Even if the state with destroyed dual use facilities had been the unjust aggressor and has the resources to repair its own facilities, the state that destroyed them must offer to repair or pay for the damages if the facilities that were destroyed are needed to secure core human rights. Doing so is consistent with right intention. Not only fighting with constraint but also limiting harm to civilians by carrying out or at least offering to pay for repairs is a necessary condition for establishing a lasting peace with justice. Doing so has the potential to facilitate reconciliation and trust between the warring parties as both states work through the postwar phase together.

In addition, there is an obligation to repair targeted dual use facilities even when the targeting satisfied necessity and proportionality criteria that included allowance for residual effects on civilians. For example, a bridge that the enemy crosses during a counterattack meets military necessity and proportionality criteria (including residual effects) and may justifiably be destroyed. The bomber pilot is a justified threat to the civilians in the area of the bridge while it is under bombardment. However, after that attack and after the war, civilians who previously used that bridge to reach the local hospital might be no longer able to reach the hospital without traveling ten miles out of their way to the nearest surviving bridge.

Although this was not only a legitimate dual purpose target but also met proportionality (to include residual effects) and necessity guidelines at the time of the bombing, a belligerent should repair that bridge after the war to the extent that allows local civilians access to their hospital. Necessary and proportionate military action poses a justified threat to civilians, but this should only be the case during the time of the war, not after. The bridge was a justified target at the time of the bombing, but after the war the bridge's destruction continually impairs civilians' chances of obtaining medical attention. And once the war is over it is no longer acceptable or justifiable to inflict harm on civilians as an unintended side effect because of a decision that was made during the war. In the postwar phase, a tactical bomber pilot can no longer be excused as a justified threat, because the war is over. However, the destruction that the pilot justifiably caused in the midst of war continues to harm civilians in the postwar phase, when such damage can no longer be claimed to be acceptable or justifiable.

Although the victor should be held morally accountable for repairing dual purpose destruction that it caused, this does not suggest that the victor is responsible for fixing the aggressor state back to the *status quo ante*. Belligerents do not have the obligation to cover the costs of destroyed infrastructure that was not essential to safeguarding core human rights. Of course, history is dotted with such cases where the victor has rebuilt, even transformed, the government of the unjust state, but this falls outside the parameters of what is morally owed by the victor to the vanquished. Many of these endeavors—where the victor rebuilt the vanquished—were based on prudential considerations and a nation-building ideology but not moral stipulations. Nation building, securing economic privileges, or using land as a power projection platform for one's own troops are beneficial to the victor, but these are not morally necessary undertakings.

It could very well be the case that by just "repairing" basic infrastructure necessary for securing core human rights instead of restoring it to the *status quo ante* civilians' quality of life will likely be much less than it was before the war. That is, the extent of nonbasic rights that these civilians enjoyed before the war will be curtailed after the war. There is a worry, though, that a victor that does not restore infrastructure, etc., to more or less the *status quo ante* will risk enmity from civilians who, when faced with the choice between blaming their own leaders or blaming another country for their losses may be all too easily baited into blaming another country. Just because the civilian populace blames the just victor for its decimated condition, it does not suggest that more is required than repairing infrastructure that protects civilians from standard threats to core human rights. However, setting the stage for a just and lasting peace, the victor might have to do more than required on account of the civilian immunity norm. Postwar norms associated with reconciliation might require more than just rebuilding dual purpose facilities and basic institutions to a level that is just "good enough" in order to assist a state return to its *status quo ante* as well as attenuate the animosity of the populace.

On another note, in a different imagined scenario, it might be the case that civilians of the unjust aggressor state did not enjoy basic human rights before the war. Maybe this outlaw regime funneled all of its money into its military and neglected its citizens' right to have a social minimum (a government implemented infrastructure that provides the rule of law, medical treatment, food and water access, shelter, and sewage and trash removal). In such a case, whatever dual purpose facilities that the just victor destroyed would have to be returned to the *status quo ante*, because even returning it to this level (*status quo ante*) is still subpar with a social minimum. Returning it to anything less than those civilians already had *ex ante* is clearly wrong because it would decrease the already inadequate capacity of that state. Human rights norms should require more from not only the victor but also the international community as the backup obligor for securing core human rights.

Larry May posits that it seems unfair to hold victors responsible for restitution and reparations; this is an undue burden. May advocates a compensation fund and proposes a "world-wide-no-fault insurance scheme," like a no fault insurance policy, from which these restoration costs would be paid. This fund would disconnect paying the costs from the question of "fault" because all states (victor, vanquished, and bystander) would pay into this fund. May states, "All parties in a war have equal responsibilities of restitution or reparations whether they were defenders or aggressors during the war."[35] May further goes on to say, "All States are complicit in war and no States can be fully said to be without fault concerning the ravages of war or mass atrocity."[36]

Although I empathize with May's attempt to develop a fund that could be used to facilitate war-torn states, I do not agree with his perspective that holding victors responsible for restitution and reparations seems unfair because it is an undue burden. States committed to setting conditions for a just and lasting peace have an obligation to repair certain infrastructure (dual use facilities that safeguard core human rights). This might be a burden on the victor but it is not an undue burden. Although this places a burden on belligerents to repair the damage *ex post* that they caused, it is warranted. Belligerents do not have to destroy dual use facilities that affect the basic human rights of the civilian population but choose to do so for the advantage to be gained. Holding belligerents accountable by incorporating an *ex post* commitment to repairing dual use facilities is fair and reasonable.

Second, on another note, maybe as a way to have all states agree to a compensation fund, we do not propose that all states are complicit in war. In some fashion we can say that states such as Switzerland, Finland, and Luxemburg, etc. have been complicit (at varying levels) in war, especially during the Middle Ages. But I think that in order to get all states to agree to contributing to a compensation fund we should approach it from a different perspective such as one that comes with realizing that our world is faced with many nonideal situations and some of those situations will inevitably lead to war. That being the case, then collectively all states should contribute to a fund that allocates reparation monies that can be used to help rebuild states that have been devastated by war as a way to help those states rebuild, secure basic human rights, and establish conditions for a just and lasting peace. This way, we do not universally place blame on all states for their warring nature. Rather, we recognize that a system is necessary, so states contribute financially to a fund that is designed to provide relief to civilians suffering from the effects of war.

Regardless of why they entered the fray (acting in self-defense or initiating an unjust war), all belligerent nations must be morally accountable for their actions. Just as a liberal democracy defending itself has a legal right to bomb dual purpose targets, so does an aggressor state, but it too then should be morally obligated to cover the *ex post* reparation costs. I am referring to belligerent's legal rights regarding the law of armed conflict. I do recognize, though, that an aggressor state can be charged with the crime of aggression because the war is unjust. However, legally speaking, in war all belligerents (whether just or unjust) are subject to the same set of legal rules governing conduct.

There is a moral requirement to provide reparations regardless of financial hardship for both victor and vanquished. Of course, suggesting that belligerents are morally obligated to cover those costs is a separate matter from devising a way to make them pay or addressing the question whether, in response to other issues, it might be best that the moral obligation go unmet, for instance, when the unjust state is left destitute after the war, or the just state, although victorious, has suffered overwhelming damage to its own infrastructure and needs to tend to it first, etc. The pragmatic consideration to forgo or temporarily suspend restitution because of financial hardship does not negate the moral obligation of belligerents. It also could be the case that when belligerents have extensive financial burdens other states might assist them.[37]

Although implementing *ex post* restoration obligations on belligerents that destroy important dual use facilities to the enemy's civilian population is important, so too is institutionalizing routine *ex post* independent review of all decisions to target dual use facilities.

EX POST OBLIGATION: BELLIGERENTS SHOULD BE RESPONSIBLE FOR GROSS MISCALCULATIONS

The international community must shore up the moral requirements for dual purpose targeting by incorporating residual effects into proportionality criteria.[38] Henry Shue and David Wippman suggest that the criteria for bombing dual purpose targets "unduly favors military efficiency over protection of the civilian population."[39] Once a target is determined to be military, its relationship to the civilian community and its concurrent civilian contribution is usually sidelined. Doing so creates an obvious tendency to find any military use in order to legitimize attacking almost any target. However, dismissing the facility's contribution to the civilian community does not change the fact that the damage to civilians, although "incidental or unintentional, is still real damage."[40]

Moreover, emphasis is placed on immediate rather than residual effects, most likely because these data are easier to ascertain. The tendency to ignore long-term effects gives the targeting of a dual use facility a misleading appearance of permissibility, at least in terms of proportionality. Shue and Wippman suggest that if military planners correctly did the analysis regarding the permissibility of attacking a dual purpose target, the "expected incidental civilian harm [to include cumulative effects] would be excessive in relation to an anticipated military advantage"[41] to be gained.

Shue and Wippman would just as soon prohibit most dual use targeting. However, their position might be too restrictive, because "if the law of armed conflict prohibited everything necessary to the effective conduct of warfare, it would simply be ignored and would quickly fall into disuse."[42] If the bombing of dual purpose targets were no longer authorized, belligerents (whether the unjust aggressor or the just liberal democracy) would not abide by these guidelines because to do so might significantly degrade their war-making ability. Some states would claim that they need to decisively engage their enemy, that is, that it is a matter of necessity to strike such dual purpose targets, while others might claim that these targets violate proportionality.[43] In order to meet the demands of both necessity and proportionality, we need a system that works and that states will also agree to. Although *ex ante* targeting criteria might be somewhat interpretative, belligerents should be accountable for gross errors in their proportionality calculations.

Discussing preventative force, Buchanan and Keohane suggest that there should be an *ex ante* impartial commission comprised of a group of states with diverse interests that can review and investigate whether preventive force is warranted. Subsequently, an *ex post* commission would review the actions taken by the initiator of the preventive war to determine whether there had been any unjust or unfounded activities, including cases of emergency actions undertaken that bypassed the strictures imposed by the *ex ante* tribunal. If force was not warranted, sanctions would follow. Sanctions are essential, because without them, as Thucydides has remarked, "The strong do what they can and the weak suffer what they must."[44]

Although Buchanan and Keohane's external commission (outside of the UN) could quite possibly be used to determine if preventive force is warranted, the same concept for the *ex ante* requirements of dual purpose targeting cannot be used. Military lawyers, versed in the law of armed conflict, are a constitutive element of military planning cells. These planning cells do not need or require outside control and oversight in determining legitimate military targets. It seems that trying to set up an *ex ante* external committee to oversee and analyze the full complement of potential dual purpose targets is way too demanding on any external committee and would severely hamper a belligerent's rapid responsiveness, which is critical in war.

Belligerents wanting to bomb dual purpose targets should not be required to provide information to an impartial commission for their approval. It is nearly impossible to see how an external commission could police the tactical decisions of belligerents during combat. Ensuring that targets meet legal criteria and requirements should be left to the belligerent and not an external commission.

With this comes the fact that we will have to basically accept belligerents' likely flawed *ex ante* judgments of proportionality given the inevitable fog of war (limited information, confusion, impulsiveness, lack of long-term [residual] effects considerations, etc.). However, an *ex post* external commission should be created which could then review dual purpose target *ex ante* proportionality judgments to determine any unjust or unfounded activities in the targeting decision, as well as to review widespread effects on civilians of legitimate attacks on dual use facilities. The bombing of purely military targets would not have to be reviewed by an *ex post* commission unless collateral damage is prima facie excessive. Furthermore, there needs to be *ex post* accountability even if legal criteria and *ex ante* necessity and proportionality requirements have been met. An *ex post* review would be used just to enforce the *ex post* obligations.

If there is no accountability *ex post* other than just repairing infrastructure, it might be the case that targeting determinations will always grossly err on the side of military advantage. That is, if the only accountability is nothing more than repairing a structure, compared to having to submit to an external commission's review and investigation of belligerents' actions, then belligerents might be apt to destroy even more dual purpose facilities. The point is that *ex post* review and sanctions will alter *ex ante* decisions/reasoning.

These stringent requirements might impact belligerents' decisions to bomb certain dual use facilities (e.g., a major highway interchange or an electrical generation plant), so belligerents might instead bomb alternative dual purpose targets (multiple smaller road junctions or electrical substations [switching units]) that would have similar effects and military gains without causing as much collateral damage (residual effects). Of course, lives will still be lost in the actual bombing, but lingering side effects would be minimized in the absence of the bombing of larger dual use facilities.[45]

If the belligerent fails to acquiesce to *ex post* requirements of repairing infrastructure or an external commission's *ex post* investigation and findings, then the belligerent should not only be vilified as morally culpable for its failure but also be subjected "to sanctions according to rules that have been established in advance."[46]

Although a belligerent that has destroyed dual purpose facilities has an obligation to ensure that the basic human rights of its enemy's civilian population is safeguarded, this does not suggest that decimated human rights conditions in a vanquished state impose duties on other states outside of the belligerent that caused the damage.

THE DIFFERENCE BETWEEN NONCOMBATANT IMMUNITY AND HUMAN RIGHTS

General human rights responsibilities should be fulfilled by backup obligors if the primary obligors cannot fulfill its responsibility. If other states that were not involved in the war want to help or assist with the rebuilding and restoring in order to secure basic human rights or other needs of the vanquished state, then these obligations are fulfilled by a commitment to realize human rights and not noncombatant immunity. Other states (those outside the parties to the conflict) that wish to help secure basic human rights are not required to do so because of the principle of noncombatant immunity. Rather, these other states, acting as backup obligors, would be driven by human rights norms, not noncombatant immunity norms.

States that are not party to the conflict can have two obligations: (1) helping the vanquished, and (2) holding the primary obligor accountable for its destruction.[47] Third-party states have the ability to pressure and push for the triggering of specified sanctions against the primary obligor (belligerent) if it fails to uphold its *ex post, jus in bello*, obligations. Backup obligors should first pressure the primary obligor to fulfill its special obligation if the primary obligor does not initiate this on its own or to the extent that is needed.

If the primary obligor refuses or needs assistance, the backup obligor should help as a matter of general human rights' assistance. States are the backup obligors for other states that need assistance in securing the basic/core human rights of their citizens. If the primary obligor refuses to fulfill its special obligation, then backup obligors should not only attempt to enact peaceful measures (public condemnation, targeted sanctions, etc.) against the primary obligor for its failure but also those backup obligors now have the obligation to assist the vanquished state in safeguarding its citizens' basic human rights.

Noncombatant immunity norms apply only to the engaged in the conflict. War is a special relationship between parties and with it comes a set of special entitlements, restrictions, and obligations. The principle of noncombatant immunity does the justificatory work and is particular to those two states—whether victor or vanquished—and their relationship in the context of the war. Of course, noncombatant immunity is derived from human rights. However, noncombatant immunity is not ubiquitous. It only manifests as the driving norm within a specific special relationship: combat, that is, war.

CONCLUSION

War promises death not only to combatants but to the innocent as well. Francisco de Vitoria stated, "To see that greater evils do not arise out of the war than the war would avert"[48] is essential to fighting a just war. During the war phase, the civilian population is vulnerable and fatally exposed to the harms of war. However, it does not end there. Months after the conflict, civilians continue to die as a result of inadequate living conditions brought about by indirect and unintended results from major combat operations, which include the bombing of dual use facilities.

There is a lot going on when two states clash in armed conflict. However, they should not acquiesce to the exigencies of war. Derived from human rights, the principle of noncombatant immunity is an essential part of the war convention. Without it, force would be unconstrained, and wanton violence and destruction would ensue. Although noncombatant immunity is derived from human rights, the distinct principle of noncombatant immunity pertains to only the determinant parties to the conflict (the belligerents).

When destroyed dual use facilities threaten or violate the basic human rights of noncombatants, then special obligations apply to belligerents. Implementing *ex post* accountability is twofold: (1) belligerents must immunize civilians *ex post* from the ills of war by repairing dual use facilities that contribute to securing basic human rights, and (2) belligerents must be held accountable *ex post* if they grossly subordinate proportionality to military necessity.

Belligerents should acquiesce *ex ante* to these *ex post* requirements in order to insulate civilians from the lingering effects of war. Otherwise, there is no moral underpinning to support dual purpose target destruction, since the residual effects of war will continue to harm the innocent long after the fighting stops. These obligations surface on account of abiding by the norm of right intention and the principle of noncombatant immunity. Although they are not particular to the *post bellum* phase, the *post bellum* or *ex post* implications of the immunity rights of civilians are more robust than we have commonly thought.

4

Negative and Positive Corresponding Duties of the Responsibility to Protect

In the spring of 1994, members of the Hutu tribe viciously slaughtered almost 800,000 Tutsis in a genocide campaign in Rwanda while the international community sat back and let the madness unfold. Not only were the Hutus morally culpable for their heinous acts, but every state (to some extent) was also morally to blame for the United Nations' failure to stop or even attempt to stop the Hutu rampage. Four years after the genocide in Rwanda, President Clinton apologized for the Western world's inaction in the face of such terrible acts. Then, a year later, as an ethnic cleansing campaign swept across Kosovo, and with the members of the United Nations Security Council (UNSC) divided on the decision to intervene, NATO decided to bring an end to the Serbian ethnic cleansing of Albanians. However, NATO's bombing campaign produced thousands of civilian deaths by bringing about a lack of potable water, electricity, and medical necessities. In both cases the UN failed to act.

Even though NATO acted in Kosovo, it caused more harm than it should have. The intervention in Kosovo only consisted of a NATO air campaign. No ground forces were used. The bombing focused on destroying dual use targets (electrical grids, highway interchanges, oil refineries, bridges, fuel depots, etc.) as a way of undermining Slobodan Milosevic's ability to wage war on the civilian population. Although this strategy brought about the capitulation of Milosevic's forces, it also caused the death of thousands of civilians due to foreseeable but unintended results as well as residual effects (lack of potable water, food, shelter, and medical attention).

In an attempt to respond to the international community's lack of response to the tragedies of genocide and crimes against humanity, Secretary-General Kofi Annan, during the 2000 United Nations General Assembly, made a plea to the international community "to try to find, once and for all, a new consensus on how to approach the issue of humanitarian intervention and to forge unity around the basic questions of principle and process involved"[1] when it is required.

In 2000, the International Commission for Intervention and State Sovereignty (ICISS) was formulated to grapple with the legal, moral, operational, and political issues surrounding the use of external military intervention for human protection. Many issues come into play when determining if using force to stop force is necessary. Nonetheless, I will focus on the moral aspects of military intervention. I will show that a state can lose its moral right to pursue a policy of nonintervention, and when a state loses its moral right to nonintervention, military intervention can be required, if further necessary conditions are met.

Aligning the just war tradition with the norm of right intention is essential in order to set conditions for a just and lasting peace. The concept of "Right Intention" is central to protecting the innocent. And so, of course, military intervention is a justified act of war and is essential in helping and protecting those people that cannot stop grievous and permanent harm from being unjustly done to them. Justice is predicated on the fulfillment of human rights, which constitute the core of international justice. Human rights are supposed to dictate a state's governance—both externally toward the citizens of other states and internally toward a state's own citizens and inhabitants. Unjust war, oppression, and genocide arise from unjust state institutions, so establishing a lasting peace is predicated on safeguarding basic human rights, fidelity to the principle of civilian immunity, and the recognition of the international responsibilities to protect.

I plan to make the case for the Responsibility to Protect as well as examine its conditions and content, in an eleven-section analysis. Section 1 shows the evolution of the emergent norm of the Responsibility to Protect but also exposes some of the worries raised by the doctrine. In sections 2 and 3, I will show that where the conditions of sovereignty fail there is no right to recognition or right to nonintervention, but that the absence of a right to nonintervention is not sufficient reason to establish either a right or duty to intervene.

In my view, there are a number of necessary conditions that are, when taken all together and fulfilled, sufficient to justify military intervention. These include not only serious, widespread violations of physical security rights, but in order for a military intervention to be called for it must have a reasonable chance of success, must be used only as a last resort, must be welcomed by those being harmed by the precipitating violations, must be all things considered proportionate, must be undertaken voluntarily by states, must not abridge the rights of the soldiers it involves, and the target state must have had ample opportunity to redress the problem itself.

The focus of this chapter turns to rights and duties in sections 4 through 8. The precedence of securing physical security rights is the topic of section 4. In sections 5 and 6, I will propose that safeguarding basic rights requires the fulfillment of both negative and positive duties and advocate that the international community can and should fulfill this duty via the UN. Later, I suggest that the duty to intervene is not exclusively a military duty. I then turn to a discussion of the rights of soldiers.

In the remainder of this chapter (sections 9, 10, and 11), I will discuss aspects of the obligation to intervene by looking at the availability of the resources that are provided by states voluntarily as bearing on whether the international community is obligated to intervene. I then explain that in the event that the international community fails to act where required, individual states may act. The chapter ends with my proposal that the UN also has a duty to improve in order to more efficiently and effectively respond to this obligation.

THE ICISS, WORLD SUMMIT, AND IMPLEMENTING THE RESPONSIBILITY TO PROTECT

In 2001, the ICISS published "The Responsibility to Protect," which replaced the term *Humanitarian Intervention* with the term *The Responsibility to Protect* (RtoP or R2P). The terminology was changed because the commission believed that arguing for or against the right of one state to intervene in another was outdated and unhelpful. Humanitarian agencies have also opposed the existing term since it militarized the word *humanitarian*. Military action, the intentional killing of others, should be seen for what it is—intervention or military intervention—but should not be called humanitarian because it denigrates the actual meaning of the word *humanitarian*, which should denote actual relief and assistance, not assistance by way of killing those who are trying to kill others. And so the ICISS replaced humanitarian intervention with the responsibility to protect because, "1) state sovereignty implies primary responsibility for the protection of citizens rests with the state itself, and 2) where a state is unable to or unwilling to avert grievous issues (*Genocide, War Crimes, Crimes against Humanity, and Ethnic Cleansing*),[2] the principle of non-intervention yields to the international responsibility to protect."[3] The Responsibility to Protect doctrine consists of three specific responsibilities: (1) the responsibility to prevent—to identify early warning signs of trouble and take action to mitigate underlying issues; (2) the responsibility to react—to respond to the situation with appropriate measures; and (3) the responsibility to rebuild—to provide (following military intervention) full assistance with restoration efforts.[4] In order to justify the use of military force (the react phase), there has to be serious and irreparable harm occurring to human beings: either (1) large-scale loss of life, actual or anticipated, and with genocidal intent or not, that is the product either of deliberate state action, or the neglect or inability to act, or a failed-state situation; or (2) large-scale ethnic cleansing, actual or apprehended, whether carried out by killing, forced expulsion, acts of terror, or rape.[5]

In addition, the ICISS stated that the UNSC should take into account that if the UN fails to discharge its R2P obligations, then the UNSC may not rule out other means (states acting unilaterally, subregionally, or regionally) to meet the seriousness of the situation. Although the ICISS states that there is no better or more appropriate body than the UNSC to authorize military intervention for human protection, it recognizes the case that other states might act if the UN fails to and that this would greatly undermine the credibility of the UN.

In 2005, at the World Summit (WS), the UN General Assembly agreed that the responsibility to protect was an important feature in safeguarding the innocent, and unanimously agreed (Resolution 63/308) to paragraph 139 of the 2005 WS regarding R2P: "The UN will be prepared to take collective action, in a timely and decisive manner, through the Security Council, in accordance with the Charter, on a case-by-case basis and in cooperation with relevant regional organizations as appropriate, should peaceful means be inadequate and national authorities manifestly fail to protect their populations from genocide, war crimes, ethnic cleansing, and crimes against humanity."[6]

The ICISS suggested that the duty to intervene existed not only in actual cases of genocide but in instances involving large-scale loss of life, even though it might have occurred without genocidal intent. However, these stipulations, which were incorporated in the 2001 ICISS, were weakened during the 2005 World Summit. Although the ICISS's proposal was discussed during the 2005 WS, member states unanimously agreed to provisions that were less demanding than what the 2001 "The Responsibility to Protect" proposed.

The 2001 ICISS publication suggests that the UNSC has a duty to intervene. However, by the 2005 World Summit, it seemed that the UNSC only had a right (not necessarily a duty) to intervene. The justification for force is no longer large-scale loss of life, "actual or apprehended," with genocidal intent or not,[7] but rather applies to cases of "actual" genocide, war crimes, ethnic cleansings, and crimes against humanity.[8] Also, reacting to a crisis does not seem as paramount as it did in 2001 when the ICISS stated that the principle of nonintervention yields to the international responsibility to protect. Instead, the 2005 WS consensus was that the UN would be prepared to act on a case-by-case basis. On another note, the World Summit did not make any reference to the international community's ability to take independent action if the UNSC fails to take action. This makes it seem as if the UN wants to position itself as the only institution that can decide when intervention is warranted.

In 2009, UN Secretary-General Ban Ki-moon issued "Implementing the Responsibility to Protect" to the General Assembly, in an attempt to transform the results of the 2005 World Summit into an R2P operational policy. The operational framework consists of three pillars: Pillar One—the protection responsibilities of the state (to secure and protect human rights and support the work of the UN Human Rights Council); Pillar Two—international assistance and capacity building (to develop mutual and active partnerships and assist those failing states that are "under stress before crises and conflicts break out");[9] and Pillar Three—to assure timely and decisive response, which can involve not only peaceful measures (UN Charter, ch. VI), but also coercive measures (UN Charter, ch. VII).[10]

Sovereignty implies responsibility. However, "It is the responsibility of the international community to take timely and decisive action to prevent and halt genocide, ethnic cleansing, war crimes and crimes against humanity when a State is 'manifestly failing' to protect its population."[11] But essential to employing coercive action when necessary is that the permanent members of the UNSC "refrain from employing or threatening to employ the veto in situations of manifest failure to meet obligations relating to the Responsibility to Protect, as defined in paragraph 139 of the Summit Outcome, and to reach a mutual understanding to that effect."[12] As of 2009, the General Assembly reaffirmed its respect for the UN Charter, citing the results it had reached for R2P during the 2005 WS, and decided to continue its consideration of R2P.

In 2010, the Secretary-General published "Early Warning, Assessment and the Responsibility to Protect," not only to inform but also to strengthen interactive dialogue in the General Assembly. This was followed in 2011 by "The Role of Regional and Sub-regional Arrangements in Implementing the Responsibility to Protect." Three key points in this document, detailed below, are: the essential nature of the regional and subregional actors, peaceful measures as a strategy to mitigate threatening situations, and the necessity of coercive means to stop genocide.

First, the UN recognizes that regional and subregional actors are not only essential in monitoring human rights violations and assisting in capacity building, but also have a stake in a neighboring state's protection of its citizens because violations or grave failures might have spillover effects (refugees and violence) on one's own state.

Second, the report recognizes that enacting peaceful measures can be a strategy to mitigate a dangerous situation; however, the UN wholeheartedly recognizes the limitations contained in these measures. "Financial tools like travel bans, targeted sanctions, and restrictions on arms and equipment often take too long to become effective, are difficult to implement and monitor, and can cause collateral damage to trading partners and neighboring countries."[13]

Third, cognizant that sanctions can be problematic and unreliable, the report recognizes (as a last resort) the importance of coercive means, while acknowledging that it lacks procedural development regarding the implementation of coercive means (military intervention) to stop genocide. "The Report notes that these methods [military intervention] are necessary but underdeveloped, needing further discussion."[14] This point is critical, since coercive means will on occasion be needed in preventing acts of genocide, but the UN has no effective standing military capacity.

Although the UN has recognized this emergent necessity and has taken steps to develop such a framework, it is still is unclear how the responsibility of using sanctions or using military force should be distributed, planned, resourced, and executed. Paragraph 139 of the 2005 WS (as the basis for the R2P doctrine) is inherently problematic because it states that the UNSC will review each violation on a case-by-case basis instead of universally declaring that it will take appropriate measures regarding all manifested failures to protect.

In addition, some of the UN literature is ambiguous. Article 2.7 of the UN Charter states: "Nothing contained in the present Charter shall authorize the United Nations to intervene in matters which are essentially within the domestic jurisdiction of any state or shall require the Members to submit such matters to settlement under the present Charter."[15] In addition, Article 138 of the 2005 World Summit (which comes before Article 139 on R2P) declares, "Individual sovereign states still bear the primary responsibility to protect their populations, and we accept that responsibility and will act in accordance with it."[16] The ambiguity in the doctrine encourages some to believe that the notion of sovereignty always entails a right to nonintervention instead of the realization that sovereignty is itself conditional on securing human rights, among other things. "Not surprisingly, governments tend to be very keen on the idea of political sovereignty; they tend to assume that they have an automatic right of military resistance to any violation of national sovereignty,"[17] or perhaps they just believe that they are in fact legitimate.

Either way, I am not discounting that states should bear the primary responsibility for protecting their own citizens. However, better articulation and clarity of that concept is needed. Articles 2.7 and 139 have been cited by countries that do not consent to external coercion. In certain situations, when the UN has contemplated the use of external force to remedy human rights violations, the states that are responsible for these violations have posited that granting the use of coercive means is too rash because it is the state that has the primary responsibility to fix the issue and not the international community. Jennifer Welsh notes that some state violators have attempted to dissuade the international community from getting involved by trying to "delegitimize external involvement in their internal crises; in the case of Darfur, for example, the Sudanese government claimed that it had not yet manifestly failed to exercise its primary responsibility to protect its population and that outside intervention was therefore premature."[18]

SOVEREIGNTY AND THE RIGHT TO NONINTERVENTION ARE CONDITIONAL

Shortly after the 1648 Treaty of Westphalia, which denounced external influence into domestic affairs and established state sovereignty, Thomas Hobbes and John Locke developed their own nuanced version of the state sovereignty concept. Hobbes suggests that since man is always competing for honor and dignity he must be subdued and coerced in order to compel his obedience and performance. Hobbes states, "Coercive power is used to compel men equally to the performance of their covenants, by terror of some punishment, greater than the benefit they expect by the breach of their covenant."[19] Establishing a common power is the only way to protect citizens against injury by others and invasion by foreigners. The only way to establish such a common power is for members of a state "to confer all their power and strength upon one man, or upon one assembly of men, that may reduce all their wills, by plurality of voices, unto one will."[20] The sovereign commands his subjects but is himself above the rule of law. All of the subjects will obey those dictates that "concern the common peace and safety, and therein submit their wills, every one to his will, and their judgments, to his judgment."[21]

What follows is that "nothing the sovereign representative can do to a subject, on what pretence [sic] so ever, can properly be called injustice, or injury,"[22] because the sovereign has ultimate power to decide what is best. Furthermore, a sovereign ruling and controlling a piece of territory has the right to rule as he sees fit, because for Hobbes the international domain is a state of nature, and no one really has secure rights in a state of nature. Not only does a powerful sovereign have absolute domestic power, but also unchecked freedom internationally, since there is no global sovereign. States can be interfered with, aggressively attacked, and so on, without any violation of a right to nonintervention. Justice does not prevail. Rather, the international domain is predicated on survival of the strongest where wealth, power, and rational interests guide actions instead of justice. Peace between states is achieved by power, impotence, or *modus vivendi*.

Locke's account of sovereignty is much different. For Locke, a state's people are not considered subjects but citizens. Men voluntarily unite into a community of government—a body politic—for public good and safety. It is the consent of the people from which a ruler derives his power. As Locke posits, "The governments of the world, that were begun in peace, had their beginning laid on that foundation, and *were made by the consent of the people*,"[23] and not by absolute unchecked power and coercion of the people, because men agree to join and unite into a community "for their comfortable, safe, and peaceable living one amongst another, in a secure enjoyment of their properties, and a greater security against any, that are not of it."[24] Some reciprocity exists between ruler and citizen and both are subject to the rule of law. Citizens not only have certain basic constitutional rights but also have the right to evaluate, criticize, dissent, and even secede from their body politic. The sovereign's rule, "in the utmost bounds of it, is *limited to the public good* of society; it is a power, that hath no other end but preservation, and therefore can never have a right to destroy, enslave, or designedly to impoverish the subjects."[25]

If a sovereign uses its power to destroy, enslave, or impoverish its citizens, then that sovereign—failing to uphold the standards of conduct that it was charged with—will not only cause alarm and concern domestically but also internationally among the free system of states. "Actions of men and of rulers must be in conformity to the laws of nature, and the fundamental law of nature is the preservation of mankind."[26] A sovereign who has renounced the way of peace and who has used force to accomplish his unjust ends, such as a despot, "renders himself liable to be destroyed by the injured person, and the rest of mankind, that will join with him in the execution of justice, [against] any other wild beast, or noxious brute, with whom mankind can have neither society nor security."[27] Locke's view, arising out of natural law, supports a conditional notion of domestic sovereignty or legitimacy, and the idea that the international order is bound by various moral norms rooted in natural law, supporting, perhaps, a right to nonintervention for legitimate sovereign states.

The Lockean notion of sovereignty has slowly taken hold of, and has begun to shape, international law and politics and practice. This constrained notion of a state's power (subjecting itself to a limited authority both domestically and internationally) would inevitably become the world order that we have today. The Lockean conception of sovereignty is conditional upon the fulfillment of certain moral criteria. That is, we have moral criteria governing the legitimacy and recognition/standing of states. "Political entities are legitimate only if they achieve a reasonable approximation of minimal standards of justice, again understood as the protection of basic human rights."[28] States that adequately protect core human rights are recognized as "a member in good standing of the system of states, with all of the rights, powers, liberties, and immunities that go along with that status."[29] Such powers and liberties include the right to territorial integrity, to self-determination, to noninterference, to make treaties, to make just war, and to enforce legal rules within its boundaries. David Luban points out: "When State A recognizes State B's sovereignty it accepts a duty of non-intervention in B's internal affairs; in other words, it commits itself to pass over what B actually does to its own people."[30] If a state does not meet this minimum standard of justice then that state loses its moral right to noninterference, because "a state must be legitimate in order for a moral duty of non-intervention in its affairs to exist."[31]

Sovereignty, insofar as it entails a right to nonintervention, presupposes legitimacy, and legitimacy presupposes the effective realization of core human rights, including physical security, subsistence, and basic liberty rights. "Human rights set a necessary, though not sufficient, standard for the decency of domestic political and social institutions."[32] This necessary standard implies a dual responsibility: "[E]xternally—to respect the sovereignty of other states, and internally, to respect the dignity and basic rights of all the people within the state."[33] A state that adequately protects and respects the human rights of its own people as well as the human rights of citizens in its external relations with other states can be a considered a member in good standing of the international community because "it successfully carries out the requisite political functions,"[34] needed in order to guarantee its legitimacy. "Human Rights fulfillment is 1) a necessary condition of the decency of a society's political institution and of its legal order, and 2) sufficient to exclude justified and forceful intervention by other peoples."[35]

INTERVENTION IS REQUIRED

Although members of the international community share principles and common ground, these states do not take interest in everything other states do. However, they do take interest when states fail (whether deliberately or not) to reasonably secure these basic rights of their citizens. The key point here is that to guarantee a state's right to political self-determination and nonintervention that state must reasonably honor the core rights of its own people.

States that manifestly violate core human rights (whether intentionally or not) lose their moral right to nonintervention because they not only violate the basic rights of their citizens but also "pose a fundamental threat to peace and stability within the international order."[36] A state that has failed to observe the moral conditions of legitimate sovereignty leaves the state system with a gap: there is a population neither organized nor represented by a legitimate state, resulting in the destabilization of the state system/international community. It is as if a population becomes "stateless," since its state fails to fulfill certain conditions necessary to recognition as a legitimate state in the international arena. The state system is a system of states. If we have moral criteria governing the recognition/standing of states, then the system is compromised where those conditions are not fulfilled.

There are many conditions, including a wide range of human rights conditions, that a state must fulfill in order to merit recognition and a right to nonintervention. The failure to fulfill any of these will leave it without a claim to recognition and without a right to nonintervention. But other states cannot justify an intervention by simply pointing out that the "state" they are intervening in has no right to nonintervention. That it has no such right is a necessary condition of the permissibility of an intervention, but not by itself a sufficient condition. Military intervention is required and so permissible only if a number of further necessary conditions are fulfilled. In my view, there are a number of necessary conditions that are, when taken all together and fulfilled, sufficient to justify intervention. I am not arguing for a view that picks out any one condition as sufficient to render intervention permissible. Rather, the only sufficient condition is the fulfillment of all the necessary conditions. In addition to a state's inability or lack of intent to secure basic physical security rights, other necessary conditions must be satisfied, that is to say, a military intervention should be a last resort, should have a reasonable chance of success, should be proportionate (all things considered judgment), should not abridge the rights of soldiers who are implemented, should be undertaken voluntarily by states that have the resources to do so, should be reasonable in supposing that the victims of the genocide campaign would actually welcome military intervention as a form of rescue, and the target state should have had ample opportunity to address/correct the problem itself.[37]

PHYSICAL SECURITY RIGHTS TAKE PRECEDENCE

Security, subsistence, and basic liberty rights, according to Henry Shue, are all necessary to the existence of any rights at all. If anyone is to have any rights at all then they must have basic security, subsistence, and liberty rights which are necessary to the existence of any rights at all. The idea is that you cannot enjoy any rights as a matter of right unless you enjoy the basic rights as a matter of right. "Basic rights, then, are everyone's minimum reasonable demands upon the rest of humanity; they are the rational basis for justified demands the denial of which no self-respecting person can reasonably be expected to accept."[38]

Although on Shue's account genocide might engender our sympathies in an especially dramatic way, the human rights violation is not any more "basic" than if subsistence or basic liberty rights were also violated. In a sense, the violation of any basic physical security, subsistence, or liberty right is equally "basic" for Shue, so if societies are committed to honoring any rights, then they must be committed to honoring security, subsistence, and liberty, since these are the most basic. Physical security rights are a person's reasonable guarantee from physical threat and harm, assault, rape, torture, enslavement, murder, etc. Subsistence rights are a person's reasonable guarantee to an adequate level of food, water, clothing, and shelter. Basic liberty rights are a reasonable guarantee of an adequate level of freedom of personal agency and autonomy by not being subjugated, shackled, chained, imprisoned, quarantined, etc. However, R2P doctrine, as it currently stands, does not support this. But as a moral matter, R2P doctrine should be extended in order to cover all basic rights (physical security, subsistence, and basic liberty) violations, because all of these rights are equally basic.

The widespread systematic violation of subsistence and basic liberty rights seems just as much a threat to agency as widespread killing, etc. Agency is "the capacity of each individual to achieve rational intentions without let or hindrance."[39] Agency is "individual empowerment."[40] When individuals have it, Michael Ignatieff states, "[t]hey can protect themselves against injustice, and they can define for themselves what they wish to live and die for."[41] Without a reasonable guarantee of protecting subsistence, basic liberty, and physical security rights there cannot be any possibility of any type of agency by a population.

However, as a pragmatic matter, we should limit military intervention to that which protects persons from widespread and systematic physical security rights violations. Resources are finite, and to expand the list of what would require R2P military intervention to include subsistence and basic liberty rights violations is beyond the scope of what the international community can muster. Instead, the international community can use lesser forms of intervention (political persuasion and pressure, sanctions, etc.) as part of the R2P platform in order to hold states accountable for their gross subsistence and basic liberty failures that do not have an immediate and irreparable impact on civilians, as acts of genocide do.

For a military intervention to be pragmatically acceptable and morally required it must be aimed at immediately occurring systemic physical security rights abuses of the most serious sort: genocide, ethnic cleansing, war crimes, and crimes against humanity. R2P military intervention should be reserved for grave cases where not only a basic right is violated but so too is agency, and the harm imposed is immediate and irreparable.

The physical act of murder cannot be undone nor can the psychological effects of being tortured, raped, or witnessing love ones being killed, maimed, tortured, or raped be undone. Not all harms are equal. Some are more destructive than others, and R2P military intervention should be reserved for the most serious of harms. The fundamental nature of the right, the irreparable, immediate, and grave harm incurred, and the deliberate stripping of agency is why the securing of physical security rights should pragmatically take precedence over all other basic rights.

Of course, lack of freedom of movement (being quarantined) or lack of food/shelter cause-harm but this is not the same kind of harm as being slaughtered. Reasonably, physical security rights should be considered as having a special status compared to other basic rights. Genocide, war crimes, and crimes against humanity impose significant physical and psychological dimensions of harm that are immediate, extreme, and irreversible. Malnourishment or lack of freedom can be fixed, not discounting the fact that extreme malnourishment and quarantine (e.g., starving a population as a form of slaughter, keeping a group captive in a camp and subjecting them to forced labor, etc.) could possibly be used as a calculated means to achieving genocide or ethnic cleansing. In such a case, R2P military intervention should still be triggered because it is still a situation in which one group intends and has enacted the physical destruction (genocide) of another group, but instead of using machetes or gas chambers, this group uses starvation and forced labor as the vehicle to accomplish it.

This does leave at odds, though, some serious physical security rights violations of ethnic cleansing (e.g., quarantine, displacement, prevention of sexual relations, deportation). These violations could be resolved through the use of other peaceful/ less coercive measures instead of military intervention because these physical security rights violations are neither immediate (as in losing one's life) nor necessarily irreparable. Rather, these types of violations require time in order to produce the desired results. Therefore, implementing measures short of military intervention has the potential to resolve the situation.

SAFEGUARDING BASIC RIGHTS

We can say that all persons have the right to life, to subsistence, physical security, and basic liberty, but, "The proclamation of the right is not the fulfillment of the right."[42] Rather, there needs to be assurance that the right is honored, because basic human rights are universal and dictate the conduct of all states to "prevent, or to eliminate, insofar as possible the degree of vulnerability that leaves people at the mercy of others."[43] The fulfillment of basic human rights is necessary for any attempt at an adequate life. All legitimate states are committed to the human rights of their citizens. This commitment requires states to do more than simply not violate the human rights of their own citizens. It actually requires the institutionalization of positive action. Otherwise, basic human rights cannot be reasonably safeguarded.

A basic right such as physical security entails both negative and positive corresponding duties in order to effectively safeguard that right and actually guarantee its fulfillment. The basic idea behind positive and negative duties is that the positive ones "require other people to act positively—to do something—whereas another kind of rights [the negative ones] require other people merely to refrain from acting in certain ways—to do nothing that violates the rights."[44] The same can be said about subsistence and basic liberty rights, which also require negative and positive corresponding duties in order to ensure that they are honored. I use physical security rights as an example to illustrate Shue's point.

The underlying distinction between the two categories is between one of action and one that involves omission of action.

Living in a polity, a person has the negative duty to refrain from intentionally harming others, "but it is impossible *to protect* anyone's rights to physical security without taking, or making payments toward the taking of, a wide range of positive actions."[45] If the fulfillment of honoring these security rights is solely based on the negative duty to avoid doing harm, the negative duty would not reasonably guarantee the fulfillment of those rights. If there is not an institutional apparatus that protects citizens against threats to physical security, then some citizens might choose to violate this precept for various reasons, for instance, because of a lack of moral education, a lack of a willingness to comply, or a lack of penalty for noncompliance.

If the right not to be killed is taken seriously then efforts to enforce its correlate duty not to kill must be made. There has to be a social guarantee against threats that jeopardize one's enjoyment of physical security rights. The institutionalization of positive duties helps enforce the negative duty. A society can safeguard the security rights of its members by way of restraint and protection against nonrestraint. To ensure that security rights are honored, positive steps must be taken, since we realize that this will be an effective and efficient way to protect persons against nonrestraint. Positive duties are used to stop and punish, and the most effective and efficient way to do this is by designing institutions that try to prevent nonrestraint and punish those for nonrestraint. Members of the polity understand that the institutionalization of positive duties is necessary because it is the best way to coordinate requirements that are essential.

Members of the polity pay taxes, which are used to fund a professional police force, criminal courts, prisons, an educational system for criminal justice professionals, and the moral education of all members. States are the primary obligor for the implementation and operation of positive duties. That is, states are obligated to protect their citizens. Insofar as the positive duties can be most reasonably fulfilled by a state, then it follows that in order for there to be any rights at all there must be states, or at least some type of social form that effectively distributes duties. Although they may not be absolutely necessary, states are the most obvious candidate, since we not only live in a world comprised of states, but they also effectively distribute duties (enforcement, remediation, backup obligors, etc.). If we are going to have states, then they must protect core rights.

Persons not only have a negative duty to refrain from doing harm, but also a positive duty not to allow such action. If a perpetrator attacks someone and others witness the attack, they do not necessarily have an obligation to stop the attack but do have an obligation to assist when required, for instance, by calling the police, providing an eyewitness account, testifying in court, etc. The negative duty to refrain from inflicting harm, coupled with a basic social structure that protects the right, provides a reasonable guarantee of a person's basic right to physical security. Murders, although tragic, will still occur; however, as long as the state is reasonably doing what it is expected to do in order to protect its citizens from violations of physical security rights, that state meets a necessary condition toward legitimacy. There are some states that fail at least to some degree because of their citizens' failure to uphold what is reasonably required of them. For example, a state might have an adequate police force and legal system, but citizens of that state never report attacks on members of minority groups (or on women), never testify in trials against those charged with attacking minority groups, etc. States that find themselves in such a position need to educate their citizenry in an attempt to mitigate ignorance and discrimination.

States that invest a reasonable amount of resources in order to arrest, prosecute, and punish perpetrators for their failure to comply with physical security rights meet a necessary condition of legitimacy, since they not only sufficiently protect the security rights of their members but the state also remedies the situation in which the victim has had his security rights violated. The state incarcerates the perpetrator as a form of retribution but also to prevent recidivism. The victim may also receive medical treatment, counseling, and even restitution. By protecting physical security rights, we can say that even a violated person's right to life/security was honored since the perpetrator has been brought to justice. Even if there is murder, or even, potentially, widespread but isolated murder (for example, murders happen daily across the United States but these do not constitute a concerted, organized event), it does not necessarily mean that these are a human rights failure by a government. If a state reasonably fulfills its duty of policing, prosecuting, imprisoning criminals and aiding the victims, then it has acted reasonably within the domestic jurisdiction.

THE INTERNATIONAL COMMUNITY SHOULD FULFILL THIS DUTY VIA THE UN

Human rights are a practical political creation based on common ground and shared principles that are "minimum reasonable demands upon the rest of humanity."[46] If states are committed to realizing human rights, then they must be committed to protecting them. This commitment requires them to do more than simply not violate the human rights of noncompatriots. States must also act together to ensure that there is some international system in place that will reliably protect the human rights of noncompatriots, remedy violations, etc.

Without any effective international system that takes positive action to protect those rights, basic human rights will be violated by governments that either do not care or that are unable to provide for their people at one time or another.

This being the case, it is not enough for a state to be the primary obligor without any backup obligors. Having backup obligors provides a level of guarantee and protection of subsistence, basic liberty, and physical security rights that could not be met otherwise. This is important because the principle of basic human rights imposes the same duties on all states. It binds us together. Human rights are what we owe each other. Every person is a duty bearer, so if a state fails in its responsibility then others have a duty to help through the auspices of their state.

In order to manage this responsibility and coordinate behavior we have two options: (1) create a new global institution to oversee the international community, or (2) use the existing global structure that we have.

The practical choice is to use an existing global structure that is familiar with human security issues. The United Nations was instituted to facilitate cooperation between states with regard to international law, trade, security, human rights, and peace. However, "one of the reasons why States may want to bypass the Security Council is a lack of confidence in the quality and objectivity of its decision-making. The Council's decisions have often been less than consistent, less than persuasive and less than fully responsive to very real State and human security needs."[47] While it does seem problematic in many ways, the UN, ideally conceived, works in conjunction with regional and subregional arrangements by supporting dialogue, education, and negotiation. One major problem of the UN is that its membership includes some outlaw states and that its charter's language is ambiguous. Also problematic is the current veto rule wielded by the permanent members of the Security Council. Furthermore, the UN's original purpose was mainly to facilitate diplomatic engagement, not to function as a vehicle for something like R2P. However, with modifications and improvements, the United Nations can make headway in order to adequately address and remedy R2P cases.

Having an organization of states reduces the burden on any one state. Using an institution that has the organization, potential military capacity, and ability to fulfill the positive duty of enabling systems in order to prevent physical harms is a plausible way to fulfill the obligation that the basic human right of physical security demands. Without any hierarchal organization to oversee the obligations, there are not any feasible strategies for most states on their own to fulfill their obligation to this basic human right. An international unified effort is more effective because it is equipped to implement a course of action that is not only necessary but also sufficient and feasible.

First, the use of a collaborative process (whether it is subregional, regional, or global) would help assuage the concern held by some states that the hegemonic United States would monopolize R2P and use it as a cover for advancing imperial ambitions. In addition, a collaborative process has the potential to encourage a state to assist that might otherwise be preoccupied by self-interested motives (economic costs, public opinion, war fatigue, national interests). Furthermore, a cooperative effort can also mitigate other forms of inaction. For example, the bystander effect is the phenomenon that happens when people witness a person in distress. As the number of bystanders increases in a given situation, the possibility that one of the bystanders will assist the person in need decreases. The more spectators, the greater the possibility of inaction because there is a false belief that someone else will intervene.

Each state waiting for another state to take the lead could lead to inaction. Moreover, entertaining the idea of conducting unilateral action might be so overwhelming (exorbitant economic costs, no clear exit strategy, lack of experience in dealing with these types of issues) that it leads to inaction. Although regional and subregional alliances, coalitions, and organizations can mitigate the bystander effect and play a considerable role in monitoring human rights violations and assisting in capacity building, they are not a global federation of states.

Regional and subregional alliances and coalitions can attempt to alleviate a particular situation, but the UN should not only be cognizant of such action but also have the ability to agree to such action. Otherwise, cases could be hit or miss if left up to regional and subregional organizations. Leaving R2P implementation to regional or subregional alliances, coalitions, and organizations could quite possibly lead to inconsistent responses and to a varying degree of assistance, depending on a state's geographical location. Hopefully, the UN as a federation of states can oversee all R2P cases and apply a level of impartiality, consistency, and uniformity in dealing with all states in duress. "The task is not to find alternatives to the Security Council as a source of authority but to make the Council work better than it has."[48]

It might also be the case that a state (in addition to supporting the actions of the UN) wants to further assist in some fashion (because of historical, political, or geographical ties). If a state decides to go above and beyond what is required of it through the UN, this is permissible, supererogatory even, provided that the state is not doing so for personal gain. Risks may be associated with states acting unilaterally. The initiation of unilateral action, particularly extensive unilateral action (e.g., sending military advisors, weapons, and equipment) should have to be agreed upon by the UN to assure that no ulterior motives are present, and if they are, to assure that those motives are not satisfied.

THE INTERNATIONAL COMMUNITY HAS A DUTY TO INTERVENE

In addition to acknowledging the existence of severe, widespread, and systematic violations of basic physical security rights, it is essential that the UN evaluate the remainder of the necessary conditions that need to manifest in order for military intervention to be obligatory. Those necessary conditions (which when taken altogether are sufficient to justify intervention) include that there exist serious, systematic, and widespread violations of physical security rights. Further, military intervention must: have a reasonable chance of success; be employed as a last resort; be welcomed by those whose rights are being violated; be proportionate to the offenses it seeks to interdict; be undertaken voluntarily by states; not abridge the rights of the soldiers it involves; and, lastly, be accompanied by a stipulated timeline in which the offending state has had an opportunity to redress its violations but failed (whether deliberately or not) to do so. Once the evidence establishes that the state has no intention to honor its citizens' basic physical security rights, then military intervention is required.

Reasonable Chance of Success

Can the R2P military force not only defeat the target regime but also accomplish such a task with limited loss and damage to its own force and resources? In cases where the offending state allows foreign military intervention or does not have a large modernized force to stop the military intervention, the peace-enforcing force[49] has a greater chance of success, because it can adequately interdict the harm to civilians without having to defeat the target state's standing army. However, in other cases, military intervention will not be successful, for example, a despot who not only refuses access to a foreign military force but also has a large modernized army with a significant air defense capability. In such a case, military intervention seems counterintuitive, and intrusive conventional coercive measures should be ruled out by the nature of the adversary, since success (if one can call it that) would come at a high cost of loss of life among soldiers of the peace-enforcing force as well as significant destruction to backup obligors' finite resources. At any rate, this does seem problematic, because the use of R2P military intervention will be preferential toward weak or failing states as compared to those that pose a moderate to powerful military.

The point I have tried to articulate throughout this chapter is that states have a responsibility to protect civilians from another state when that state has failed in its responsibility to protect its own inhabitants. And those inhabitants are the victims of serious and widespread grievous harms. Intervening and stopping those grievous harms is congruent with the principle of right intention. But just as some scenarios in war—such as the Korean War (1950–53) and the first Gulf war (1990–91)—did not result in regime change, such can also be the case in R2P scenarios. However, armed military intervention could be used to secure some measure short of a just and lasting peace. The rights that were violated by an outlaw regime against a group of people in its state or the rights that were violated by a nonstate actor operating inside of a burdened society will have been redressed to an extent although for other compounding reasons there wasn't an occupation or regime change.

Last Resort

Have all alternatives been tried before initiating a military intervention? The initiation of a military intervention should not be premature. Less intrusive (peaceful) measures should first be initiated in order to hold the offending state accountable. In addition, the offending state must be given an adequate amount of time to redress the situation. The UN should make every effort to achieve a pacific settlement, because it recognizes that a full-scale military intervention is the last resort. However, this does not suggest that other, less intrusive coercive measures are a last resort. It could be the case that peaceful measures coupled with less intrusive coercive measures (no fly zones, naval blockade, drones, etc.)[50] are employed as a way to stop a state's conduct after initial diplomatic, cultural, and economic sanctions have failed to work.

Just because a state (as the primary obligor) has manifestly failed to protect the physical security rights of its citizens does not suggest that there is no other recourse for the UN (as the backup obligor) than to take on the actual task of protecting the human rights of those whose rights are violated. Rather, the UN as the backup obligor can fulfill its duty by either pressuring the failing state to fulfill its primary obligation or by rescuing the victims of the state's failure.

Given these two choices, the UN/international community will, of course, first attempt to persuade (e.g., negotiations, public criticism or condemnation—what James Nickel refers to as *jawboning*)[51] and then if it has to, try to compel or coerce the state (e.g., through economic sanctions, withholding of assets, denying trade, etc.) to fulfill its primary obligations before undertaking any attempt at implementing military force to rescue the innocent and physically force the culprit to change its behavior.[52] The UN cannot license intervention at the very first sign of a state's failure to secure basic human rights. This would essentially undercut a state's status as the primary obligor.

Although "the primary aim is to rescue not to punish,"[53] I feel that this language lacks specificity. Establishing refugee camps or no fly zones could temporarily rescue civilians from harm, but this does not solve or stop the problem; it just creates different problems. Any adequate long-term solution will have to address the rehabilitation of degraded political and social institutions as well as try offenders in the International Criminal Court. Military intervention should not be a never-ending commitment or blank check, rather, only what is required to adequately remedy the situation.

Welcome the Intervention

Do civilians who are being harmed by their own state actually welcome the military intervention? That is, would civilians reasonably subject themselves to further danger knowing that the force that is intervening is there to stop the genocide and ultimately protect them? I believe that in such an imagined scenario, when other implemented actions (negotiations, sanctions, etc.) have not worked, civilians must realize that they will continue to be harmed by acts of genocide, and so must willingly accept a military intervention, even if there is a possibility of being unintentionally killed by UN forces, as their best chance to be saved from the horrors they currently suffer. Civilians in this dire circumstance must recognize that if there is not a military intervention the murder of the innocent will continue.

Stipulated Timeline

Military interventions should not be launched prematurely. States that have failed in their duty to reasonably safeguard the physical rights of their citizens must be pressured to fulfill their duty to protect. The notion that states be allowed to remedy internal issues is important. Giving states a chance to fulfill their duties as primary obligor of their citizens' human rights seems consistent with R2P and the Lockean conception of sovereignty.

However, a reasonable assessment and timeline must be stipulated to the offending state. If a timeline is not dictated to a state, then it is the state once again that has unlimited authority over its citizens, and this should not be the case. The question, though, is how much of an opportunity a state should have to bring itself into compliance with human rights before it loses its right to nonintervention. It seems reasonable to suggest that a state's moral right to nonintervention is questionable until the evidence establishes that the state either has no intention to fulfill or cannot fulfill its members' human rights.[54] We should assume no right to intervene unless it can be shown that there are widespread human rights failures and that there is no prospect of their being corrected in a reasonable time frame. Once we are in possession of facts sufficient to establish a right to intervene, the offending state has lost its right to nonintervention, and military intervention is required (as long as all necessary conditions have been met). A military intervention would not only be used to stop the irreparable, immediate, and grave harm but also to secure the rights of those people. The international community only fulfills that obligation after the attempt to pressure the state has not worked and systematic and widespread harm remains.

All Things Considered Proportionate

Will military intervention save and protect more lives than it will harm? If the intervening military force has to first defeat a large standing army, the bombing of dual use facilities will be the lynchpin of such an operation in order to degrade its adversary's ability to communicate, resupply, and move forces. Such action would most likely kill thousands of civilians as a consequence of unintended results and residual effects, which clearly would undermines the reasons the UN used military force in the first place. This might violate the notion of proportionality. Of course, this depends on what good is achieved on the other side of the balance. However, prima facie, this type of strategy seems overly destructive.

In addition to analyzing the proportionality at the tactical level, an "all things considered" analysis must be conducted as well. The proportionality analysis should not only pertain to the states that are about to take up arms. The proportionality criteria must be applied in an all things considered analysis that not only encompasses the effects on the warring parties but also takes into account subregional, regional, and global strategic ramifications. The proportionality analysis pertains to the ability to secure the just cause in light of the harm (to include accounting for destructive second- and third-order effects not only to the parties to the conflict but to other states in the region as well). I call this an "all things considered" analysis to draw attention to the fact that second- and third-order effects (instigating greater regional instability, escalating a subregional conflict into a regional war, etc.) need to be accounted for instead of myopically restricting the proportionality analysis to the initial belligerents in the conflict.

It might be that the UN has *pro tanto* reasons in favor of committing forces. However, in conducting a thorough all things considered analysis, the UN recognizes that although it has a genuine reason for committing troops it could very well instigate a larger conflict in the region or even a World War III–type scenario. The UN might have adequate reason for action, but the inclination to employ force does not necessarily override competing reasons that are also present. In this case, the expected good to be achieved does not outweigh the harm that might result.

In sum, military intervention is required and so permissible when all necessary conditions have been met. If any of the necessary conditions is not met, then a full-scale military intervention is not justified. However, just because a robust military intervention is not justified, this does not suggest that the UN is excused from acting in situations that fall within the scope of R2P. The UN must fulfill its duty to protect and aid as best as possible in every situation. However, the extent of the intervention can vary depending on the situation. It is possible that lesser coercive forms (naval blockade, weapon caches, drones, etc.) may be employed (if they do not trigger worse results) even though a conventional R2P military intervention might not be justified. There will also be cases where pacific means will be applied but with little effect, although they are really the only reasonable options to pursue. Sometimes, the UN as the backup obligor—although it might have both peaceful and coercive measures at its disposal—will not be able to fully intervene to the extent necessary to stop severe physical security rights violations because one or more of the necessary conditions have not been met. However, the UN is, all things considered, required to intervene to some degree for all R2P cases.

The UN has a positive duty to protect and aid in every case of genocide, ethnic cleansing, war crimes, and crimes against humanity, but this leaves unanswered the question of how other states ought to treat a state's failure of sovereignty when it arises out of something other than a systematic widespread violation of physical security rights. One possibility is to link failure to meet the conditions necessary to sovereignty to certain sanctions designed to persuade the delinquent state to reform its current practices or failures, for instance, by creating a kind of sanctions scale ranging from low- to mid- to high-level sanctions/actions that might be applied to compel a state to redress its widespread and systematic violations. R2P peaceful measures are appropriate and permissible in response to certain categories of failure of sovereignty (widespread and irreparable violations of basic rights [physical security, subsistence, and basic liberty]) but R2P coercive measures (military intervention) are only appropriate/permissible in response to widespread and systematic violations to physical security rights: genocide (some forms of) ethnic cleansing, war crimes, and crimes against humanity. Designating measures as either peaceful or coercive is consistent with R2P doctrine terminology. As stated earlier, some peaceful measures are coercive in nature. However, the distinction between the two categories lies with the use of military force, which is deemed a "coercive measure." Everything short of implementing military force falls into the "peaceful measures" category (see Table 1). I will

Table 1. Sanction Scale

Human Rights Violation	Initial Response	Follow-up Response
Religious discrimination, violations of free speech rights, arbitrary arrests and imprisonment, sexual and gender-based violence, summary executions, etc.	**Low-level Peaceful Measures** Diplomatic and cultural sanctions—e.g., expressed concern, nonrecognition, refusal to participate in cultural exchanges, exclusion from various undertakings within global civil society, etc.	These human rights violations although serious do not justify military intervention. Depending on their severity, the international community measures, as a result of triggering R2P.
Large-scale recruitment and use of child soldiers, refusal of humanitarian aid, widespread gender-based violence, and R2P-specific issues: genocide, ethnic cleansing, war crimes, and crimes against humanity	**Mid-level Peaceful Measures** Diplomatic, cultural, and economic sanctions, including public criticism and condemnation, denial of trade, freezing assets, etc., in addition to implementing low-level peaceful measures	**Low-level* Coercive Measures** Include implementing peacekeeping, naval blockades, providing arms and supplies to the civilians who are being harmed, etc.
		Mid-level Coercive Measures Include establishing no fly zones, disabling electronic network systems, using drones and special forces advisors, in addition to low-level coercive measures
		High-level Coercive Measures Include destroying the targeted state's air assets (jet fighters and attack helicopters), increasing to a full-scale military intervention in addition to implementing both low- and mid-level coercive measures

*Coercive measures are only employed once all necessary conditions have been met. They range from low- to mid- to high-level depending on what level of force is reasonable and proportionate and in alignment with all things considered.

elaborate on the implementation of armed drones as a justified use of force (*jus ad vim*) in the following chapter.

At the less intrusive end are various low-level forms of diplomatic and cultural sanctions (nonrecognition, refusal to participate in cultural exchanges, exclusion from various undertakings within global civil society, etc.) that would be initiated in order to demonstrate the international community's intolerance for violations of free speech rights, arbitrary arrests and imprisonment, sexual and gender-based violence, etc. These infractions would trigger R2P peaceful measures designed to deal with the aforementioned human rights violations. While a state that widely denies free speech rights will fail to satisfy the conditions of sovereignty, and thus will have no right against intervention, other states may not permissibly intervene militarily since that is not the kind of human rights violation that justifies military intervention, though it might justify cultural, diplomatic, or economic sanctions or some other sort of response.

Mid-level sanctions focus on curtailing serious widespread and systematic violations such as large-scale recruitment and use of child soldiers, refusal of humanitarian aid to the population, widespread gender-based violence, and R2P-specific issues: genocide, ethnic cleansing, war crimes, and crimes against humanity. In these sort of scenarios, both low-level (diplomatic and cultural sanctions) and mid-level (public criticism and condemnation) and economic sanctions (from denial of trade to freezing assets, etc.), would be implemented in order to pressure the state in violation to redress the situation.

Cases of genocide might invite high-level action, but mid-level sanctions could be initiated right away. It is not that genocide only calls for mid-level sanctions. Rather, the UN implementing its R2P doctrine could start pressuring the failing state by imposing peaceful but stringent mid-level measures right from the start. Implementing these measures would show the state in question that the international community does not tolerate a state's failure to safeguard core physical security human rights. It would have the added benefit of giving the UN time to evaluate that state's compliance with the international community's demands before deciding whether some level of military intervention is called for.

If the targeted state does not redress its violations, and widespread and systematic violations continue, such as genocide and crimes against humanity, then in addition to the previous sanctions listed, coercive sanctions as the most intrusive form of correction should also be implemented. Coercive sanctions range from low level (peacekeeping envoys, blockading sea routes, supplying weapons to the civilians that are being harmed, etc.) to mid-level (creating no fly zones, disabling electronic network systems, using armed drones and special forces advisors, etc.) to high level (from destroying the targeted state's air assets to a full-scale military intervention).

It would be difficult, if not impossible, to develop detailed account of the sorts of failures that could jeopardize or revoke a state's moral right to nonintervention, along with the various sorts of sanctions that should be applied at each level of transgression. Rather, these suggestions offer a framework for the proposed R2P military intervention previously defined. The international community led by the UN has access to a series of sanctions (peaceful and coercive) that it can implement depending on the given situation. When there is a case of genocide, ethnic cleansing, war crimes, or crimes against humanity, intervention of some sort by the international community is required. Sometimes, peaceful measures will be the only viable actions. At other times, it might be possible to implement mid-level peaceful sanctions along with low-level coercive measures (naval blockade and providing weapons).

Although it would be nice to think that the UN would always initiate military intervention to stop acts of genocide, this is more of an ideal than an expectation. However, in cases where the UN has done what it reasonably can and the killing continues, the moral stain—blame—rests with the state (primary obligor) that is killing its citizens rather than with the international community, which as the backup obligor has fulfilled its positive obligations as fully as could reasonably be expected.

Although the UN is required to intervene, "how much sacrifice can reasonably be expected from one person for the sake of another, even for the sake of honoring the other's right?"[55] This question leads to the two remaining necessary conditions that must be addressed—not abridging the rights of the soldiers it involves and using one's resources for someone else.

RIGHTS OF SOLDIERS

Charles Beitz indicates, "The experience of the period since 1990 is mixed and suggests that the prospects for success vary with the particular political aims of an intervention, the circumstances of the society intervened in, and the military capabilities and political will of the intervening agent."⁵⁶ As Beitz suggests, the political will of those that intervene plays a serious role in determining if intervention will even take place or if it does, then to what extent. Thomas Hill and Kok-Chor Tan both raise points about this issue. Tan posits that "[t]he right of a state not to intervene, or its right to remain neutral, is an aspect of its sovereignty."⁵⁷ And Hill raises a broader point: "Should we use the state's resources to help others?"⁵⁸ Additionally, it may be one thing to spend money and provide supplies to another state in order to assist its population, but it is quite another—as Larry May notes—to jeopardize/sacrifice the physical security of one's own soldiers in order to protect noncompatriots. In military intervention scenarios, Jeff McMahan notes, it would not be hard to imagine that soldiers would want to resist taking part in such an operation, even by falsely claiming to oppose it on moral grounds.

No doubt, if coercive means are used, the UN peace-enforcing force will sustain casualties, but this should not be seen as a reason to forgo coercive measures if they are warranted. However, a state's soldiers dying on behalf of noncompatriots raises some concerns that need to be addressed. May states, "It is especially problematic for one state to abridge, or risk of abridging, the special human rights of its own citizens so as to protect the general human rights of the citizens of another state."⁵⁹ May further advances, "A State's soldiers and other citizens have human rights that may, and sometimes should, be taken into account whether to wage humanitarian war,"⁶⁰ because "the justness of the cause does not mean that the rights of those that serve in defense of that cause should always be overridden."⁶¹ It is not that the rights of soldiers should be an overriding concern, but they should not be dismissed, either. Rather, they should factor into the analysis of whether initiating a military intervention is morally acceptable. Some believe that sacrificing the basic rights of soldiers to save noncompatriots—in most cases—seems like a disservice to a state's soldiers. For this reason, May believes, "[i]t is especially difficult to justify jeopardizing the lives of soldiers and the basic interests of civilians when we are talking not about wars of self-defense but about wars undertaken for humanitarian reasons."⁶²

Fundamentally, the role of soldiers is to defend their own state from acts of aggression by other state or nonstate actors. Nonstate actors are organizations that have the capacity and capability to influence and/or coerce states, subregions, regions, or even the international community. By defending their state's political sovereignty and territorial integrity, they protect the lives of their innocent compatriots. Another way that soldiers protect the lives of their innocent compatriots is by participating in R2P military interventions. The volatility of an outlaw regime has the potential to affect the stability and order of the international domain. Outlaw regimes do not abide by arrangements or treaties, nor do they effectively keep their population from instigating aggressive and criminal acts domestically. So soldiers that are implemented as a R2P military intervention force to stop acts of genocide and end an outlaw regime's reign are—in a sense—defending their own homelands and the rest of the international community against instability and spillover effects.

Multiple states working in tandem form a collective self-defense force that may be used not only to stop acts of genocide but also to protect the international community. However, there is a limit. The actual threat that Nazi Germany posed internationally by its systematic and widespread violations of physical security rights cannot be generalized to all cases, since most cases of systematic and widespread physical security violations—such as those involving Rwanda, Darfur, and Cambodia—did not truly affect the international community. In most cases, soldiers used in an R2P mission will not be even indirectly defending their own homelands, and they will have been placed in harm's way to save noncompatriots. Although we recognize that soldiers accept risk in helping others, it is one thing to volunteer for military service. That is, the volunteer agrees to a commitment of possibly being placed in harm's way. However, it is quite another to be dragooned into military service. That person never volunteered to be placed in harm's way in order to protect others.

Russia, Austria, Brazil, Turkey, and Norway, among other nations, have compulsory military service for all males. As a rule, the period of enlistment is limited to twelve months of service. The officer corps of these states comprises an all-volunteer force. A state might have the right to force its citizens into military service and make them fight to defend their compatriots and government; however, it seems unreasonable to suggest that they should fight in a distant land to save civilians of another country when they never volunteered for military service in the first place.

A volunteer force is different. Some believe that there is a high level of patriotism among citizens who freely elect to enlist. Whether there is a high level of patriotism or not, one can reasonably understand why, as McMahan suggests, "[p]rofessional soldiers would not be tempted to try to exploit a provision for selective conscientious objection as a means of evading service in a just war of national defense,"[63] because by fulfilling one's role as a soldier in a just war of national defense, that soldier not only has fulfilled his professional obligation but more importantly has protected his friends and family, compatriots, and his way of life. However, key factors such as protecting one's compatriots and one's way of life in a just war of national defense are immaterial when it comes to R2P military intervention into another state.

For this reason, McMahan suggests that, even if the military intervention is just, "it would not be surprising if some soldiers sought to exempt themselves from fighting in such a war by spuriously claiming to be opposed to it on moral grounds."[64] That is, some soldiers might attempt to shirk their professional obligation in the belief that protecting people in a distant land is not what they enlisted for and falls outside of the scope of their responsibility. In order to hold these soldiers accountable for their lack of willingness to fulfill their professional obligation, McMahan indicates that a partial solution is "to impose significant penalties on active-duty conscientious objectors; soldiers granted selective conscientious objector status after receiving wages, training, and so on from the military would have to submit to these penalties as a means of demonstrating their sincerity; penalties could range from forfeiture of the benefits of military service, such as educational assistance and retirement funds, through compulsory public service to imprisonment."[65] McMahan does go onto to say, "If, on the one hand, he refuses to fight and the war is in fact just, he will fail in his duty, as a soldier, to protect innocent people."[66] If he refuses, then someone else will have to replace him. "Perhaps the real victim of his refusal to fight would be the person who would have to replace him and be exposed to the risks of war in his stead."[67] Therefore, they might figure out how not to participate. I understand McMahan's concern. Soldiers, at least those conscripted and perhaps those who have volunteered seeking to escape poverty, or even acting out of ignorance of what they are volunteering for, might deny that they have any obligation to risk their lives for the human rights of noncompatriots.

However, before we rush to impose significant penalties against those soldiers, as McMahan advocates, I think that we should take into account the basic human rights of the soldiers themselves, as Larry May does. Out of respect for those rights, the peace-enforcing force should be comprised only of volunteers, a detailed mission analysis should be conducted prior to disembarkation, and the necessity for military intervention should have been decided in advance by the international community. Fulfilling all three of these requirements will not protect soldiers' basic rights, but it diminishes the chances of unnecessary risk or rights abridgment. Only if these three conditions have been met might we be justified in subjecting soldiers to penalties for refusing to participate in military operations.

My own view is that states have an obligation to participate in R2P efforts to protect noncompatriots, but that sending troops to save noncompatriots is only permissible if a state's soldiers have actually volunteered for military service and that before they enlisted they were aware of the types of missions that they might be involved in. That is, soldiers have a duty to save noncompatriots, but only when they have freely volunteered and are cognizant of the fact that they might be assigned for R2P efforts.

Although there has been a trend over the last few decades of states (e.g., the United States, United Kingdom, France, China, Canada, New Zealand, Sweden, Poland, Japan, and Australia, among others) adopting the model of an all-volunteer military, the term *volunteer* is problematic in two ways: (1) wherever conditions imposed by social inequality are particularly harsh, we can infer that low-income citizens with limited opportunities will in particular be attracted to military service, and (2) those who do enlist may join without fully understanding the role (in addition to providing national self-defense and natural disaster relief) that they might be called upon to play.

Citizens might enlist for patriotic reasons. However, there are other reasons that attract low-income persons to join the military, such as to earn college money or other financial benefits, for the job security a military career affords, for occupational training, to acquire family medical insurance, or even to provide a ticket out of an economically depressed home environment. In such cases, have these citizens freely decided to enlist or do they feel that they really do not have many alternatives to joining the military?

To be a soldier defending one's own country or assisting one's compatriots is one thing; to be attached to a UN peace-enforcing or peacekeeping force in a distant land as a part of a collective defense force assisting an ally is quite another. We can give some weight to the fact that they have voluntarily enlisted, but in order for a citizen to be truly considered a volunteer, that citizen would not only have to reside in a country where equitable living conditions are the norm, but would have to be aware of all of the potential roles that a soldier might fill.

Recruiting materials would have to highlight this reality in order for it to be pervasive in public culture. There would have to be a shared understanding on the part of both state and citizen regarding all of the potential operations (police force, intervention, etc.) the enlistee might anticipate, so that citizens who were thinking about enlisting understood the multifaceted nature of a state's military. Soldiers should not be significantly penalized for not wanting to contribute in a military intervention if at the time of their enlistment they were not even aware the possibility of being involved in such a role. Defending one's state is by far the first priority, but if one's compatriots are secure from harm (they are not being attacked by another state), then it is possible that soldiers could be implemented in a peace-enforcing/peacekeeping force if such a situation arises.

Maybe currently there are only a few countries that have just background conditions (social, economic, and political institutions). If citizens, as co-legislative members of the state (with just background conditions and fully understanding what they are volunteering for) freely consent without mental reservation to enlist to serve their state, then we can say that those soldiers actually comprise an all-volunteer force. Therefore, in either case, defending their state and compatriots or defending noncompatriots in a distant land, an all-volunteer force is not being used against its will. However, as it currently stands, the preponderance of military forces will most likely be comprised from states that have substantial militaries like those of the United States and China, but the United States and China do not have just background conditions.

Second, a detailed mission analysis is needed. Subjecting soldiers to risks is one thing; sending them to their death is quite another. As Michael Walzer states, "Risking one's life is not the same as losing it."[68] By suggesting that troops should be committed to a peace-enforcing force in a distant land, I do not believe that states should not give special weight to the human rights of its own soldiers, but giving special weight to the rights of soldiers does not entail that soldiers should not be implemented when needed. Rather, a state honors the rights of its soldiers not only by using military intervention as last resort but also by developing clear attainable military objectives, fully analyzing the risks and costs associated with the operation, and having a coherent exit strategy that avoids an endless entanglement. Development of a unified and synchronized plan helps achieve political and military aims and saves soldiers' lives, because it neither needlessly places soldiers in harm's way nor continually exposes them to the ills of war while politicians figure out what the next step is.

Third, the choice to initiate military intervention should be decided by the international community. Not only is this decision the result of collective reasoning but also such a decision may in fact epistemically provide a justified belief that assisting is warranted to the soldiers that are to be involved in the intervention. McMahan suggests, "We should offer soldiers a source of guidance about the morality of war that would be more impartial and more authoritative than their own government, this could provide a basis for holding them accountable for their participation in unjust wars—perhaps accountable in law but certainly accountable to their own consciences."[69] Although McMahan's point is about establishing an impartial international court that would review all matters of *jus ad bellum* (justice of war) for all wars in an attempt to prevent the initiation of unjust wars by eliminating skewed excuses available to unjust combatants, we can also use an international collective body to provide facts and judgments that should reinforce the justness of R2P military intervention.

A collective body, or the UNSC, might on some level seem more authoritative than a state's own government, but it is highly unlikely that soldiers from State A would agree to serve the international body requiring military intervention if their own state did not. State A's soldiers are not going to agree to go to war if the political leadership and even popular consensus of State A does not agree with it in the first place. In addition, if State A does not endorse the intervention, then its soldiers are not going to war. There is little prospect that an international commission will order a state to participate in an R2P mission against its own will, and so soldiers will never face the prospect of going into an R2P mission solely because an international commission has judged it warranted.

However, a collective body (the international community) deciding all things considered that military intervention is warranted provides some assurance to soldiers that the intervention their state is asking them to undertake really is justified and is not just an attempt to pull off some sort of imperialistic land grab, etc. This assumes that it is reasonable to suppose that the international community, or UNSC, can be trusted. Even if it can be trusted more than any one state or one's own state, it may still not be particularly trustworthy. However, if there is a level of trust, then soldiers might reasonably believe that what they are doing is morally justified. Soldiers acting as part of a R2P force would be able to satisfy their own consciences regarding the moral justification of the operation that they were involved in, since the international community, in addition to their own state, has collectively recognized that action needs to be taken.

THE VOLUNTEERING AND AVAILABILITY OF MILITARY RESOURCES

Kok-Chor Tan's point is broader and focuses on whether a state has the right to remain neutral. The international community has an obligation as a backup obligor to protect and aid civilians when a state has failed to do so, regardless of whether that state is unable or unwilling to avert grievous acts. However, each state should be left to judge for itself if it can assist or not. The international community should in good faith defer to a state's own judgment about its ability to assist. Within this decision-making process there must be some scope for reasonable disagreement. That is, if a state decides that it is not able to assist, then the international community should accept this answer. Reasonable disagreement parameters encompass a state's capability to assist. If a state believes that by assisting another state it might jeopardize the fulfillment of basic human rights (such as subsistence rights) to its own people, then it is not required to assist. If states claim that they do not have the ability to assist so as to "free ride" on the willingness of other states to bear the burden, then those states are morally culpable for their inaction. Assuming states have a right to decide for themselves whether they have the ability to assist, and even to make a (reasonable) mistake about whether they have such ability, there is still the problem of states making an unreasonable mistake or simply refusing to assist so that others bear the burden of R2P. When this is the case, those states that are assisting have the right to jawbone or publicly criticize those states that prefer to free ride or make an unreasonable mistake. If states simply refuse to contribute to R2P efforts although they have the resources to do so, then these states are morally culpable for their inaction. Refusing to assist is unreasonable, and such states should be publicly criticized for their refusal. Although a capable state has a duty to act, other states do not have the right to compel/coerce that state to fulfill its duty.

Even if a state is not capable of supporting an R2P mission with money, soldiers, or supplies, it can still show solidarity by publicly supporting the UN's decisions to implement R2P efforts. To remain absolutely neutral—neither denouncing a state that is committing acts of genocide nor supporting UNSC resolutions to stop such a state—is reprehensible.

Some states might disagree, because this places R2P efforts and the rights of others ahead of one's own compatriots. However, "The objection that a state can never have a duty to sacrifice some of its own for others no matter how grave the situation is rests on the false premise that moral duties begin and end at the border of states."[70] Kok-Chor Tan declares that (of course) states have a responsibility to their own people. Nevertheless, if a state's people are adequately cared for (this includes its army being comprised of a volunteer force) and somewhere in the world innocent people are being slaughtered, then that state's ability to assist and protect should be focused toward those that need its assistance urgently, since its own members have already been provided for.

There may be cases where citizens of a certain state want to invest in a space program or attempt to find a cure for cancer. These are great programs. However, R2P should not be discounted on account of these projects. I recommend that a portion of the monies and resources that would go to these projects be diverted and then allocated to R2P. If states do not recognize the importance of protecting persons against widespread physical security rights violations, then R2P is a hollow concept. Tan does not specify what he means by "adequately cared for," but if a state reasonably protects its members' basic rights, then this is the tipping point where those states should help those whose basic rights are being violated. States in this position might have the potential to assist. However, I recognize that some states that secure their own members' basic rights might have very few military resources.

In such a case, "our priority ought to shift from our immediate community to the larger community of humanity."[71] That is, "our general duties to humanity in these cases ought to override our special duties to compatriots."[72] I adopt Shue's position here. Shue argues for the priority of basic rights (physical security, subsistence, and basic liberty) over nonbasic rights (for example, right to cultural and scientific advancements, paid vacations, property ownership), such that states such as the United States must take measures in their conduct of international relations aimed at securing the basic rights of others around the world before they can permissibly invest in the nonbasic rights of their own citizens.[73] Wealthy states such as the United States would be not only able to fund R2P efforts but also secure the nonbasic rights of its own citizens. Most likely, U.S. citizens and citizens of comparable states aiming at securing the basic rights of others around the world would only lose some of their own preference satisfaction. (Possibly certain textiles, food, industry and automotive products are only manufactured to help other nations so they are not readily available to U.S. citizens. Therefore, U.S. citizens would have to choose between items A, B, and C instead of items A through N. Additionally, there might be fees or larger fees at museums and national parks and other federally funded programs might incur reductions.) Of course, as Shue suggests, there must be limits and guidelines. Otherwise, "it is possible for the costs to be unreasonably high if the scope and magnitude of alleged duties is indefinite and open-ended,"[74] and able states would deny assistance because it would be a never-ending commitment to help others in every way imaginable.

More than two and one-half centuries ago, Emmerich de Vattel, a distinguished thinker whose writings are influential on international law and political philosophy, recognized this fundamental point. Vattel posited a similar concept: "Hence whatever we owe to ourselves, we likewise owe to others, so far as they stand in need of assistance, and we can grant it to them without being wanting ourselves."[75] No state can invoke the nonbasic rights of its citizens as grounds for not acting to secure the basic rights of others, because in the case of basic rights, "the duty to avoid deprivation must be universal."[76] So states that affirm R2P might be putting the nonbasic rights or at least preference satisfaction of their citizens at risk. Most likely, many states and their citizens will not be happy about this, especially those states that provide extensive nonbasic rights and many privileges to their citizens.

What I conclude from these critical points that both May and Tan present, is twofold: (1) there is no algorithm for determining whether a particular state ought to contribute, as often the issue at hand will be difficult and subject to reasonable disagreement, and (2) given the voluntarist nature of the international community, states have a right to act on their own reasonable judgments, even if those judgments are viewed, even correctly viewed, by others as incorrect. The international community has no right to compel any state to contribute militarily to an intervention that the international community has a duty to undertake. This is one sense in which one might say that states retain a right to remain neutral. However, it is not the traditional idea of neutrality in the sense of taking no moral stance.

IF THE UN FAILS TO ACT, INDIVIDUAL STATES MAY ACT

States in the international context are analogous to individual persons in the domestic context. Just as individual persons cannot fulfill their duties to secure and protect the rights of one another except through coordinating their efforts together and constituting/acting as a domestic state, so too individual well-ordered states cannot fulfill their duties to secure and protect the rights of persons beyond their borders except through coordinating their efforts together and constituting/acting as an international community or federation of states (e.g., the UN). A world state is not required since we already have a system of states, and most of those states adequately protect their citizens' basic human rights.

Forcing states into a nonvoluntary global/international order is similar to conscripting civilians into military service. It violates their autonomy. In addition, it does not seem any more practical than the system of states that we already have. Both the strength and weakness of the UN comes from the voluntary aspect of it. If the international community or federation of states fails in its duties, then individual well-ordered states may have a duty to act individually; indeed, it was their duty to act individually that they were rationally fulfilling by coordinating their efforts with other well-ordered states.

This is, presumably, analogous to the domestic case: if a state is functioning as it should, then a person has no duty perhaps to do more than call the police or testify in court as a contribution to protecting the rights of his fellow citizens. But if the state fails, then a person may have a duty to do more to actually come to the aid of those whose rights are being violated. For example, if there was a house fire and if members of the local fire department were on strike, then citizens would have to attempt to alleviate the situation without state assistance.

THE UN'S DUTY TO IMPROVE

"The solution is not to reduce the United Nations to impotence and irrelevance: it is to work from within to reform it."[77] Awareness goes a long way. The international community recognizes that R2P is a positive duty, and with that the UN has a duty to improve. The UN recognizes that one of the best ways to reduce R2P cases is by not only working directly with countries but by also involving regional and sub-regional communities which assist in the education and monitoring of neighboring states. The UN has made positive gains by addressing its concern for physical security rights of all people. Just as there is legal enforcement at the state level—a positive obligation to protect—there needs to be legal enforcement at the international level as well. Beitz states, "It is unrealistic to believe that analogous conditions are likely to be satisfied at the global level in the absence of global institutions that enforce them."[78] I believe what Beitz is referring to is that there is a strong demand for competent global institutions that decisively enforce positive duties when states fail to. Human rights are supposed to be capable of guiding political action. If states not only fail to adequately protect basic human rights but, even more, commit genocide, there needs to be a global institution that is capable of stopping the situation.

Recognizing that R2P is a positive duty also gives impetus to develop operational—not just conceptual—doctrine, because if the UN recognizes that it has a positive duty to act in every case (using peaceful or a combination of peaceful and coercive measures), then it would want to develop a system that could plausibly do just that by responding to grievous violations in an efficient and effective manner. As it currently stands, the UN is more prepared to implement peaceful measures although these are less effective, so it would need to operationalize coercive measures. However, the practical problem is the fact that the UN does not have a standing military. The state system constrains what sort of military capacity the UN can have at its disposal. States have argued about an array of military concerns: command structures issues, costs, unclear mission objectives, troops committed to the UN *ex ante*, etc.[79] Although working out this issue is no small task, it needs to be done in order for the UN to effectively and efficiently handle military intervention if warranted.

McMahan points out that one possibility would be to create "a special force under international control whose only purpose would be to carry out humanitarian military operations."[80] He further goes on to say that "[t]his would have to be a volunteer force composed of individuals who would not be members of any national military force."[81] Along with McMahan, I believe that there needs to be a specific force for R2P. However, I believe that his concept is impractical.

It is difficult to imagine that many countries would fund such a force. In addition, what soldiers get paid in the United States and in the UK is much different from what they get paid in countries such as Bangladesh and the Republic of Sudan. Whatever salary the UN would be able to muster for this special force (a result of state contributions) would most likely only draw enlistment from third world countries. The result would be as if the UNSC had outsourced R2P missions: first world nations would pay third world enlistees to fight in order to implement their policies. In addition, such an international volunteer force would lack expertise, top-notch training, and state of the art military equipment. It would be comprised of a motley lot of people from some of the poorest nations on earth looking for work. In addition, who would lead such a force?

Like McMahan, I believe that there is a need for a standing R2P force. However, the preponderance of money, special equipment, and military trainers for this force should come from the permanent members of the UNSC. Fair cost sharing definitely needs to be thoroughly addressed; however, I will only briefly mention that a plausible way forward would be to institute an international tax system to support R2P missions. Although there has been a lot of discussion about changing/updating the UNSC, I do not foresee the five permanent members' status as changing in the near term. That is, I believe that they will remain permanent members. Maybe additional members (e.g., Germany, India, Brazil, etc.) will be added as permanent members. Regardless of what changes to the UNSC will occur, the permanent members will continue to play a decisive role in global politics. On another note, the UN's Military Staff Committee (which consists of the chiefs of staff of the permanent members of the Security Council) can advise in the development of such a R2P force.

The benefit of having more political control and power should also come with the burden of funding, equipping (to some extent), and training the military force for R2P missions. The permanent members of the UNSC would equip the R2P force with state of the art equipment for intelligence, surveillance, and reconnaissance and also with armed drones. In addition, the permanent members of the UNSC would incorporate their own air assets (fighter, bomber, and refueling aircraft) into an R2P campaign. Soldiers (from the five permanent members of the UNSC) would be used in an advisory and trainer role in order to develop this cosmopolitan R2P force (of which the preponderance of soldiers would come from third world nations) with the skills needed to be implemented successfully. Other first world nations would also be required (but to a lesser extent than permanent members of the UNSC) to contribute monies and equipment to funding this R2P force. In addition, the ten nonpermanent members of the UNSC should be tasked to provide logistical support (sea and airlift capabilities, training facilities, etc.) for the R2P force. Soldiers for R2P would remain as members of their own state's military but would be assigned to an R2P role under the direction of the UN.

One benefit of this type of approach would be that the R2P force composed of soldiers from third world states might have regional or subregional commonalities with the failed state that they are to militarily intervene in. An R2P force having cultural, historical, and/or political ties with the failed state as well as, possibly, a common language would only further benefit the situation. On another note, not having American soldiers deployed to some distant country for an R2P mission might actually help the situation, because many states view the hegemonic United States as unjustifiably having its hand in everything. Many people view U.S. soldiers deployed in other states as agents of imperial expansionism or as representing the desire to secure natural resources for American use.

An earmarked R2P force that is properly funded, trained, and equipped would not only be operationally ready to engage in military intervention in a timely and decisive manner, but even more, it might be seen as a deterrent to states that intend to deliberately harm a group of people in their own state.

CONCLUSION

The honoring of basic rights (physical security, subsistence, and basic liberty) can only be adequately upheld by institutionalizing positive measures that provide protection from and punishment for nonrestraint. It is essential to the very idea of a right that there are not only negative duties not to harm but positive duties to create institutions to protect and that these often involve the institutionalization of backup obligor responsibilities to protect and aid where primary addressees fail to protect their members.

The Lockean notion of state sovereignty and right to nonintervention is predicated upon securing core human rights. Sovereignty implies responsibility. States that violate any basic rights in a systematic way lose their standing as states with a right to nonintervention.

However, military intervention is not considered permissible just because a state has lost its moral right to nonintervention. In addition to widespread systematic violations of physical security rights, there are further necessary conditions (a last resort, a reasonable chance of success, all things considered proportionate, the rights of soldiers, undertaken voluntarily, welcomed, and a reasonable timeline) that would have to be satisfied before a military intervention was required and so permissible. Intervention is all things considered required, although depending on the situation the response might be limited, but that does not change the fact the back-up obligor (the UN) must assist in some fashion (negotiations, condemnation, sanctions, etc.) when military intervention is not a viable option.

Having an institution that can reasonably deal with every nonideal case is a step toward this goal. The UN is an organization that is united to protect and promote the basic human rights of all persons. As Vattel states, "Nations or states are bodies politic, societies of men united together for the purpose of promoting their mutual safety and advantage by the joint efforts of their combined strength."[82] Over the past decade, the R2P norm has emerged and is continuing to evolve. When a state does not reasonably safeguard the basic rights of its citizens, the international community, headed by the UN, must make timely decisions and take decisive action (either peaceful or a combination of both peaceful and coercive) in order to protect and aid those who have been targeted. Regardless of what group is the victim of these atrocities or omissions to protect their physical security rights, all persons should be respected and their basic human rights should be observed with equal weight and equal concern, because "basic human rights bind all states regardless of their consent."[83]

5

Justified Drone Strikes are Predicated on Responsibility to Protect Norms

The United States has conducted personality and signature drone strikes[1] into Afghanistan, Pakistan, Iraq, Syria, Yemen, Somalia, and possibly other states. The United States conducts drone strikes in these areas in order to disrupt, dismantle, and defeat terrorist organizations (such as al-Qaeda and associated groups/forces),[2] because, "At this moment, the greatest threats come from the Middle East and North Africa, where radical groups exploit grievances for their own gain."[3] In some of these attacks, states have given their expressed (e.g., Afghanistan, Iraq, Yemen) or tacit (e.g., Pakistan) consent to the United States to conduct these armed drone strikes. However, some states do not consent to the United States conducting kinetic drone strikes within their territory. In these cases, it seems prima facie reasonable to suggest that these acts are unjustified because they violate the political sovereignty and territorial integrity of a nonconsenting state. Furthermore, the United States is not at war with these states, so to suggest that the United States has a right to conduct these operations against another state seems unjustified.

Traditional just war principles regarding going to war (*jus ad bellum*) specify a state's moral responsibility in resorting to armed conflict. Based on contemporary just war doctrine, a state can resort to war as a matter of enforcing individual or collective self-defense when that state's political sovereignty, territorial integrity, or the human rights of its people have been violated. This is a state's inherent right in seeking to protect its government, land, and people or those of an ally. Extending this concept, the United States has declared that drone strikes may be used to stop imminent threats abroad, because doing so is consistent with a state's inherent right to self-defense.[4] However, doing so constitutes a violation of traditional *jus ad bellum* principles (just cause and last resort) according to just war theory. In addition, and even more alarming, conducting drones strikes in a state that the United States is neither at war with nor morally entitled to be at war with, since that state or a nonstate actor (operating in that state)[5] does not *actually* constitute an imminent threat is problematic. This stance seems to violate the traditional concept of self-defense and is not congruent with right intention.

As previously discussed, St. Augustine of Hippo declared that military acts should only be pursued out of necessity, and that the harms of war should be restricted as best as possible. Augustine's claim that "we fight so we can live in peace"[6] constitutes the norm of right intention and should not only inform the motivation behind the resort to war and influence and guide reconstruction and reconciliation after a war ends but also inform and guide how a state fights. Fighting in accordance with right intention demands certain reforms to just war theory, which includes a morally permissible approach to the use of armed drones.

In order for drones to work effectively they should be a cog in a much larger comprehensive strategy involving all elements of national power (military resources, economic rewards and pressure, information campaigns and cyber management, and political negotiation). The use of drones doesn't necessary set the conditions for a just and lasting peace. Rather, drones are an instrument that can be used as part of a much larger strategy that can be implemented to achieve a just and lasting peace. Establishing a lasting peace is predicated on the concept of "right intention," which is a central theme to protecting the innocent. The use of drones as a justified act short of war might obtain, if certain conditions are met regarding the safeguarding of basic human rights.

In order to address the current, problematic U.S. policy regarding the use of armed drones, I would like to address these concerns and put forth what might be a plausible framework from which the United States can make a moral argument (that is, be morally justified) for its use of armed drone strikes in those states that do not consent to such action. Following this framework would be consistent with right intention. Implementing such a framework would require a change to the current policy, and would primarily focus on five areas: (1) Current

U.S. policy addressing the question of imminent threat is too permissive and does not constitute self-defense; (2) A more plausible account of justified drone strikes would be one in which such strikes were predicated on the Responsibility to Protect (R2P) norms; (3) If the use of armed drones were thus predicated on R2P norms, there would be other conditions (right intention, reasonable chance of success, proportionate response, and voluntary use) that must obtain; (4) Using James Pattison's Moderate Instrumental Approach, the United States is the most reasonable choice to intervene in such scenarios; And, lastly, (5) The United States—whether it wants to or not—has already established the precedent regarding armed drones for the rest of the world to follow, and, therefore, must be proactive, disciplined, and consistent. Focusing on short-term goals can have serious ramifications. There are second- and third-order effects arising from current U.S. policy, which, if they are not addressed, will require that conditions be imposed that might cause the United States' armed drone program to be overshadowed by serious long-term problems that will undermine the whole program.

IMMINENT THREAT

Although Congress authorized the use of military force (AUMF) against those responsible for the attacks on September 11, 2001, which granted the president the authority to use all necessary and appropriate force against those he determined had planned, authorized, committed, or aided in those attacks, this does not suggest that every use of military force that the United States implements is morally justified. More recently, the United States has implemented a policy regarding the targeting of U.S. citizens abroad who are considered to be senior members of al-Qaeda (e.g., Anwar al-Awlaki) or associated groups/forces. This policy sets forth the most rigorous criteria to justify targeting U.S. citizens; if the target is not a U.S. citizen, the criteria are lower and at times may be employed to justify signature strikes (in which the purported targets are engaged in what is considered suspicious activity).[7]

Current U.S. policy regarding remotely piloted aircraft (also known as RPAs or drones) is so malleable that it essentially sanctions any drone strike. According to the United States, the target is lawful when it poses an imminent threat, capture is not possible, and the attack is conducted in accordance with international law/law of armed conflict. CIA director

John Brennan was the first administration official to publicly acknowledge drone strikes in a 2013 speech, calling them "consistent with the inherent right of self-defense."[8] And Attorney General Eric Holder specifically endorsed the constitutionality of targeted killings of Americans, saying, "They could be justified if government officials determine the target poses an imminent threat of violent attack."[9]

However, the underlying concern is the United States' definition of imminent threat. According to a Justice Department "White Paper," "The threat posed by al-Qa'ida and its associated forces demands a broader concept of imminence."[10] That is, "'Imminent' threat of violent attack against the United States does not require the United States to have clear evidence that a specific attack on U.S. persons and interests will take place in the immediate future."[11] Since the United States cannot be aware of all plots, in essence it cannot be confident that none are about to occur, so "imminent threat" does not entail actual intelligence about any plot against the United States.

According to just war theory, just cause is defined by an act of aggression (armed violence against the political sovereignty, territorial integrity, and human rights of the people of a state). Some suggest that preemption is morally permissible in the event of an imminent threat (seriousness and closeness of the actual threat)[12] and that waiting or doing nothing other than fighting greatly magnifies the risk to a state's people. However, the United States' imminent threat policy is both porous and malleable, and I believe does not actually define what constitutes imminent threat because of the breadth of interpretation it invites.

RESPONSIBILITY TO PROTECT

The use of armed drones is a recent phenomenon that will continue to evolve, and as it does there will come a need to establish a set of moral guidelines regarding itsimplementation. We ought to consider drone strikes not as acts of war but as measures short of actual war and then elaborate on what constitutes the just use of force (*jus ad vim*), since this technology is not only here to stay but will only become more prevalent in the twenty-first century.

It is reasonable to suggest that states have the right to use force in limited ways, but how and when those limited ways may be justified has not really been concluded. Currently, "actual" imminent threat, a state's consent (to drone strikes within its own territory in order to defeat a hostile nonstate actor), or UN Security Council authorization are the only three reasons a state can justifiably use force. However, can drone strikes be morally justified in situations involving other than these? I would propose that drones strikes may indeed be morally justified as acts short of war in situations in which the justification for those acts is predicated on the Responsibility to Protect (R2P) norms. Incorporating the R2P norms into a *jus ad vim* account provides a framework within which states can morally resort to the use of force short of war.

The justification for using force short of war may be found in a state's failure (intentional or not) to honor basic human rights. First, I will discuss R2P and explain that when a state does not comply with certain necessary conditions then that state loses its moral protection against intervention. This alone does not justify the use of force short of war. It only indicates that that state has lost its moral entitlement to be spared from intervention. Because my argument turns on an R2P account of when force short of war is justified, I will briefly explain why this is the case (a more robust argument can be found in the preceding chapter) and then offer an account of all necessary conditions to conduct justified drone strikes into another state.

According to the Responsibility to Protect doctrine, "1) state sovereignty implies primary responsibility for the protection of citizens rests with the state itself, and 2) where a state is unable to or unwilling to avert grievous issues, the principle of non-intervention yields to the international responsibility to protect."[13] According to the R2P doctrine, in order to justify the use of military force there has to be serious and irreparable harm occurring to human beings: genocide, war crimes, ethnic cleansing, and crimes against humanity. It can be argued that terrorist activities are consistent with the definition of acts that constitute crimes against humanity. Crimes against humanity "are namely, murder, extermination, enslavement, deportation, and other inhumane acts committed against any civilian population, before or during the war, or persecutions on political, racial or religious grounds in execution of or in connection with any crime within the jurisdiction of the Tribunal, whether or not in violation of the domestic law of the country where perpetrated."[14] A state that is unable or unwilling to prevent such grievous acts fails in regard to its legitimacy. A state's legitimacy is conditional upon the fulfillment of certain moral criteria, comprising "a reasonable approximation of minimal standards of justice, again understood as the protection of basic human rights."[15] A state that adequately protects core human rights is recognized as "a member in good standing of the system of states, with all of the rights, powers, liberties, and immunities that go along with that status."[16] Such powers and liberties include rights to territorial integrity, self-determination, and noninterference, and the right to make treaties, to make just war, and to enforce legal rules within its boundaries.

Sovereignty, insofar as it entails a right to nonintervention, presupposes legitimacy, and legitimacy presupposes the effective realization of core human rights, including physical security, subsistence, and basic liberty. The achievement and protection of basic human rights sets the minimum standard for decency in a state, which implies a dual responsibility: "externally—to respect the sovereignty of other states, and internally, to respect the dignity and basic rights of all the people within the state."[17] A state that adequately protects and respects the human rights of its own people as well as citizens in other states may be a considered a member in good standing in the international community because "it successfully carries out the requisite political functions"[18] needed to guarantee its legitimacy.

The international community should, and does, take interest when states fail to reasonably secure these basic rights of their citizens. This pertains not only to the state's committing acts such as genocide, ethnic cleansing, war crimes, and crimes against humanity, but also to the state's failure to deter terrorist groups that not only deliberately strip civilians of their basic human rights but also plot and scheme to strip civilians in distant places of their rights as well.

States that manifestly violate core human rights, whether by committing injustice, by allowing terrorist organizations to operate within their borders, or by abnegating the responsibility to protect their own populations, forfeit their moral right to nonintervention, because any state that violates the basic rights of its citizens also "poses a fundamental threat to peace and stability within the international order."[19]

A state that has failed to meet the moral conditions of legitimate sovereignty creates a gap in the roster of states that make up the international community, for it embodies a population neither organized nor represented by a legitimate state, which has the effect of destabilizing the state system/international community. It is as if that population has become "stateless." Our global structure is a system of states. If we have moral criteria governing the recognition/standing of states, then the system is compromised when those criteria are not fulfilled. The failure of any state leaves its own population exposed, even as it provides significant cause for concern by laying the groundwork for further acts of aggression into other areas that might threaten, for instance, American citizens and other U.S. interests.

There are many conditions, including those that address a range of human rights, that a state must fulfill in order to merit recognition and a right to nonintervention. Failure to satisfy any of these will leave it without a claim to recognition and without a right to nonintervention. But other states cannot justify the use of force by simply pointing out that the state they are intervening into has no right to nonintervention. That is a necessary condition for the use of force, but not a sufficient condition.

ADDITIONAL NECESSARY CONDITIONS

Military force short of war, i.e., drone strikes, may be justified only if a number of necessary conditions are fulfilled. I am not arguing that any single condition is sufficient to render strikes permissible; rather, the only sufficient condition is the fulfillment of all the necessary conditions. In addition to a state's inability or lack of intent to secure basic physical security rights, other necessary conditions must be satisfied, such as right intention, reasonable chance of success, proportionate response, and voluntary participation by states that have the resources to do so.

Commitment to *right intention* is the overarching constraint on war, as right intention aims at a just and lasting peace. A lasting peace is not achievable unless certain standards of basic justice have been secured. This should be no different with regard to the use of force. Implementing signature and personality drone strikes should not negate the responsibility to use political discourse and pursue peaceful measures to resolve the conflict. Right intention also includes incorporating a reasonable timeline, by which the offending state might be given time to redress the precipitating violations before the coercive measures/drone strikes are initiated.

I am not denying the need to neutralize such high-value targets as members of the ISIL and al-Qaeda leadership. Using drones to do this is only one viable course of action, which should complement a much broader strategy aimed at rendering these terrorist organizations ineffective. Drone strikes—although permissible when all of the necessary conditions are met—should be complemented before, during, and after their deployment by diplomatic communications and negotiations between states. That is, the use of drones needs to be a part of a comprehensive program that employs diplomatic, informational, economic, and military resources, including negotiations with the states (Syria, Iraq, Pakistan, Somalia, Yemen, etc.) where we operate drones.

However, I do not suggest negotiations with ISIL. There is really no point. Most states privilege and realize human rights; ISIL does not. ISIL manifests widespread and systematic rights violations including acts of genocide, ethnic cleansing, war crimes, and crimes against humanity. Its adherents commit murder and rape, and show no respect for human life. ISIL poses a fundamental threat to justice, peace, stability, and humanity. It has to be rendered ineffective. Its degradation will enable the Iraqi and Syrian governments' to regain control of their land, consolidate their power, and focus on creating better conditions than previously in order to establish a just peace.

Any implementation of the use of force should have a *reasonable chance of success*. Conducting drone strikes in order to disrupt terrorist organizations could be considered reasonably successful in multiple ways. "Compared to acts of war, *jus ad vim* actions present diminished risks to one's own troops, have a destructive outcome that is more predictable and smaller in scale, severely curtail the risk of civilian casualties, and entail a lower economic and military burden."[20] There are significant advantages to using drones instead of trying to mobilize men, materiel, and resources to fight. Public support is easier to obtain when using drones instead of deploying soldiers into harm's way. Additionally, drones have the ability to avoid detection, have extensive loiter time, can gather up-to-date intelligence and conduct surveillance and reconnaissance before a kinetic strike, and are able to operate in remote areas and inhospitable terrain. Finally, drones are a precision-strike munition that "under the Obama administration, have avoided civilians about 86 percent of the time."[21]

Another significant advantage is that using armed drones can be efficient at reducing the effectiveness of terrorist groups. "When experience [terrorist] leaders are eliminated, the result is 'the rise of lower level leaders who are not as experienced as the former leaders' and who are prone to miscalculations. And drones also hurt terrorist organizations when they eliminate operatives who are lower down on the food chain but who boast special skills: passport forgers, bomb makers, recruiters, and fundraisers."[22] Drones—loitering and circling overhead—dissuade men from gathering in groups for fear of being targeted and killed. Dissuading these men "undercut[s] terrorists' ability to communicate and to train new recruits."[23]

The use of force must be *proportionate*. By its nature, the use of drone strikes is more proportionate than full engagement in war, and has a capability that is more restricted in scope and intensity. A proportionality analysis should entertain and abide by principles of discrimination, military necessity, proportionality, and due care to the civilian population.

MODERATE INSTRUMENTAL APPROACH

The final necessary condition is that force short of war should be *undertaken voluntarily* by states that have the resources to do so, and these states' actions should be seen as legitimate. Before I go farther into this concept, let me address the point that the UN has recognized that it "need[s] to be prepared to be much more proactive on these issues [of the use of force and coercive measures], taking more decisive action earlier, than it has been in the past."[24] The UN recognizes that there are legitimate and justified reasons for the use of force/coercive actions such as when it is "necessary to maintain or restore international peace and security."[25] Because of this, the Security Council has adopted seriousness of threat, proper purpose, last resort, proportional means, and balance of consequences as its criteria for sanctioning coercive force to stop an injustice.[26] However, the Security Council also recognizes that while identifying these criteria is essential, they "will not produce agreed conclusions with push-button predictability, but should significantly improve the chances of reaching international consensus on what have been in recent years deeply divisive issues."[27] And so, this is a significant step in the direction of progress. This provides the UNSC a framework by which its members can objectively determine when coercive measures are necessary regardless of the agendas, ideologies, and jockeying that at times cause inaction. Additionally, the implementation of the UNSC's five basic criteria of legitimacy for the use of force has the potential to "maximize the possibility of achieving Security Council consensus around when it is appropriate or not to use coercive action and to minimize the possibility of individual Member States bypassing the Security Council."[28]

Although the international community recognizes that it has a responsibility to respond to the situation in question with appropriate measures, it also recognizes that—according to the International Commission for Intervention and State Sovereignty (ICISS)—the UNSC should take into account that if the UN fails to discharge its R2P obligations, then the UNSC may not rule out other means (states acting unilaterally, subregionally, or regionally) to meet the seriousness of the situation. That is, there are cases in which states acting independently should be allowed to do so.

The U.S. Senate Committee on Foreign Relations endorsed the U.S. Genocide and Atrocities Prevention Act of 2016, which is the United States' attempt to identify early warnings about at-risk communities as well as coordinate the full range of its diplomatic, political, financial, and intelligence capabilities. A U.S. high-level atrocity prevention board with interagency participation will attempt to do the following: "Engage allies and partners, including the United Nations Office on Genocide Prevention and the Responsibility to Protect and other multilateral and regional institutions; build capacities and mobilize action for preventing and responding to atrocities; encourage the deployment of civilian advisors to prevent and respond to atrocities; increase capacity and develop doctrine for the United States foreign service, civil service, armed services, development professionals, and other actors to engage in the full spectrum of atrocity prevention and response activities; develop and implement tailored foreign assistance programs that address and mitigate the risks of atrocities; and ensure intelligence collection, analysis, and sharing of appropriate information."[29]

Human rights are a practical political creation based on common grounds and shared principles, which consitute "minimum reasonable demands upon the rest of humanity."[30] If states are committed to realizing human rights, then they must be committed to protecting them. This commitment requires them to do more than simply not violate the human rights of noncompatriots. States must also act together to ensure that there is some international system in place that will reliably protect the human rights of noncompatriots, remedy violations, etc. Without an effective international system that takes positive action to protect those rights, basic human rights will be violated by governments and/or terrorist organizations that either do not care or, in the case of governments, are unable to stop terrorist organizations.

This being the case, it is not enough for states to only be the primary obligors without any backup obligors. Back-up obligors guarantee and protect subsistence, basic liberty, and physical security rights that might not be met otherwise. This is important because basic human rights impose the same duties on all states. They bind all of us together. Human rights are what we owe each other. Every person is a duty bearer, so if a state fails in its responsibility, then others have a duty to help through the auspices of their state.

Critical to this is that coercive measures/force short of war are viable actions that should be implemented when justified. Although peaceful measures provide options, they often fail to accomplish what they intend. Not only is it important to recognize that coercive measures/force short of war are necessary, but just as important is recognizing that force short of war should not depend exclusively on UNSC authorization. As Michael Walzer mentions, "Collective security depends on collective recognition."[31] This not only means that states, collectively speaking, are responsible for providing protection and defense to others but that states must also collectively agree that in fact force needs to implemented, and this can be inherently problematic. Both the strength and weakness of the UN comes from its voluntary aspect. If the international community, or any federation of states, fails in its duties, then individual states may have a duty to act individually.

There is a strong demand for competent global institutions that can decisively enforce positive duties when states fail to. Human rights are supposed to guide political action. If states fail to adequately protect basic human rights, there needs to be a global institution that can act in their stead.

As it currently stands, the UN is better prepared to implement peaceful measures, although these are less effective, and faces the need to operationalize coercive measures. However, the practical problem that the UN does not have a standing military and the state system constrains the sort of military capacity the UN can have at its disposal. This being said, we should acknowledge the legitimacy of unilateral action. Given the voluntaristic nature of the international community, states have a right to act on their own reasonable judgments here. That is, a state is justified to implement force short of war when all necessary conditions obtain.

I would like to implement James Pattison's moderate instrumental approach as the principle that applies not only to R2P intervention but to justified drone strikes as well. The moderate instrumental approach stipulates which states may intervene against a state that forfeits its moral right to nonintervention. The primary responsibility for a state's population is that state. However, issues surface when that responsibility transfers to the international community. Although human rights are the fundamental value behind any attempt to intervene in the affairs of another state, the moderate instrumental approach holds that "achieving good consequences is necessary—and sometimes sufficient—for an intervener's legitimacy."[32]

Moral philosophy regarding just war is an amalgamation of different emphases and values: just cause and right intention (deontological), proportionality and chance of success (teleological), and legitimate authority and formal declaration (procedural). And since war is an amalgamation of these different perspectives it seems plausible to suggest that a state that has the ability to maximize the good in any situation would be a legitimate intervener. This approach "takes the good to be increased as the enjoyment of human rights."[33] That is, "an intervener that increases the enjoyment of human rights of those currently suffering is effective."[34] Four measures of the effectiveness of the intervener's actions are: the intervener secures the peace; the intervener fulfills its R2P obligation, the intervener's actions protect civilians, and the intervener's actions end not only the killing but the other precipitating human rights violations.

If a state allows or cannot stop terrorist organizations from doing harm and neither that state consents to drone strikes nor the UNSC authorizes coercive measures, then a state acting as a backup obligator can be substantiated to intervene because of its actual capability to assist as long as the other necessary conditions obtain.

PRECEDENT

The United States is setting the precedent for the rest of the world regarding the use of armed drones and therefore has to be proactive, disciplined, and consistent. Additional issues that accompany current U.S. drone implementation practices include the psychological strains on the target population incurred by drones, the need for secrecy and program control, the restriction of UAV capabilities on the part of allies, and the unilateral and subjective nature of the United States' definitions of imminent threat. All of these considerations attach long-term risks to current short-term U.S. gains. U.S. political leaders should not only be cognizant of these concerns and their ramifications, but they should waste no time in implementing sound policies in order to address them.

Psychological Strain

Although there are short-term benefits to using drones, they can cause disastrous side effects. A population subjected to surveillance 24/7 suffers psychological and mental duress. The "eye in the sky" is a form of repression. People who are constantly watched by drones become fearful that one day a drone will come for them. Drones are so ingrained in the lives of some groups in the Middle East and South Asia that parents tell their children to be home by a certain time or a drone will come for them.[35] Constantly surveilled, these people do not feel safe. As previously mentioned, signature strikes require only a low threshold of identification. An innocent person in the wrong place at the wrong time is at risk of death from a signature drone strike. The fear this causes gives way to animosity and animosity to hatred. Hatred may be externalized as an excuse to seek vengeance for their friends, families, and themselves for living in fear of death hovering from above them at all times. Although the use of drones facilitates the gathering of intelligence, it has the potential to incite populations that were not originally anti-American to become so, and to fight back.

A population under constant surveillance has no way to confront the threat they experience. Villagers have no way to directly engage a Predator or Reaper high in the sky; instead, these locals (or their friends or contacts in another part of the world) might confront the threat indirectly, by attacking easier and softer targets such as American civilians abroad.

In addition, some terrorist organizations have become adept at the use of social media, and while they might lose a military engagement, they can compete in the informational war by using video clips, Facebook, Twitter, etc. Social media are a great way to spread propaganda and an effective recruitment tool for terrorist organizations. Using social media outlets to portray drone strikes as indiscriminate weapons of the West, terrorist organizations incite violence, garner support for their cause, and recruit new members. Although drone strikes against al-Qaeda have been successful to some extent, "[t]argeted killings have not thwarted the group's ability to replace dead leaders with new ones, nor have they undermined its propaganda efforts or recruitment. Even if Al Qaeda has become less lethal and efficient, its public relations campaign still allow it to reach potential supports threaten potential victims, and project strength."[36]

"In short, the picture is mixed: drones are killing operatives who aspire to attack the United States today or tomorrow. But they are also increasing the likelihood of attacks over the long term, by embittering locals and cultivating a desire for vengeance."[37]

Secrecy and Program Control

U.S. policymakers are currently wrestling with the question whether the Central Intelligence Agency (CIA) or the Department of Defense (DoD) should control the country's UAV program. Some, such as Senator Diane Feinstein, suggest that "the drone program is a covert one and is best run by a clandestine organization. In addition, the CIA has developed the kind of careful and methodical approach to the program that the military has yet to show."[38] However, others, such as Senator John McCain, suggest that since "the targeted killing program, of which America's drone fleet is the workhorse, has reached the point where it is an integral part of the conflict and a very essential one, its control should shift to the Department of Defense and the military."[39]

Ally Restriction

Although the UK and the United States are the only two states that currently deploy armed drones, this is bound to change.[40] "Over the last several years, it has become clear that the technical know-how and production capability to develop and sustain UAS [unmanned aerial systems] are not unique to the U.S. One estimate puts the number of different drone programs worldwide at nearly 700."[41]

The 2015 Paris Air Show was full of UAV technology, on display to wow military personnel and civilians alike. There seems to be no limit on the roles UAVs can play, which include, "ground surveillance radars, direction finders, acoustic sensors, command and control, electronic support, jamming, and even drone interceptors into mid-air defense systems."[42] Overwhelmingly, the majority of the nearly seven hundred worldwide UAV programs consist of unarmed drones that are used for many purposes, including reconnaissance, surveillance, and intelligence gathering for both domestic and international objectives. However, armed drone research and development programs do exist in many countries, including Israel, Turkey, Russia, India, China, Germany, Italy, and France.

Regardless of whether U.S. policymakers are cognizant of the ramifications of employing armed drone strikes, U.S. policy will surely inform other states' actions regarding the use of armed drones. Currently, only the UK is authorized to purchase the armed version of the MQ-9 Reaper. "Italy would like to arm its machines [MQ-9 Reapers] but so far has failed to get approval of the U.S. government for such a move."[43] Italy, a NATO partner and strong ally, is working directly with the United States in order to take advantage of U.S. technology, training, and know-how, as well as to gain authorization from the United States in order to arm its U.S.-supplied drones.

At present, the United States restricts the exports of its armed drones to the UK, but this in no way encourages the conclusion that armed drone programs in other countries will not eventually proliferate. We must be aware that we do not have a monopoly on the technology of armed drones, or on their use. For example, Italy, Germany, and France have announced plans to jointly fund and develop a medium altitude, long endurance (MALE) UAV project.[44] The announcement "provides additional evidence that advanced UAV proliferation is likely inevitable even if the US continues restricting UAV exports to its closest allies and partners."[45]

Elsewhere, China, Israel, and Iran already have armed drones. And Russia, Pakistan, India, and Turkey are pursuing their own armed drone programs and have achieved varying stages of research and development and testing. If the United States fails to take charge of the process, the world will be left with a hodge-podge of policies from many countries, representing many different goals, perspectives, and values. The United States ought to at least collaborate with its NATO partners to develop a system based on interoperability, communication, partnership, intelligence sharing, and training as a response to the current situation of global disorder and unpredictability. Intelligence sharing and collaboration among NATO countries is essential to developing and maintaining a common operating picture and system from which terrorist organizations may be tracked. However, if U.S. policymakers remain aloof, the possibility presents itself that our allies and partners will seek assistance and partnership from other states. China, for example, is interested in having a greater influence not only in the Pacific region but in Europe as well. If the United States withholds collaboration from its allies in areas such as armed drone technology, it might lead to some European governments working more directly with China, thereby helping China enhance its presence in Europe.

Precedent

The United States is setting the standards for drone strikes and defining by its actions where and when they can be conducted. The implied precedent is that the threshold to initiate an armed strike is low, which invites danger in the presence of other states that are developing their own armed drone programs. The United States risks encouraging countries such as Russia, China, Iran, and others to implement the same guidelines that we use, particularly with regard to defining imminent threat.

The United States' belief that some terrorist organizations (such as al-Qaeda, its associated forces, and ISIL) demand a broadened definition of imminence is likely to be mirrored by other countries. As it stands, the concept of imminence or imminent threat against the United States "does not require the United States to have clear evidence that a specific attack on U.S. persons and interests will take place in the immediate future."[46] As the United States cannot be aware of all plots, in essence it cannot be confident that none are about to occur. So "imminent threat" does not have to refer to actual intelligence about any ongoing plot against the United States.

This being the case and the precedent, China and Russia might well follow the exact same policy as the United States and start engaging organizations in other countries with armed drone strikes. The United States would be hard-pressed to condemn any armed drone strikes conducted by China, Iran, or Russia if, like the United States, those states use an open definition and malleable concept of imminent threat.

If the United States did condemn Chinese or Russian armed drone strikes, China or Russia would justifiably cry foul, because they would only be doing what the United States has been doing for years. The United States' imminent threat policy is porous and malleable, and does not always confront actual imminent threat because of the breadth of interpretation it employs in defining a necessary condition. Other countries, echoing our policy, have no reason not to adopt the same porous and malleable policy on the use of armed drones in order to protect their national interests and sphere of influence. However, protecting what one wants does not necessarily entail that it is a moral cause, nor that the means to accomplish it are moral. Rather, armed drones strikes need to be predicated on R2P norms in order to be morally justified, instead of operating in what is—based on current precedent and policy—a Wild West–type environment.

CONCLUSION

U.S. drone strikes are morally justified when they are employed against terrorist organizations (such as al-Qaeda, its associated groups, and ISIL), provided that all necessary conditions have been satisfied. The only sufficient condition is the fulfillment of all the necessary conditions. In addition to the target state's inability or lack of intent to secure basic physical security rights for its people, other necessary conditions (a right intention, a reasonable chance of success, a proportionate response, and a voluntarily act) must exist. If even one of the necessary conditions is not met, a drone strike is not justified.

Although the UN has a responsibility to protect all of the world's people, inherent complexities and competing interests at times leave the UNSC unable to commit to justified action. However, when the UN fails to act or does not act adequately, any state, acting as a backup obligor, may claim the moral responsibility to protect the life of innocent people. The justification to use force short of war is predicated on the responsibility to protect norms. According to the responsibility to protect and the moderate instrumental approach, the United States is justified in using force short of war (including drone strikes) to disrupt, dismantle, and defeat terrorist organizations. However, the United States must be cognizant that the privileging of short-term goals can lead to serious long-term issues.

6

Updating the Fourth Geneva Convention

The postwar phase has an established history in just war theory, and it has received a considerable amount of attention over the last decade. Although the postwar phase seems to be the focus of many current just war debates and philosophical works, law and practice concerning the postwar phase has received considerably less attention over the same period. International law regarding the *ad bellum* and *in bello* (of and in war) phases is currently more developed than international law stemming from the moral principles that are relevant to the *post bellum* (after war) phase.

For instance, in the prewar phase, the international community, represented by the United Nations, oversees the conduct of war according to the UN Charter, which specifically defines when a state has the moral and legal right to resort to war (in cases requiring either collective defense or self-defense, according to Articles 2.4 and 51). States recognize that they should petition the UN for approval before initiating any military endeavor that is different from the traditional definitions of acting in collective or self-defense, which include preemption, law enforcement, military intervention, etc. Regarding the war phase, the international community has signed treaties (Hague and Geneva Conventions) derived from moral norms and customary law regarding how and when states and their armies can morally and legally engage in war.

Both the *ad bellum* and *in bello* phases operate within moral and legal guidelines, but the *post bellum* phase lacks these directions. This can be rectified not only by expanding the range of *jus post bellum* moral norms to include fighting with right intention but also by giving legal embodiment to those norms. That is, obligations stemming from the norm of right intention should be realized not only as morally prescribed but as legally binding as well. If civilians/noncombatants are to be "at all times humanely treated, and protected against all acts of violence or threats thereof,"[1] then belligerents should attempt to indemnify civilians from the harmful effects of war as comprehensively as possible. Although it is accepted that civilians are to be protected in wartime, belligerents' obligations to civilians can be ambiguous, because the current international treaties regarding the treatment of civilians do not adequately define those obligations.

This shortcoming needs to be addressed, because when their basic human rights are abrogated, it is the civilians who suffer the consequences most harshly, often fatally. Their core human rights must be safeguarded in a fashion that will guarantee their access to life-sustaining goods and services, including food and water, shelter, security, and medical attention. There needs to be a guarantee of a social minimum, the absence of which signals a failure to secure human rights.

States that act with right intention do so recognizing that basic human rights must be reasonably safeguarded during and after war. Fighting with right intention entails a robust account of securing core human rights, which the principle of noncombatant immunity already recognizes. Immunizing civilians from harms that threaten basic human rights fits into any plausible account of what the principle of noncombatant immunity requires, because noncombatant immunity entitles civilians to protection of more than just their basic human rights (e.g., respecting religious conviction and practices, honoring manners and customs, and barring threats and insults). Therefore, belligerents acting with right intention and in accord the principle of noncombatant immunity are required to protect civilians from the harms of war. I am not suggesting that war cannot be waged when civilians are in the proximity. Article 28 (Part III: Status and Treatment of Protected Persons) of the GCIV states that "the presence of a protected person [noncombatant/civilian] may not be used to render certain points or areas immune from military operations."[2] However, belligerents should be accountable for the destruction they cause and should take reasonable measures (as the situation dictates) to at least insulate civilians from standard threats to their basic human rights (physical security, subsistence, and basic liberty).

Although there has been a lot of attention paid to the moral principles of *jus post bellum*, standards governing the transition[3] and postwar phases of war should be expanded to include not only the goal of lasting peace but also the ideals of justice.[4] Legal embodiment of these standards is also essential. Without legal embodiment of those relevant moral norms in place to govern the transition phase, postwar obligations are left to the interpretation of the victor.

Furthermore, occupation law, which codifies the primary legal regulations for governing during the postwar period, is outdated, inadequate, underdeveloped, and vague. As it currently stands, there is a normative gap (that is, what is morally required has not yet been codified) in the law of transition from war to peace. Although current occupation law provides a framework that, if fulfilled, might achieve some level of peace, it does not aim at peace with justice. Moreover, if the long-term aim of just war is to establish a just and lasting peace, substantive legal embodiment of the relevant moral principles is necessary to bring occupation law into line with this goal. This is necessary not only to point the parties involved more squarely in the direction of justice but also to inform them of what is required of them. If we do not have clear legal rules, justice becomes difficult to secure and maintain and a state's duties, obligations, and restrictions are left to interpretation and bargaining.

As it currently stands, occupation law fails to adequately address the positive efforts needed both for basic human rights fulfillment and for reasonable political self-determination—both of which give content to peace with justice. As a result, "the law of occupation is inadequate to the realities of modern occupation, and to the demands of modern peacebuilding and post-conflict reconstruction."[5]

My argument will entail a three-section analysis of relevant postwar moral norms and their legal embodiment. In the first section, I intend to show that the Geneva Convention Relative to the Protection of Civilian Persons in Time of War,[6] which is the treaty that covers the treatment of civilians during and after war, does not reflect current moral norms regarding human rights. Therefore, the Fourth Geneva Convention needs substantive reform in order to set forth the legal embodiment of relevant moral principles. In the second section, I will argue that ad hoc legal arrangements are problematic because these obligations are determined *ex post*, which is too late. Rather, overarching legal rules (ones that always pertain to any conflict) should be formulated and instituted ahead of time. In addition, ad hoc legal arrangements cite specific treaties that belligerents should comply with, but those very treaties favor the victor and do not allow for political self-determination. In the third section, I will propose that the UN needs to take a larger role in postwar operations. The reason is twofold: (1) the UN is the global entity whose mandate is to foster the cooperation of states regarding issues of peace and security; and (2) the UN has the responsibility to monitor and report compliance failures, as it already does with regard to human rights violations.

REVISED GENEVA CONVENTION

The 1907 Hague Convention IV and the 1949 Fourth Geneva Convention (Section III: Occupied Territories) comprise what is commonly referred to as occupation law. At the conclusion of a conflict, an occupation force may or may not be deployed, because it is not always evident that such a force is permissible or required for an effective transition to peace with justice in every case. Moreover, I am not suggesting that every war that has a clear victor is followed by the installation of an occupation force. For example, the 1991 Gulf War did not result in Coalition forces leaving behind an occupation force, but the 2001 war in Afghanistan and the 2003 war in Iraq did.

The placement of an occupation force (if warranted) can play an essential role in enabling a war-torn state to become autonomous once again. The functions of an occupation force is generally express themselves in six main areas: conduct of combat operations against any hostile state or nonstate actors that have refused to surrender; reestablishment of the rule of law; training the vanquished state's internal defense forces; repair and restoration of essential facilities and infrastructure that uphold core human rights; fostering legitimate governance; and promoting economic pluralism. The final *post bellum* goal is restoration of the losing state as an independent sovereign state that is internally legitimate and externally peaceful. Depending on the situation, an occupation force may or may not contribute to bringing about this end.

Occupation law "establishes the rights and duties of the occupier, the duties of the civilian population of the occupied lands, the limitations on exercises of power against the civilian population, and the continuing rights of the ousted sovereign."[7] However, these stipulations only help maintain the *status quo ante* (negative duty of do not harm) and focus on conflict termination but not on peacebuilding. But, as Kristen

Boon notes, "peace is no longer limited to a minimalist negative core but increasingly contains positive duties linked to the conditions that make peace practicable."[8]

Although occupation law, in particular the GCIV, was ratified in 1949 after the implementation of the 1948 UDHR, the GCIV needs to be revised so it is consistent with the human rights movement that has gained considerable momentum over the last forty years. The realization that human rights are essential to developing and maintaining international peace and stability has since been slow and intermittent. It has taken decades to move from the UDHR to the two main conventions,[9] and then decades more for those conventions to become anything close to effective. But human rights standards have taken hold, and "the rise of human rights obligations have set certain benchmarks for behavior."[10]

Human rights "provide protections of basic human interests against standard threats to those interests; the character of the standard threats and what serves as adequate protections against them both reflect the nature of the kind of social world in which human beings now find themselves."[11] Just as human rights should be realized not only as moral but also as (international) legal rights in order to hold states accountable for providing adequate protection against standard threats, so too the norms of just war that follow from right intention should be realized not only as moral norms but as (international) legal rights. If we can adequately identify the character of standard threats in our social world then we can also adequately identify the character of standard threats that harm civilians during and after war.

Empirical evidence provides plenty of reliable information "about what makes for human misery and degradation"[12] in modern war. As Allen Buchanan notes, "Once we appreciate the importance of factual premises, it becomes clear that the task of specifying human-rights norms is *ongoing*: as conditions change, new threats to basic interests may present themselves and new institutional arrangements for countering them may be needed."[13]

Just as we have updated and revised human rights treaties in order to better reflect our world, we must do the same with treaties that concern human rights and the welfare of civilians in the postwar period. The point is that we need to update and revise international treaties regarding war in order to adequately accommodate our commitment to right intention and human rights. Moreover, if resorting to war justly is more than vindicating a just cause but is also conducting war in such a manner that will set necessary conditions for a just and lasting peace, then new (updated) institutional arrangements are needed in order to counter those new or at least newly recognized threats to basic interests.

On another note, institutionalizing norms is not "merely a mechanism for translating independently justified moral rights into legal ones."[14] Rather, these institutions constitute, as Buchanan notes, "modes of public practical reasoning [structured by legal institutions] that contribute to our understanding of moral rights and to their justification."[15] Public practical reasoning allows for greater "inclusive representation of interests and viewpoints than is likely to be available at the domestic level and to that extent can mitigate the risk of culturally biased understandings of basic human interests, of what threatens them, and of what institutional arrangements are needed to counter the threats."[16]

Allowing for public practical reasoning structured by legal institutions can help us know "what our obligations are regarding human rights by providing principled, authoritative specifications of human rights when there is a range of reasonable alternative specifications."[17] Of course there will be differences, even reasonable disagreement, but public practical reasoning provides a forum to discuss the issues of occupation and transition law as the two components of a legally embodied *jus post bellum* regime. Engaging in such a discussion would not only shed light on the current inadequacies of legal protection that the GCIV specifies for civilians in the postwar phase, but also address the question of what authoritative specifications are needed in order to adequately account for protecting civilians' core human rights (physical security, subsistence, and basic liberty).[18]

Historically, the GCIV was instituted as a way to capture considerations that the 1907 *Hague Convention IV Military Authority Over the Territory of the Hostile State* never addressed, because, "The experience of Axis belligerent occupation during World War II made it clear that more precise standards and enforcement mechanisms were necessary for the security of civilians and their property in occupied territories."[19] But the 1907 Hague Convention IV left much open to interpretation regarding the rights of the civilians in occupied territory. Articles 43 and 46 of the Hague Convention IV state that the "lives of persons must be respected, private property cannot be confiscated, and that the Occupying Power shall take all measures to ensure as far as possible public order and safety,"[20] but it does not provide a specific account of what constitutes public order and safety. In addition, it does not make any reference to ensuring that the civilian population has food, water, shelter, or medical supplies or that the occupying power has any positive obligation to facilitate the delivery of these necessities.

The primary focus of occupation law is the following: "The occupier must take necessary steps to identify and register children in an attempt to reunite families, ensure food and medical supplies of the populations, maintain public health and hygiene services, ensure that penal laws of the occupied state remain, allow relief schemes by other states and/or the Red Cross, not compel protected persons (civilians) to work unless they are over eighteen years of age, not restrict employment opportunities, and must not conscript protected persons into its own army."[21]

Since the ratification of the CGIV in 1949, occupation law has applied in the Six Day War (1967) where Israel occupied former territories of Egypt (the Gaza Strip), Jordan (the West Bank), and Syria (the Golan Heights); the 1976 Syrian occupation of Lebanon; the invasion of Kuwait by Iraq (1990), the U.S. invasions of Grenada (1983) and Panama (1989), as well as the invasion of Afghanistan (2001) and Iraq (2003) by the United States and UK.

Some states have flat out denied their obligations under occupation law. For example, Israel believed that occupation law was not relevant because it had a legitimate claim in annexing the occupied territories that it gained during the Six Day War, and "Iraq did not apply the law of occupation to Kuwait, insisting that it was the nineteenth province of Iraq."[22]

Though more explicit than the Hague Convention IV, the CGIV neither fully reflects nor aligns with the human rights movement. Article 55 of the GC IV states, "To the fullest extent of the means available to it, the Occupying Power has the duty of ensuring the food and medical supplies of the population; it should, in particular, bring in the necessary foodstuffs, medical stores and other articles if the resources of the occupied territory are inadequate."[23] In addition, Article 56 states, "The Occupying Power has the duty of ensuring and maintaining, with the cooperation of national and local authorities, the medical and hospital establishments and services, public health and hygiene, with particular reference to the adoption and application of the prophylactic and preventive measures necessary to combat the spread of contagious diseases and epidemics."[24]

Although Articles 55 and 56 of the GCIV are clear improvements to the Hague Convention IV, this still is inadequate. For example, ensuring the food and medical supplies of the population does not mean that the occupying power has to provide any particular sort of access to these supplies. It just suggests that the occupying power has to provide these supplies, most likely at centralized locations such as refugee or displaced persons camps. In addition, Article 56 notes that prophylactic and preventive measures must be enacted in order to combat the spread of contagious diseases and epidemics. But this article does not elaborate on what that actually entails. Administering vaccinations, washing hands, breast feeding, and eating fruits and vegetables are all prophylactic and preventive measures. Is an occupation force that only supplies vaccines, hand soap, and fruits and vegetables doing all that is required within the spirit of the law?

It may be the case that articles rarely specify details because that is left to other documents and procedures. However, again this sounds like a bargaining process where powerful states have the upper hand in negotiating those procedures. I am not suggesting that articles in a general convention must incorporate all details. This would not only be overly taxing but most likely impossible. The level of specificity appropriate to a general convention must be at least at a level that addresses essential requirements. Otherwise, the article fails to give any definitive guidance. For example, articles governing the conduct of an occupation must include baseline criteria such as identifying the rudimentary prophylactic and preventive measures that are required, as well as provide more detail about what supplying "access" to food and medical supplies actually requires.

Infrastructural services are an essential element of prophylactic and preventive medicine, but the CGIV makes no reference to this. I would suggest that both Articles 55 and 56 need to be significantly revised or additional articles ought to be added to the GCIV that articulate the need for the occupying power to assist the host state with sewage disposal, trash removal, and electricity. These basic services are essential to a state's ability to safeguard the core human rights of its people. In addition, the civilian population must have access to potable water, food, and medical supplies, which the occupying power is responsible for providing if the defeated state cannot. This means that roads, highways, bridges, and rail lines will have to be repaired in order to grant the civilian population access to these necessities.

Article 64 of the GCIV states, "Penal laws of the occupied territory shall remain in force."[25] Just because these penal laws remain does not entail that they can be reasonably enforced when the infrastructure has been decimated. Rather, the occupying power would have to assist in repairing the infrastructure necessary to enable the rule of law, but the current GCIV does not address this.

Civilians should reasonably be immunized from harms that compromise their basic human rights. Civilians should have potable water, food, shelter, physical security, sewage and trash removal, and access to medical attention. In addition, civilians require a state that can effectively secure those rights for them, which is to say, road networks, power grids, courts, police stations, etc. are going to have to be operational. We cannot leave the civilian victims of war without these institutional prerequisites to their human rights.

The 1977 *Geneva Protocol I Additional to the Geneva Conventions (1949) and Relating to the Protection of Victims of International Armed Conflicts* calls for additional protection of the civilian population of a war-torn state.[26] Article 69 of Protocol I states, "In addition to the duties specified in Article 55 of the Fourth Geneva Convention concerning food and medical supplies, the Occupying Power shall also ensure the provision of clothing, bedding, means of shelter, and other supplies essential to the survival of the civilian population of the occupied territory."[27] This is clearly an improvement, because the original GCIV does not mention anything about the occupying power being responsible for clothing, bedding, or shelter. However, as stated previously, infrastructure needs to be operational in order for civilians to have their basic human rights reasonably secured. Furthermore, neither the GCIV nor Protocol I address other serious issues such as the repatriation and resettlement of refugees and displaced persons, children returning to school, and integrating combatants into the civilian population. Maybe it is believed that all of these issues will work themselves out in due time. However, not addressing or implementing positive measures in order to accommodate these issues is a serious shortcoming. Civilians returning home, children attending school, and former soldiers and other civilians finding work are essential to a country striving to return to a state of normalcy.

AD HOC LEGAL ARRANGEMENTS

Historically, international law regarding the relationship between states has been broken into two categories: war and peace. The problem is that this binary split does not properly account for the period of transition from conflict to peace, which creates a normative gap in the law.

Twentieth-century pre and post–World War II international law focused on developing and demarcating two sets of rules (the law of war and the law of peace). Consequently, "the transition from war to peace was not treated as a paradigm in terms of law."[28] International law should not be binary (war or peace), because both International Humanitarian Law and International Human Rights Law apply in war's aftermath.

Although human rights law applies before, during, and after war, International Humanitarian Law (IHL) is a set of international rules that are specifically intended to solve humanitarian problems directly arising from international or noninternational armed conflicts. IHL's main treaty sources are the four Geneva Conventions (1949) and their Additional Protocol I (1977). International Human Rights Law (IHRL) is a set of international rules on the basis of which individuals and groups can expect and/or claim certain behavior or benefits from governments. IHRL's main treaty sources are the International Covenants on Civil and Political Rights and on Economic, Social and Cultural Rights (1966) as well as the Convention on Genocide (1948). While IHL and IHRL have historically developed separately, recent treaties, such as the Participation of Children in Armed Conflict and the Rome Statute of the International Criminal Court, include provisions from both.[29]

The period between conflict termination and the establishment of a just and lasting peace cannot adequately be subsumed by the laws of war and the laws of peace because these laws do not adequately address either the positive efforts needed to secure human rights in the postwar phase or the moral right to political self-determination and international toleration needed to establish peace with justice. Postwar is a confluence of both categories (war and peace) and needs its own division and classification of transitional law.

Attempting to address postwar issues by incorporating them into the laws pertaining to the conduct of war is insufficient because that corpus of law is centered on fighting and not on rebuilding. Ad hoc legal arrangements are insufficient because constituting such legal arrangements after the conflict not only delays postwar implementation but also creates shortfalls. In addition, before a war begins, states and international organizations (the UN, IMF, World Bank, WHO, etc.) are sometimes unaware of their respective postwar obligations and responsibilities, which leads to inadequacies. "These inadequacies have created complexities on the ground because the duties and obligations of the various international actors are uneven and often unclear."[30]

Furthermore, because "there is not a consensus on the obligations that unilateral or multilateral actors incur when they engage in transformative occupations and interventions; powerful states jockey for resolutions that favor their own interests."[31]

Working through and establishing a legal framework that could be implemented in all postwar scenarios would greatly reduce issues that surface in the postwar phase.[32] In addition to its political or practical application of having a legal document that encompasses all specific rules, regulations, and responsibilities of all parties regarding postwar, an updated convention on postwar would bring international focus onto the importance of the postwar phase. It would also provide a comprehensive listing of what is required of warring parties before states ever resort to war, instead of waiting until after the war to see and agree upon what is required. Agreeing to postwar stipulations after the conflict seems too late. Rather, rules need to be developed and articulated before the conflict.

Having an updated preexisting legal document would (hopefully) guide a state's actions. For example, if the United States had been more willing to consider its obligations in the postwar phase, it would not have disbanded the Iraqi civil service after the 2003 invasion of Iraq. Disbanding the civil service created a nonfunctioning government almost overnight, which fostered animosity, chaos, fear, and lack of physical security and exposed the civilians of that state to greater harms than necessary.

It can be argued that the United States did not adequately anticipate the consequences of disbanding the civil service. But the decision that the United States made was a problem of principle and not just misjudging the facts on the ground. There was no preplanning or planning for the postwar period until immediately before the six week war began. This is too late. In addition, there was not any interagency planning and coordination between the state and defense departments, although the U.S. State Department would oversee the political rehabilitation of Iraq. On another note, Iraq is an example of why it is important to have an updated, preexisting codification of the relevant moral norms regarding occupation and postwar obligations. Given the existence of such a document, every state would know ahead of time what was required of it in the postwar phase. If anything, an updated Fourth Geneva Convention regarding occupation law might quite plausibly have informed U.S. planners that the effects of disbanding the Iraqi civil service would have been catastrophic where any attempt to enabling any form of governance in that defeated country was concerned.

Additionally, the absence of a preestablished fixed legal framework gives rise to the very real potential of the exercise of undue influence by powerful states or a hegemon, which has historically been the case during postwar negotiations. That is, "peacemaking itself largely was conceived as a process governed by the discretion of states"[33] with the victor having the largest degree of discretion. Negotiation between victor and vanquished does not exactly facilitate a neutral, evenhanded approach to securing peace with justice. As a result, the terms of agreement are, essentially, "set by a bargaining process of the victors of the rights and obligations of the vanquished."[34] Carsten Stahn posits, "Self-determination was not viewed as a binding legal principle, but as a flexible principle; it had to yield where it conflicted with overriding strategic interests of the victorious powers."[35] Victors have been prone to make extensive internal legal and institutional reforms of the vanquished state most of which have had nothing to do with improving the war-torn state but have been imposed because "the occupant usually wishes to export its own institutions, or to establish a regime that will be friendly to its security interests."[36]

If anything, "the presumption of neutrality during occupations has generally been disproved in practice."[37] Citizens of the war-torn state do not necessarily agree to the reform but welcome it as a "pragmatic desire for the rule of law."[38] In other words, citizens want physical security, so they acquiesce to the occupier's reforms. However, we need to put limits on powerful states in the *post bellum* context. One way to do this is by having an updated, preestablished, and fixed legal framework that embodies the relevant moral norm of reasonable political self-determination and will foster political inclusiveness, popular legitimacy, and international toleration. As it currently stands, resolutions (formulated *ex post*) cite outdated treaties, which favor the victor. The GCIV was written shortly after the formulation of the UN Charter (Chapter 1, Article 1.2), which "calls for respect for the principle of equal rights and self-determination of peoples."[39] However, the norm of reasonable political self-determination has "evolved from a principle into a right under international law,"[40] and that evolution should be reflected in the GCIV.

After a conflict, a United Nations Security Council Resolution (UNSCR) is usually drafted and adopted as a way to encapsulate all of the considerations to be applied to postwar justice. However, these resolutions cite outdated and unhelpful regulations. For example, both the 2003 UNSCR 1483 on Iraq and the 2009 UNSCR 1885 on Liberia "[call] upon all concerned to comply fully with their obligations under international law including in particular the Geneva Conventions of 1949 and the Hague Regulations of 1907."[41] But the Fourth Geneva Convention and Hague Convention IV, which are referenced specifically as the treaties that need to be fully complied with, do not reflect human rights standards of the twenty-first century (as discussed earlier).

In addition, UNSCR 1483 "stresses the right of the Iraqi people freely to determine their own political future and welcomes the commitment of all parties concerned to support this."[42] However, Article 54 of the Fourth Geneva Convention (which is the primary reference for an occupying power) gives "the right of the Occupying Power to remove public officials from their posts."[43] The GCIV does not provide any additional information for what would constitute reasonable removal of public officials from their positions; it just gives the occupying force permission to do so. In other words, the GCIV allows the occupying power to decide what is best. Thus, clearly, the authority given to the occupying force can obstruct a peoples' right to reasonable political self-determination. Article 54 favors the victor and the victor's interests. Article 54 of the CGIV does not reflect Part I, Article 1 of both the International Covenant on Economic, Social, and Cultural Rights (ICESCR) and the International Covenant on Civil and Political Rights (ICCPR), which states, "All peoples have the right of self-determination; by virtue of that right they freely determine their political status and freely pursue their economic, social and cultural development."[44] In many cases, the defeated state or government did not itself express or constitute the reasonable political self-determination of the population over which it ruled, and so if the occupying force is to foster reasonable political self-determination, it may have to remove officials and provide for a transitional process such as a new constitutional convention. However, the GCIV does not adequately address this concept. It states only that the victor may remove public officials from their posts, instead of making explicit the stipulation that the victor may remove public officials from their posts as a way to help facilitate a people's right to freely choose their own form of governance.

I am not discounting the importance of resolutions arrived at after a conflict, but these should be used to address specific case-by-case issues, whereas an updated Geneva Convention might be used as a uniform legal document to regulate the postwar phase to the level at which the prewar and war phases are currently regulated. I suspect that there will always be a need for ad hoc legal arrangements that cover the specific issues of a given case. However, currently ad hoc legal arrangements reference outdated treaties (CGIV and Hague Convention IV) as the primary legal documents by which belligerents must abide. This is unhelpful if we are trying to establish conditions for a just and lasting peace. Rather, we need to allow for political self-determination as well as protect the basic human rights of the civilian populace and enable or repair the institutions that can reasonably do just that.

Fostering political self-determination is consistent with right intention and establishes conditions that aim at a lasting peace with justice. In order permissibly to go to war, a state having right intention must not only have a just cause and limit its war-making activity to the steps necessary to vindicate the just cause, but it must also seek to vindicate its just cause in a manner likely to yield a just and lasting peace. Vindicating a just cause with right intention means vindicating it in a way that brings about a lasting peace with justice, and the only way to secure a lasting peace with justice is to allow a significant degree of political self-determination to be exercised by peaceful peoples that respect human rights.

Some scholars, lawyers, and politicians might suggest that a substantive legal framework for *post bellum* obligations is not necessary on the grounds that every *post bellum* context or circumstance is unique, so that only ad hoc responses make sense. I grant that every war is different from every other war and has its own unique intricacies. However, I would think that we might all agree that at minimum the treaty (GCIV) that is referenced by ad hoc legal arrangements should be updated in order to better reflect the positive efforts needed to reasonably secure the core human rights of the civilian populace.

THE UNITED NATIONS POSTWAR OBLIGATIONS

The UN is the appropriate institution not only to facilitate this process but also to play a role in institutionally expressing and adjudicating any relevant treaty. First, the UN is the global structure that specifically deals with fostering the cooperation of states regarding issues of peace and security. Second, the UN should monitor and report compliance failures, much as it already does when it comes to human rights violations.[45]

Regardless of the states involved in a conflict, the UN should oversee the postwar phase. Although the international community (signatories to the UN Charter) has delegated to the UN this power in Article 39 (Chapter VII, UN Charter),[46] which stipulates that the UN can decide what measures shall be taken in order to maintain or restore international peace and security, there are still shortcomings that need to be addressed.

For example, the UN primarily focuses on peace and security, rather than peace with justice. In addition, the states that comprise the UN have heterogeneous political perspectives, which can lead to inaction, competing interests, and even adversarial relationships within the community of states. Members of the UNSC have different conceptions of domestic and international justice, as is evidenced by the two most powerful states in the Council: the United States and China. But although member states have different political perspectives, the UN is still the best international organization to oversee the implementation of an updated and revised GCIV as long as there exists a common definition of international justice that all members of the UN might be expected reasonably to accept.

Given the various disagreements between nations over what justice requires, it might be difficult to designate what a commitment to an enduring peace with justice requires in terms of a specific legal embodiment of noncombatant immunity and *post bellum* norms. However, the GCIV should at least reflect a commitment to safeguarding basic human rights to physical security, subsistence, and basic liberty, as well as the right of people to self-determination in an occupied territory. In a sense, this would provide a baseline definition of what justice requires, given that, at present, a consensus on the application of such a requirement to any but the most obvious cases would be difficult to formulate, adopt, and ratify in the international arena.

Although the international community adopted the Genocide Convention in 1948 as a way to define and punish genocide in legal terms so as better to prevent it, it still saw a need to develop the Responsibility to Protect (R2P) in 2001 as a complementary legal doctrine. R2P is a holistic attempt to stop genocide by understanding all three phases of conflict (before, during, and after): the Responsibility to Prevent, React, and Rebuild. The recognition of these three phases is very important because it "implies the responsibility not just to prevent and react, but to follow through and rebuild."[47] This means that if military intervention is undertaken "there should be a genuine commitment to helping to build a durable peace and promoting good governance and sustainable development."[48] That is, R2P is not just a commitment to stopping egregious human rights abuses, but also a commitment to securing institutions necessary to assure peace with justice.[49] This is important because the International Commission on Intervention and State Sovereignty (ICISS), which was commissioned by the UN to find the best way to implement R2P, recognized that "[c]onditions of public safety and order have to be reconstituted by international agents acting in partnership with local authorities, with the goal of progressively transferring to them authority and responsibility to rebuild."[50]

One can reasonably infer that this is not only essential to cases of genocide but to other conflicts, in addition to R2P military intervention. Non-R2P wars and conflicts must also incorporate a rebuilding (postwar) phase in which there needs to be genuine commitment to building a durable peace and promoting good governance. Conditions of public safety and order have to be reconstituted by international agents acting in partnership with local authorities, with the goal of progressively transferring authority back to the host state.

If the UN and the ICISS have recognized that there needs to be a genuine commitment to building a durable peace and promoting good governance and sustainable development for R2P cases, then surely the same must apply to all postwar scenarios. The UN is currently the only organization with sufficient scope to orchestrate a concerted effort of states to review, update, and amend the CGIV so that that international treaty might readily articulate the legal embodiment of the relevant moral norms. This would be much like what the UN and international community have done regarding their analysis on genocide, developing doctrine that focuses on preventing, reacting, and rebuilding in order to adequately deal with the situation from beginning to end. R2P doctrine has significantly evolved from its original sourcing document (the 1948 Genocide Convention) and so must the Fourth Geneva Convention of 1949.

This does raise questions, though, regarding a *post-bellum* legal order that aims squarely at peace with justice, which might prove controversial or problematic, as the R2P platform has. Just as there are questions and concerns regarding what level of "justice" R2P actually aims at, so will there be concerns regarding an updated *post-bellum* legal order. However, a commitment to safeguarding civilians' core human rights and a people's right to political self-determination should not be controversial, and I believe that this level of justice is one that liberal and decent well-ordered states could reasonably affirm. Although the R2P doctrine is oriented toward peace with justice, it is centered on only intervening in order to protect persons from grave physical security rights violations. However, the R2P doctrine would also have to protect other core rights (subsistence and basic liberty), as I have suggested in chapter 3, if it is to be truly oriented toward peace with justice.

On a different but related note, the ICISS also recognizes, "Too often in the past the responsibility to rebuild has been insufficiently recognized, the exit of the interveners has been poorly managed, the commitment to help with reconstruction has been inadequate, and countries have found themselves at the end of the day still wrestling with the underlying problems that produced the original intervention action."[51] This is also analogous to postwar scenarios. If the ICISS and UN recognize this shortcoming when it comes to military intervention, surely it recognizes that these issues are commonplace in other types of conflict as well and should position itself as the multilateral organization that is best situated to oversee postwar guidelines and as the appropriate institution at the center of this process—presumably, its offices being used to monitor, report, and even adjudicate the relevant law.

The UN has also recognized that it should assist in reestablishing the rule of law in postconflict situations outside of just R2P cases. UN Secretary-General Kofi Annan stated, "The modern international legal system comprised of international human rights law, international humanitarian law, international criminal law, and international refugee law represents the universally applicable standards adopted under the auspices of the United Nations and must therefore serve as the normative basis for all United Nations activities in support of justice and the rule of law."[52]

As a result, in 2005, the UN instituted the Peacebuilding Commission (PBC) as a way to help advance the rule of law in postconflict states.[53] The PBC has a "mandate to integrate peacebuilding strategies from the outset of UN interventions and is emerging as a coordinating power dedicated to peacebuilding strategies that have a more representative basis than traditional UN activities."[54] Although this is a step in the right direction, the PBC comes with significant drawbacks. First, it needs to focus on peace with justice instead of peace and security.

In addition to helping secure basic human rights, the PBC also needs to support reasonable political self-determination and just institutions. Second, the PBC is only an advisory board, and it is not designed to operate in an environment where security is lacking. "Therefore, they [the PBC] support countries in a situation of positive peace not those in a situation of negative peace, the latter being the starting point of application of a *jus post bellum* framework."[55] In order for the UN to be able to effectively monitor and assist in all postconflict situations, the PBC must be implemented in a negative peace situation right after cessation of major combat operations. The occupation forces could provide security for the PBC, and the PBC could help provide direction to both victor and vanquished.

CONCLUSION

Although belligerents must abide by the existing occupation law, it is outdated, vague, favors the victor, and fails to adequately address many issues that peacebuilding and establishing a just and lasting peace require. The legal embodiment of the relevant *jus post bellum* norms ought to be welcomed by states committed to the idea that undergirding and unifying just war theory is the idea that military force must be deployed always and only with the right intention of achieving an enduring peace with justice.

Updating the Fourth Geneva Convention would point parties more squarely toward justice and also would inform parties (states as well as international organizations) of their role and what is required of them. If we do not have clear legal rules then justice becomes much more difficult to secure or maintain. Without clear governing rules, a state's duties, obligations, and restrictions are left to interpretation and bargaining. An updated convention would articulate the conditions necessary for establishing a just and lasting peace, and would provide legal accountability for a state's failure to abide by relevant governing norms. Although ad hoc legal arrangements will most likely always be necessary, this does not entail that the Fourth Geneva Convention should not be updated in order to institute legal rules that would apply in all situations, for instance, the securing of basic human rights and allowing for political self-determination.

The UN is the organization best suited to oversee the facilitation of a revised Fourth Geneva Convention, because the UN is specifically charged with the responsibility of fostering the cooperation of states regarding issues of peace, security, and international justice. Second, the UN should monitor and report compliance failures, much as it already does in instances of grave human rights violations. In addition to having developed the Responsibility to Protect and the Peacebuilding Commission as instruments to assist in the rebuilding of war-torn states, the UN has proven experience dealing with postwar issues and provides the forum for instituting a multilateral approach to rebuilding. With some adjustments, the UN could assist in establishing conditions for a just and lasting peace.

Conclusion

Just war theory not only establishes a framework regarding when the use of force is morally justified (such as in cases of self-defense) but also sets limits to the destructive acts of war by appealing to standards of conduct that incorporate discrimination (distinction), proportionality, and necessity. Just war theory also frames what is morally required of both the victor and the vanquished regarding rebuilding, reparations, and reconciliation during the postwar period.

Just war theory has been a constitutive part of Western political philosophy for the past two thousand years because it has remained germane to the conversation vis-à-vis declaring, fighting, and ending war justly. Just war theory has remained relevant because of constant evaluation, analysis, critique, and contribution by philosophers, theologians, soldiers, state leaders, and civilians alike. And what is absolutely relevant and critical to the ethics of war in the twenty-first century is human rights, and aligning just war theory with human rights, because human rights are a class of rights that play a special role in foreign policy. "They restrict the justifying reasons for war and its conduct, and they specify limits to a regime's internal autonomy."[1]

Political control of a territory and population no longer guarantees the moral right to nonintervention. Although this was thought sufficient to underwrite political sovereignty and so a right to nonintervention, it is now thought merely necessary. The additional requirement of meeting basic human rights is also necessary. The idea of sovereignty is still tied to the right to nonintervention. However, we have come to recognize and accept that sovereignty is something that depends on certain moral conditions being met, to include basic human rights reasonably safeguarded. Unjust war, oppression, and genocide arise from unjust state institutions in which those states (deliberately or not) encourage, allow, or fail to prevent the systematic and widespread violation of human rights. In addition, resorting to war for reasons of self-defense does not just entail fighting until a state's rights have been vindicated. Rather, "the aim of a just war waged by a just well-ordered people is a just and lasting peace."[2] There can be no lasting peace without justice, and justice is predicated on the fulfillment of human rights, which constitute the core of international justice.

Although recognizing that human rights are essential to developing and maintaining international peace and stability is foundational, this realization has been slow and intermittent at times. For example, although the Universal Declaration of Human Rights was ratified in 1948, it took almost twenty years after that to develop and ratify its two main conventions: the 1966 International Covenant on Economic, Social, and Cultural Rights and the 1966 International Covenant on Civil and Political Rights. And then it has taken decades more for those conventions to become anything close to effective in guiding state behavior. However, the human rights movement that marked the latter half of the last century shows little sign of losing its history-shaping force and momentum, and that is because human entitlements are fundamental to life. The honoring of human rights provides reasonable protections against standard threats to the basic necessities that are needed in order for people to live. Human rights advocates prescribe a two-pronged approach. That is, human rights obligations dictate how a state acts domestically, toward its own people, and how a state acts internationally, toward people of other states.

Although war or the use of armed force is justified when specific events unfold as a response to severe injustice, this does not suggest that those who are warranted to use force can do so without limitations. The nonideal conditions we face often involve circumstances leading to unjust international attacks and/or unjust domestic institutions that might seem to call for war as a just response. While war might be permissible as a response to severe injustice, there are limits on the conduct of war even when it is a warranted response, and a state pursuing a just war or just use of force must do so with right intention. The idea of right intention not only is the overarching constraint on war but is also what unifies *ad bellum*, *in bello*, and *post bellum* (of, in, and after phases of war).

Fundamental to achieving or at least setting the conditions for a just and lasting peace is having a right intention. Although right intention has been a guiding principle in just war, it has lost some traction over the years. But as I have tried to show, aligning the just war tradition with the norm of right intention is essential in order to set conditions for a just and lasting peace. The Augustinian concept of right intention is a fundamental principle of the entire just war tradition and all phases of war, not just the *ad bellum* phase. Right intention, is an essential part of war and needs to be further explored and revitalized as not only a mainstay in the just war tradition but in fact the only principle that unites all three phases of war.

Constitutive of having a right intention is that a state's political leadership and military set the goal of achieving a just and lasting peace. A lasting peace is not possible unless certain standards of basic justice are secure—primarily, the honoring of basic human rights. And so fighting with right intention and establishing conditions for a just and lasting peace demand certain reforms to just war theory, because the ethics of war are predicated on honoring human rights. Vindicating a just cause and doing so in a just manner, which respects human rights and takes due care to insulate noncombatants from the ills of war but also recognizes and honors human rights throughout the postwar period, will reliably serve as a means to a just and lasting peace.

The intent of this book has been to analyze the concept of right intention and attempt to formulate and articulate all that right intention requires. By engaging in discourse about right intention, I have attempted to ascertain what policies and courses of action are consistent with right intention and the privileging of human rights. A just war tradition that places significant emphasis on human rights can and should be squarely made part of a state's foreign policy.

I have focused on six main areas: that just war is governed by an overarching principle of right intention; that having right intention compels states to proactively analyze postwar obligations before they arise; that the residual effects of war continue to kill civilians after the fighting is over, so there are obligations to mitigate these harms; that states are morally required to intervene when a state has failed in its responsibility to protect its own citizens' physical security, subsistence, and basic liberty rights; that justified drone strikes can be predicated on responsibility to protect norms; and that the Fourth Geneva Convention needs to be updated in order to reflect right intention and the human rights movement. The aim of this book has been to explore certain key elements of the claim that a just war is one fought with the right intention of not only vindicating a just cause and doing so in a just manner but also reliably serving as a means to a just and lasting peace. These issues are not only timely but pressing and can all be argued for from the root idea that if force is to be governed by a right intention oriented toward peace with justice, various reforms are required. However, even if these issues that I have elaborated do not incorporate all of the necessary changes, their discussion here will spark further interest, discourse, and contributions.

Notes

PREFACE

1. Brian Orend, *Morality of War* (Ontario: Broadview Press, 2006), 33.

INTRODUCTION

1. John Rawls, *The Law of Peoples* (Cambridge: Harvard University Press, 1999), 79. This is just one view of human rights and their role, and the view that I endorse.
2. Ibid., 94.
3. Ibid., 89.

CHAPTER 1. RIGHT INTENTION AND A JUST AND LASTING PEACE

1. Annalisa Koeman, "A Realistic and Effective Constraint on the Resort to Force," *Journal of Military Ethics* 6, no. 3 (2007): 201.
2. *Stanford Encyclopedia of Philosophy*, http://plato.stanford.edu/entries/war/#2.1.
3. Joseph Boyle, "Just War Thinking in Natural law," in *The Ethics of War and Peace: Religious and Secular Perspectives*, ed. Terry Nardin (Princeton: Princeton University Press, 1996), 45.
4. Ibid.
5. Ibid.
6. Ibid.
7. Thomas Aquinas, *Summa Theologica* II-II, Q. 40: Of War (circa 1270); http://www.op.org/summa/.
8. Michael Walzer, *Just and Unjust Wars* (New York: Basic, 1977), 51.

9. Ibid.
10. Orend, 35.
11. Walzer, 5.
12. Ibid.
13. Ibid., 51.
14. Article 2.4 of the UN Charter states: "All Members shall refrain in their international relations from the threat or use of force against the territorial integrity or political independence of any state, or in any other manner inconsistent with the Purposes of the United Nations. http://www.un.org/en/sections/un-charter/chapter-i/index.html. And Article 51 of the UN Charter declares, "Nothing in the present Charter shall impair the inherent right of individual or collective self-defence if an armed attack occurs against a Member of the United Nations, until the Security Council has taken measures necessary to maintain international peace and security. Measures taken by Members in the exercise of this right of self-defence shall be immediately reported to the Security Council and shall not in any way affect the authority and responsibility of the Security Council under the present Charter to take at any time such action as it deems necessary in order to maintain or restore international peace and security." http://www.un.org/en/sections/un-charter/chapter-vii/index.html.
15. Aquinas.
16. Orend, 2.
17. Ibid., 189.
18. Ibid.
19. Louis Swift, *The Earthly Fathers on War and Military Service* (Delaware: Michael Glazier, 1983), 115.
20. Herbert Deane, *The Political and Social Ideas of St. Augustine* (New York: Columbia University Press, 1963), 154.
21. Ibid., 155.
22. St. Augustine, *De Civitate Dei (The City of God)*, trans. Marcus Dods (New York: Random House, 1950), Book XVII, Section 13, 594–95.
23. Ibid., Book XIX, Section 17, 695.
24. Ibid.
25. Ibid., Book XV, Section 4, 481.
26. Ibid., Book XIX, Section 13, 690.
27. Ibid., Book XIX, Section 12, 687.
28. Ibid., 689.
29. John Finnis, "The Ethics of War and Peace in the Catholic Natural Law Tradition," in *The Ethics of War and Peace: Religious and Secular Perspectives*, ed. Terry Nardin (Princeton: Princeton University Press, 1996), 16.
30. Ibid.
31. St. Augustine further states, "It is therefore with the desire for peace that wars are waged. And hence it is obvious that peace is the end sought for

by war. For every man seeks peace by waging war, but no man seeks war by making peace" (Book XIX, Section 12, 687).

32. Swift, 115.
33. Ibid., 114.
34. Immanuel Kant, *Perpetual Peace and Other Essays* (1784–95), trans. Ted Humphrey (Cambridge: Hackett, 1983), 109.
35. Immanuel Kant, *Metaphysical Elements of Justice* (1797), trans. John Ladd (Cambridge: Hackett, 1999), 155.
36. Ibid., 162.
37. Ibid., 163.
38. Rawls, *The Law of Peoples*, 37.
39. In the following section, I address the fact that public acts are our best evidence for interpreting a state's intention, whereas in the fourth section I make the case that an overall assessment regarding whether a state has met the requirements of right intention can only be reached after the totality of that state's conduct has been completed.
40. William O'Brien, *The Conduct of Just and Limited War* (New York: Praeger, 1981), 34.
41. Rawls, 96.
42. Steven Lee, *Ethics and War: An Introduction* (Cambridge: Cambridge University Press, 2012), 84.
43. Ibid.
44. *The Harvest of Justice is Sown in* Peace; http://www.usccb.org/beliefs-and-teachings/what-we-believe/ catholic-social-teaching/the-harvest-of-justice-is-sown-in-peace.cfm.
45. B. H. Liddell Hart, *History of the Second World War* (New York: Da Capo, 1970), 144.
46. Walzer, *Just and Unjust Wars*, 268.
47. Lee, 84.
48. Finnis, 17.
49. Ibid.
50. Boyle, 45.
51. Ibid.
52. Rawls, 96.
53. Allen Buchanan, *Justice, Legitimacy, and Self-Determination* (Oxford: Oxford University Press, 2004), 5. Here, I adopt Allen Buchanan's view regarding legitimacy. Buchanan goes on to say, "The state is not merely an instrument for advancing the interests of its own citizens; it is also a resource for helping to ensure that all persons have access to institutions that protect their basic human rights" (ibid., 8).
54. Rawls, 82.
55. Ibid., 94.

56. Larry May, *After War Ends: A Philosophical Perspective* (Cambridge: Cambridge University Press, 2012), 13.

57. Rawls, 96.

58. Although I recognized that there are specific *jus post bellum* norms relating to apology, forgiveness, reconciliation, etc., I will not be taking them up in this chapter.

59. Walzer, 156.

60. Ibid.

61. Ibid.

62. Ibid.

63. Eric Schmitt, "NATO Sees Flaws in Air Campaign against Qaddafi"; http://www.nytimes.com/2012/04/15/world/africa/nato-sees-flaws-in-air-campaign-against-qaddafi.html?pagewanted=all&_r=0.

64. Thomas Aquinas, *Summa Theologica* II-II, Q. 64: On Murder, Art 8: Whether One Is Guilty of Murder Through Killing Someone by Chance; http://www.op.org/summa/.

65. Rawls, 96.

66. Cole, 182.

67. James Turner Johnson, *The War to Oust Saddam Hussein: Just War and the New Face of Conflict* (New York: Rowman and Littlefield, 2005), 22.

68. Rawls, 52–53.

69. Ibid.

70. Terms of Surrender; http://www.pbs.org/behindcloseddoors/pdfs/Terms Of German Surrender.pdf.

71. Potsdam Declaration; http://www.ibiblio.org/pha/policy/1945/450729a.html#1.

72. Walter J. Riker, "The Democratic Peace Is Not Democratic: On Behalf of Rawls's Decent Societies," *Political Studies* 57 (Oct. 2009): 5.

73. Ibid., 21.

74. Walter Riker, "Democratic Legitimacy and the Reasoned Will of the People," in *Coercion and the State*, ed. David Reidy and Walter Riker (Netherlands: Springer Science and Business Media, 2008), 80.

75. Ibid., 87.

76. Riker, "The Democratic Peace Is not Democratic," 19.

77. Ibid.

78. Ibid., 14.

79. Ibid., 2.

80. Rawls, 68.

81. Ibid., 75.

82. I do not intend to give a full defense of the Rawlsian position here, because that is not my focus. Instead, I appeal to the Rawlsian position precisely

because his position allows for the possibility of illiberal or nondemocratic but still well-ordered decent polities. It is not that Rawls is a relativist about justice or does not stand foursquare with liberal democracy. Rawls does think that liberal democratic regimes are superior to other forms of government. However, he also thinks that those committed to liberal democracy ought to reject the use of force to bring about liberalization and/or democratization where the conditions of well-ordered decency are fulfilled, and that informs his understanding of the right intention of a just and lasting peace and aim of war. Rawls's viewpoint expresses a liberal democratic vision of just international relations. But it is also a vision that at least well-ordered nondemocratic or nonliberal peoples could also reasonably affirm. Rawls's assumption is that decent peoples could reasonably accept the Law of Peoples (respect basic human rights; respect freedom and independence; obey treaties and restrictions in war; treat other states as equals; and honor the right to nonintervention and the duty of assistance), and so, therefore, liberal democratic peoples have sufficient reasons to extend recognition/respect to decent peoples.

Rawls holds that a just and lasting peace is a peace between decent well-ordered states, whether liberal democratic or otherwise, who have just relations with one another. It does not require that all states be just, so it is less demanding (in that sense) than many other views. While some theorists think a just and lasting peace demands more than Rawls thinks it demands (that is, they think it demands that all states be just), all or nearly all theorists agree that it requires at least what Rawls says it requires. Therefore, I believe that the Rawlsian position can be realized as a more sensible view, something like the lowest common denominator among reasonable views. Others might demand more but everyone demands at least what Rawls demands regarding human rights. It is less demanding and so arguably less controversial and more likely to be taken up within just war theory as part of global public reason. Some will still suggest that international justice demands more than Rawls seems to think. However, one may still think it is wrong to aim at the more demanding notion of coercive regime change/denying political self-determination when going to war.

83. Andrew Altman and Christopher Wellman, *A Liberal Theory of International Justice* (Oxford: Oxford University Press, 2009), 16.

84. Ibid., 17.

85. Allen Buchanan, "Democracy and Secession," in *National Self-Determination and Secession*, ed. Margret Moore (Oxford: Oxford University Press, 1998), 17. Buchanan goes on to say that individuals are governed by the majority: "Unless one (unpersuasively) defines self-government as government by the majority (perhaps implausibly distinguishing between the individual's apparent will and her 'real' will, which the majority is said to express), an individual can be self-governing only if he or she dictates political decisions. Far from constituting self-government for individuals, majority rule, under conditions in

which each individual's vote counts equally, excludes self-government for every individual" (ibid., 18).

86. Rawls, 59–60.
87. Altman and Wellman, 41.
88. Rawls, 62.
89. John Locke, *Second Treatise of Government*, ed. C. B. Macpherson (Cambridge: Hackett, 1980), 55.
90. Rawls, 62.
91. Ibid., 102.
92. Ibid., 101.
93. Ibid., 102.
94. Ibid.
95. Walzer, 256.
96. Rawls, 102.
97. Ibid., 37.
98. Richard Regan, *Just War: Principles and Cases* (Washington, DC: Catholic University of America Press, 1996), 85.
99. St. Augustine of Hippo wrote in the *De Praesentia Dei Ep.* 187 (*On the Presence of God: Letter 187*), "Peace should be your aim; one does not pursue peace in order to wage war; he wages war to achieve peace." Quoted in Swift, *The Earthly Fathers*, 114.

CHAPTER 2. REASONABLE CHANCE OF SUCCESS

1. Walzer, *Just and Unjust Wars*, 121.
2. May, *After War Ends: A Philosophical Perspective*, 13.
3. Brian Orend, "Justice after War," *Ethics and International Affairs* 16, no. 1 (2002): 46.
4. Gary Bass, "Jus Post Bellum," *Philosophy and Public Affairs* 32, no. 4 (2004): 390.
5. May, 226.
6. Walzer, 129.
7. Richard Miller, "Legitimation, Justification, and the Politics of Rescue," *Just War Reader* (2004): 126.
8. Richard Hass, *War of Necessity, War of Choice* (New York: Simon and Schuster, 2009), 257.
9. Ibid., 260.
10. "The U.S. Administration uncritically accepted what a small number of academics and exiles had told them, namely that the Iraqi people would welcome Americans as liberators and there would be no need for a heavy occupation force" (ibid., 254).
11. Ibid.

12. The Powell Doctrine was named after General Colin Powell, chairman of the Joint Chiefs of Staff at the time of the first Gulf War (1990–91). The doctrine is based in large part on the Caspar Weinberger Doctrine; see M. Cohen, "The Powell Doctrine's Enduring Relevance," *World Politics Review*. Caspar Weinberger was Ronald Reagan's secretary of defense (1981–87) and Powell's former boss. The Powell Doctrine states that a list of questions must be answered affirmatively before military action is taken by the United States: (1) Is a vital national security interest threatened? (2) Do we have a clear attainable objective? (3) Have the risks and costs been fully and frankly analyzed? (4) Have all other nonviolent policy means been fully exhausted? (5) Is there a plausible exit strategy to avoid endless entanglement? (6) Have the consequences of our action been fully considered? (7) Is the action supported by the American people? (8) Do we have genuine broad international support? Although it also seems that the United States could not have answered question number eight in the affirmative, this falls outside the scope of my project. Another item that will not be addressed in this chapter is whether the United States was justified in invading Iraq. The United Nations Security Council Resolution 1441 declared that Iraq was in material breach of previous UN resolutions and that Iraq "will face serious consequences" as a result of its continued violations of UN resolutions. *UN Security Council*; http://www.un.org/News/Press/docs/2002/SC7564.doc.htm. However, UNSCR 1441 was ambiguous about the characteristics of the serious consequences. UNSCR 1441 did not specifically authorize the use of force to bring about Iraqi compliance. However, the U.S. policymakers believed that it did.

13. *Joint Operation Planning 5-0* (Dec. 2006): IV-5.

14. Haas, 254.

15. I am not suggesting that a military use limited force when engaging enemy combatants. The U.S. military's mindset is to gain the initiative and use decisive overwhelming force to impose its will on the enemy. I concur with this principle. However, what I do suggest is that operations continually be planned to mitigate, as best as possible, collateral damage as well as for combatants to accept more risks while reducing harm or potential harm to civilians on the battlefield.

16. Altman and Wellman, *A Liberal Theory of International Justice*, 105.

17. George Lopez, 17.

18. Richard Stein, "100,000 Civilian Deaths Estimated in Iraq"; http://www.washingtonpost.com/wp-dyn/articles/A7967-2004Oct28.html.

19. Emmerich Vattel, *The Law of Nations* (London: Robison Paternoster-Row, 1797), Book III (Of War), Ch. V, 321–22.

20. Ibid., 352.

21. Immanuel Kant, *The Metaphysics of Morals* (Cambridge: Cambridge University Press, 1996), 118.

22. Kant, *Perpetual Peace*, 111.

23. Kant, *Metaphysical Elements of Justice*, 30.
24. Ibid.
25. NBC News, "US: Insurgents using teens in Iraq attacks," 2009, 1.
26. Ibid.
27. Walzer, 121.
28. Louis Swift, *The Earthly Fathers on War and Military Service* (Wilmington, DE: Michael Glazier, 1983), 114.
29. I would like to suggest that although the UN has the potential to oversee the occupation and reformation of dysfunctional institutions, the questions still remains as to whether the UN is in fact such an apparatus. The UN has been very ineffective regarding similar past issues, so the UN should only be considered as one example of such a multilateral force. It is quite possible that a regional, Genocide and Atrocities Prevention Act of 2016, or other coalition might be better suited to handle such an endeavor.
30. Haas, 251.
31. John Lee, "Iraq Auditor Questions $636m in Costs," *Iraq-Business News*; http://www.iraq-businessnews.com/tag/corruption/.
32. Ibid.
33. Orend, *The Morality of War*, 210.
34. Hass,182.
35. Barack Obama, *Nobel Peace Prize Speech*; http://www.huffingtonpost.com/2009/12/10/obama-nobel-peace-prize-a_n_386837.html.
36. This quote is usually misattributed as Plato's. However, George Santayana is the rightful author. Santayana's remark was in response to President Wilson's comment that the World War I was the war to end all wars. George Santayana, "Tipperary," *Soliloquies in England and Later Soliloquies*, 1922; http://platodialogues.org/faq/faq008.htm.
37. Obama *Nobel Prize Speech*.
38. "The Responsibility to Protect," *International Commission on Intervention and State Sovereignty* (ICISS) (Ottawa: International Development Research Centre, 2001), 37.

CHAPTER 3. *POST BELLUM* OBLIGATIONS OF NONCOMBATANT IMMUNITY

1. Rawls, *The Law of Peoples*, 94–96.
2. By stating *jus ad bellum* and *jus in bello* civilian immunity norm, I am referring to the *jus in bello* principle of noncombatant immunity and the *jus ad bellum* principle of right intention.
3. Walzer, *Just and Unjust Wars*, 121.

4. Guerrillas or insurgents blur the line of this distinction and want the privileges of both categories. Further discussion of this issue falls outside the scope of this chapter.

5. Walzer, 36.

6. I recognize the case of the naked soldier: a soldier tending to personal hygiene that is caught off guard by the enemy. Sure, it is legally permissible for a combatant to kill a naked enemy combatant, but morally it raises questions. I prefer to bracket that topic for now.

7. Jeff McMahan, *Killing in War* (Oxford: Oxford University Press, 2009), 157.

8. Ibid.

9. In some cases, civilians do pose a threat of varying levels (in some cases even as much or potentially more than soldiers do, e.g., a scientist designing advanced munitions or a key propagandists generating popular support for the war compared to an average citizen buying war bonds to help finance the war, etc.), but these civilians still fall into the category of noncombatant and as such are not supposed to be intentionally targeted. Maybe there is more culpability with some civilians over others, and some philosophers believe that it is morally permissible to intentionally target those civilians that are culpable. I do not agree with this perspective. However, for now, I do not plan on addressing this topic.

10. David Rodin and Henry Shue, "Introduction," in *Just and Unjust Warriors: The Moral and Legal Status of Soldiers*, ed. David Rodin and Henry Shue (Oxford: Oxford University Press, 2008), 3.

11. The principle of noncombatant immunity declares that intentionally targeting civilians is forbidden, because civilians are currently harmless. However, civilians can impose a direct threat (riots, unruly crowd, hitting soldiers, etc.) to military forces. When this occurs, those civilians can be intentionally targeted with nonlethal munitions (rubber bullets, paintballs, sting grenades, tear gas, etc.). This would not only be a proportionate response, since it would only cause temporary incapacitation without leaving permanent side effects, but also nonlethal munitions provide a way of subduing aggressive civilians and deescalating the current situation. Soldiers that do not have nonlethal options would mostly err on the side of using lethal force. Killing or permanently maiming civilians only leads to straining and compounding the current relations between both states. The use of nonlethal munitions is relatively new, so much more analysis needs to be done. However, nonlethal munitions are potentially useful and permissible.

12. In some cases, civilians play an informed role when it comes to the decision for a state to go to war, but I am focusing on the typical citizen of a state, not political leaders who make decisions without the approval of the civilian populace.

13. Department of the Army, Field Manual 27-10, *The Law of Land Warfare* (July 1976), 108.

14. Additionally, when the war is officially over, combatants lose their authority to kill and liability to be killed. They *en masse* join the civilian population and are afforded the same rights: life and liberty. These former combatants require the same basic necessities as well.

15. Walzer, 135.

16. *The Law of Land Warfare*, 5.

17. Thomas Nagel advocates "[t]hat hostility or aggression should be directed at its true object; this means both that it should be directed at the person or persons who provoke it and that it should aim more specifically at what is provocative about them" ("War and Massacre," *Philosophy and Public Affairs* 1, no. 2 (1972): 88. Nagel's point is that soldiers should be attacking enemy soldiers and that bomber pilots should be bombing purely military targets (military vehicles, army headquarters, army combatants, etc.).

18. Ibid., 87.

19. I am not suggesting that a military use limited force when engaging enemy combatants. A military's mindset is to gain the freedom to maneuver and use decisive overwhelming force to impose its will on the enemy. However, operations need to be thoroughly planned to mitigate, as best as possible, collateral damage (to include residual effects).

20. *The Law of Land Warfare*, 5.

21. George Lopez, "Iraq and Just War Thinking: The Presumption Against the Use of Force," *Common Wealth Magazine* 129, no. 16 (2002): 17.

22. Richard, Miller, "Legitimation, Justification, and the Politics of Rescue," in *Just War Reader*, ed. Louis Schwartz (Mason, OH: Thomson Custom Publishing, 2004), 126.

23. Media coverage has abounded with questions of the legitimacy of drone attacks (e.g., do they violate a nonbelligerent nation's airspace; is it permissible to use a drone to kill a suspected terrorist, or to target the family of a terrorist; can the secret authorization to kill U.S. citizens deemed by the U.S. government to be terrorists be justified, etc.). Stories of drone attacks that strike or miss their intended targets and cause collateral damage such as killing innocent civilians are routinely broadcast on the nightly news. Although the use of drones has brought attention to unintended but foreseen consequences (as well as many other issues), belligerents are not held accountable for their destructiveness of dual purpose facilities. There has been neither significant media coverage nor a demand by the international community for stringent accountability of belligerents' actions regarding the targeting of dual purpose facilities, especially ones that seem to contribute significantly to the welfare of civilians.

24. McMahan, 173.

25. Ibid.
26. Ibid.
27. Ibid.
28. Ibid.
29. Ibid., 174.
30. Ibid.

31. These are independent reforms. *Ex post* review might be warranted apart from the issue of repairing damages that violate the basic human rights of noncombatants.

32. My viewpoint is analogous to Allen Buchanan and Robert Keohane's regarding the preventive use of force without Security Council approval. Although I am not discussing preventive use of force, Buchanan and Keohane's concept fits nicely with my point.

33. Allen Buchanan and Robert Keohane. "The Preventive Use of Force: A Cosmopolitan Institutional Proposal," *Ethics and International Affairs* 18, no. 1 (2004): 11. Buchanan and Keohane's paper revolves around comparison of international bodies (the UN, as opposed to an external commission). Although I use their framework, I am more focused on the moral aspects than the legal aspects.

34. Covering *ex post* repair costs can be accomplished multiple ways. Most likely, it would include a combination of not only monies but also the use of the victor's internal assets, that is, some implementation and integration of the army corps of engineers, local construction, fabrication, and supply companies of the vanquished state, international and local contractors, outsourcing to private firms, etc. I wish to bracket this subject in order to stay on topic.

35. Larry May, "Reparations, Restitution, and Transitional Justice," in *Morality Jus Post Bellum, and International Law*, ed. Larry May (Oxford: Oxford University Press, 2012), 43–44.

36. Ibid., 46.

37. I will discuss this in more detail in the seventh section.

38. Shue and Wippman indicate that "the indirect costs stemming from the long-term effects . . . are less visible and more difficult to ascertain and so often ignored" (Henry Shue and David Wippman, "Limiting Attacks on Dual-Use Facilities Performing Indispensable Civilian Functions," *Cornell International Law Journal* 35 (2002): 564.

39. Ibid., 560.
40. Ibid.
41. Ibid., 574.
42. Ibid., 559.

43. I believe that Shue, in a more recent article, attempts to press his point too far. Shue suggests that "[c]urrent doctrine represents at least in part a daring attempt to return to moral-bombing." *Targeting Civilian Infrastructure with*

Smart Bombs: The New Permissiveness, 6. The goal of morale-bombing (directly bombing populated areas) is to break the will of the people, hoping that the citizens will in turn demand that its government sue for peace. This tactic was used by the Allies and Nazi Germany during World War II. One of the reasons that this tactic was accepted as part of war was that collateral damage was incredibly high even when bombing military targets, because of the limited technology associated with bombing at the time. In the 1940s there were not any smart or precision guided munitions, so belligerents used carpet bombing. At best, American bombers could reasonably guarantee that only 25 percent of their payload would strike within three city blocks of the desired military target. Dropping hundreds if not thousands of bombs during a bombing run increased the likelihood that the military target would be destroyed. Collateral damage and incidental loss of civilian life was extremely high. It many cases, it would have been hard to tell if a specific bombing run was focused on a military or a civilian target, because civilian deaths would be very high in both cases.

Shue wants to suggest that military forces—in particular those of the United States—are now resorting again to indiscriminate bombing tactics like those used in World War II. In his article, Shue reveals the United States' joint targeting ("joint" refers to all military forces: Army, Navy, Air Force, and Marines) doctrine, which states, "Civilian populations and civilian/protected objects, *as a rule*, may not be intentionally targeted, *although there are exceptions to this rule*" (6). However, the U.S. *Joint Targeting* doctrine further stipulates what qualifies as *an exception to the rule*. "Acts of violence solely intended to spread terror among the civilian population are prohibited; the protection offered civilians carries a strict obligation on the part of civilians not to take an active part in armed combat, become combatants, or engage in acts of war; civilians engaging in combat or otherwise taking an active part in combat operations, singularly or as a group, *lose their protected status*." *Joint Targeting*, E-2; emphasis added. That is, *the exception to the rule* that allows for the bombing of civilians is that those civilians have lost their protected status because they have picked up a weapon and joined the fight similar to the role of a militia member, an insurgent, or a thug.

Shue's point does have some merit, though, because the bombing doctrine does seems to suggest that bombings are permitted to cause terror, so long as there is some military advantage that can be cited. Then again, it seems hard to suggest that there would not be terror associated with any bombings. Even bombing a purely military target such as a munitions factory, whose destruction killed civilian workers as an unintended side effect, would cause unease, fear, terror, and duress among the civilian population because civilians have neither control nor insight into what will happen next.

U.S. doctrine does attempt to mitigate harming the civilian population by incorporating a military lawyer (staff judge advocate [SJA]) into the target planning. "The SJA should be immediately available and should be consulted at all levels of command to provide advice about law of war compliance during planning and execution of exercises and operations; early involvement by the SJA will improve the targeting process and can prevent possible violations of international or domestic law." *Joint Targeting*, E-6. In addition to having a military lawyer review targets for legal permissibility, a plausible way forward is to better train and educate intelligence analysts (the military staff personnel who determine the facilities to be targeted) about the civilian contribution and residual effects imposed on the civilian population if specific facilities are targeted and destroyed.

44. Buchanan and Keohane, 12.

45. On another note, there will be hard cases. There will be cases that need to be reviewed to determine whether damage to a dual use facility caused by an attack or some other action is what threatens human rights. For example, suppose State A destroyed a power plant that is dual use (it provides civilian electricity but also provides the energy for a major munitions plant) in State B. After it is destroyed, State B opts not to divert power from another electric plant to its civilian population previously dependent on the damaged facility but rather to divert that power to the munitions plant. State B should be held accountable for taking electricity away from its own citizens to power the munitions plant. It is possible that State A will be obligated to repair the power grid if it decides to bomb it again in order to render no electricity to the whole geographical vicinity. Or if State A decides to bomb and destroy the major munitions factory, State B can then divert that power back to its civilian populace since the major munitions plant has been completely destroyed.

46. Buchanan and Keohane, 11. How institutionally to take up that moral terrain is through the use of some sort of international body, which would review potential injustices. However, the organization and composition of such an external commission, along with its rules and authoritative nature, would have to be worked out.

47. But also, it is possible that if the victor was destitute after the conflict, other states would volunteer to assist the victor with repairing the dual purpose facilities in order to protect civilians from residual harms.

48. James Brown Scott, *The Spanish Origin of International Law: Francisco De Vitoria and His Law of Nations* (Oxford: Clarendon Press, 1934), 231.

CHAPTER 4. NEGATIVE AND POSITIVE CORRESPONDING DUTIES OF THE RESPONSIBILITY TO PROTECT

1. "The Responsibility to Protect," International Commission on Intervention and State Sovereignty (ICISS), December 2001, vii.

2. In order to justify the use of military force, there has to be serious and irreparable harm inflicted on human beings. "Grievous issues"—in this context—refers to genocide, war crimes, ethnic cleansing, and crimes against humanity. Genocide is "any of the following acts committed with intent to destroy, in whole or in part, a national, ethnical, racial or religious group including: killing members of the group; causing serious bodily or mental harm to members of the group; deliberately inflicting on the group conditions of life calculated to bring about its physical destruction in whole or in part; imposing measures intended to prevent births within the group; and forcibly transferring children of the group to another group" (The 1948 Convention on the Prevention and Punishment of the Crime of Genocide [Article 2]; http://www.un.org/en/preventgenocide/adviser/genocide_prevention.shtml). War Crimes "are namely, violations of the laws or customs of war; such violations shall include, but not be limited to, murder, ill-treatment or deportation to Wave labour [foreign forced labor] or for any other purpose of civilian population of or in occupied territory, murder or ill-treatment of prisoners of war or persons on the seas, killing of hostages, plunder of public or private property, wanton destruction of cities, towns or villages, or devastation not justified by military necessity." Charter Nuremberg Trial 1945 [Article 6]; http://www.icrc.org/ihl.nsf/WebSearch?SearchView&Query=war+crimes&SearchFuzzy=TRUE&SearchOrder=4. Crimes against Humanity "are namely, murder, extermination, enslavement, deportation, and other inhumane acts committed against any civilian population, before or during the war, or persecutions on political, racial or religious grounds in execution of or in connection with any crime within the jurisdiction of the Tribunal, whether or not in violation of the domestic law of the country where perpetrated" (ibid). Furthermore, "Leaders, organizers, instigators and accomplices participating in the formulation or execution of a common plan or conspiracy to commit any of the foregoing crimes are responsible for all acts performed by any persons in execution of such plan" (ibid). Ethnic Cleansing is "the planned deliberate removal from a specific territory, persons of a particular ethnic group, by force or intimidation, in order to render that area ethnically homogenous." Genocide Prevention Project, 2009; http://www.preventorprotect.org/overview/definitions.html. However, *"there is no formal legal definition of 'ethnic cleansing,' though its scope is within the definitions of war crimes and crimes against humanity"* (ibid.).

3. ICISS, xi. Although the ICISS states that the principle of nonintervention yields to the international responsibility to protect, I will make the case for an international responsibility to protect based on basic human rights as being what we all owe to one another.

4. Ibid.

5. Ibid., xii.

6. United Nations General Assembly 2005 World Summit, para 139; http://www.un.org/ summit 2005/documents.html.

7. ICISS, xii.

8. UN GA 2005 WS, para 139.

9. "Summary of the Report of the Secretary-General on 'Implementing the Responsibility to Protect,'" International Coalition for the Responsibility to Protect (ICRtoP), 2009; http://www.responsibilitytoprotect.org/files/ICRtoP%20Summary%20of%20SG%20report.

10. While measures such as freezing assets might be "peaceful," they do seem to involve coercion. Within the context of the R2P doctrine, "peaceful measures" refers to actions that do not involve military intervention. Peaceful measures—depending on how intrusive they are—can be used as a form of persuasion or as a form of coercion; although possibly coercive, they are a lesser form of coercion than military intervention.

11. Ibid., 3. Additionally, "The Security Council and the General Assembly can appoint fact-finding missions to investigate and report on alleged violations of international law; the Human Rights Council may also deploy a fact-finding mission as well as appoint a special rapporteur to advise on the situation" (4).

12. Ibid., 4.

13. "Summary of the Report of the Secretary-General on 'The Role of Regional and Sub-regional Arrangements in Implementing the Responsibility to Protect,'" International Coalition for the Responsibility to Protect (ICRtoP); http://www.responsibilitytoprotect.org/7%20July%20Summary%20of%20the%20SG%20report.pdf.

14. Ibid., 4.

15. Charter of the United Nations; http://www.un.org/en/documents/charter/.

16. UN GA 2005 WS, para 138; http://www.un.org/summit2005/documents.html.

17. Richard Norman, *Ethics, Killing, and War* (Cambridge: Cambridge University Press, 1995), 156.

18. Jennifer Welsh, "A Normative Case for Pluralism: Reassessing Vincent's view on Humanitarian Intervention," *International Affairs* 87, no. 5 (2011): 1200.

19. Thomas Hobbes, *Leviathan*, ed. J. C. A. Gaskin (Oxford: Oxford University Press, 1998), 95.

20. Ibid., 114.

21. Ibid.

22. Ibid., 141.

23. Locke, *Second Treatise*, 55.

24. Ibid., 52.

25. Ibid., 71.

26. Ibid.

27. Ibid., 90.

28. Allen Buchanan, *Justice, Legitimacy, and Self-Determination: Moral Foundations for International Law* (Oxford: Oxford University Press, 2004), 5.

29. Ibid. 261–63.

30. David Luban, "Just War and Human Rights," *Philosophy & Public Affairs* 9, no. 2 (1980): 165. Luban uses this statement to explain that once a government is recognized as having authority and control over a piece of land, the UN observes the duty of nonintervention toward that state and does not interfere into its domestic affairs. The UN's indifference toward what constitutes authority is problematic because it excludes the moral dimension of legitimacy. Rather, it should be that when State A recognizes State B's sovereignty, it implies that State B has met necessary conditions that give it the moral right to nonintervention.

31. Ibid.

32. Rawls, 80.

33. ICISS, 8.

34. Andrew Altman and Christopher Wellman, *A Liberal Theory of International Justice* (Oxford: Oxford University Press, 2009), 3.

35. Rawls, 80.

36. David Reidy, "Political Authority and Human Rights," in *Rawls's Law of Peoples: A Realist Utopia?*, ed. Rex Martin and David Reidy (Oxford: Blackwell Publishing, 2006), 175.

37. I will elaborate further on these necessary conditions in sections 7, 8, and 9.

38. Henry Shue, *Basic Rights: Subsistence, Affluence, and US Foreign Policy* (Princeton: Princeton University Press, 1980), 19.

39. Michael Ignatieff, *Human Rights as Politics and Idolatry* (Oxford: Oxford University Press, 2001), 57.

40. Ibid.

41. Ibid.

42. Shue, 16.

43. Ibid., 30.

44. Ibid., 36.

45. Ibid., 37.

46. Shue, 19.

47. United Nations, *A More Secure World: Our Shared Responsibility* (*report of the High-Level Panel on Threat, Challenges and Change*) (United Nations Foundation, 2004), 64.

48. Ibid., 65.

49. *Peace-enforcing* and *peacekeeping* forces are terms used by the UN and NATO. A peace-enforcing mission usually involves nonpermissible borders. That is, at least one party to the conflict (the targeted state) does not welcome outside intervention, so the foreign military force is not given permission to enter the target state's territory. As a result, the peace-enforcing military unit enters the target state by force. A peace-enforcing mission will most likely involve combat

operations in order to subdue forces that not only have failed to follow UNSC resolutions but also continue to pursue their unjust and aggressive aims. Peacekeeping missions are usually welcomed by the parties to the conflict. These parties have usually agreed to an armistice and prefer the assistance of UN-sponsored troops to keep the peace between the two parties. Both peace-enforcing and peacekeeping missions are not necessarily about peace but about enforcing rights. R2P military intervention is limited to severe violations of physical security rights, so there is a sense in which it secures some measure of peace (in the sense of stopping a certain sort of violence), but the goal is vindicating the rights, not merely securing peace (which could be obtained perhaps by making large cash payments to despots, etc.).

50. I will elaborate much more on the use of armed drones (unmanned aerial vehicles—UAVs) as justified uses of force short of war (*jus ad vim*) in the next chapter.

51. James Nickel, "Are Human Rights Mainly Implemented by Intervention?" in *Rawls's Law of Peoples: A Realist Utopia?* ed. Rex Martin and David Reidy (Oxford: Blackwell, 2006), 271.

52. Larry May, *Genocide: A Normative Account* (Cambridge: Cambridge University Press, 2010), 231.

53. Ibid.

54. I endorse the existing R2P doctrine, which limits application to only actual rather than apprehended widespread violations of physical security rights. This seems to be a better choice than allowing belief or perception to dictate that R2P intervention is necessary. It is not just enough that the state (primary duty bearer) fails the duty but that persons *actually* lack the object of the right. That is, the content or object of the right is not secured for them. Persons that are the victims of a genocide campaign are denied the object of the right, namely the right to life. Specifically, civilians are *actually* being harmed by acts of genocide, ethnic cleansing, war crimes, or crimes against humanity.

55. Shue, 114.

56. Charles Beitz, *The Idea of Human Rights* (Oxford: Oxford University Press, 2009), 39.

57. Kok-Chor Tan, "Military Intervention as a Moral Duty," *Public Affairs Quarterly* 9, no. 1 (1995): 31.

58. Thomas Hill, "Kant and Humanitarian Intervention," *Philosophical Perspectives* 23 (2009): 230.

59. May, "Conflicting Responsibilities to Protect Human Rights," 7.

60. Ibid., 1. May states that not only are soldiers' rights being affected but citizens' rights as well since they will have to bear the financial burden of the military intervention.

61. Ibid., 11.

62. Ibid., 13.

63. Jeff McMahan, *Killing in War* (Oxford: Oxford University Press, 2009), 100.
64. Ibid.
65. Ibid., 101.
66. Ibid., 141.
67. Ibid.
68. Michael Walzer, *Obligations: Essays on Disobedience, War, and Citizenship* (Cambridge: Harvard University Press, 1970), 83.
69. McMahan, 154.
70. Tan, 39.
71. Ibid.
72. Ibid.
73. Shue, 111–18.
74. Ibid., 111–12.
75. Emmerich de Vattel, *The Law of Nations*, trans. and ed. C. G. and J. Robison Paternoster-Row (London, 1758, trans in 1797) (Bk II, ch. 1), 135.
76. Shue, 112. Shue states, "One is required to sacrifice, as necessary, anything but one's basic rights in order to honor the basic rights of others" (ibid., 114).
77. *A More Secure World: Our Shared Responsibility*, 64.
78. Beitz, 151.
79. For example, "During the 2004 Presidential election, candidates Bush and Kerry raised concerns about any measures that might tie U.S. hands in advance, thereby compromising the sovereign right of the U.S. to decide when to go to war." Jennifer Welsh, "The Security Council and Intervention," in *The United Nations Security Council and War* (Oxford: Oxford University Press, 2008), 557. On another note, state autonomy is probably one of the key factors that led to "state representatives failing to endorse the Secretary-General's set of criteria for the use of force at the UN Summit of World Leaders, held in September 2005," and instead unanimously agreed to relegate intervention to a case-by-case basis (ibid., 557).
80. McMahan, 100–101.
81. Ibid., 101.
82. Vattel (Preliminaries, lv).
83. Reidy, 185.

CHAPTER 5. JUSTIFIED DRONE STRIKES ARE PREDICATED ON THE RESPONSIBILITY TO PROTECT

1. Personality strikes are those that are directed against a specific person. Signature strikes are those that are directed against a person(s) who is engaged in suspicious behavior, e.g., digging a ditch near a road, armed men meeting or traveling in a convoy, etc. A person's behavior or action at a particular moment

is consistent with actions or behaviors of what an insurgent or terrorist would be doing that would justify defense. The surveilled person emits a threatening signature. Therefore, that person—although not positively identified as an insurgent or terrorist—can be legally targeted with an armed (kinetic) drone strike because of an action that is actually or construed to be a justified threat.

2. Although the September 14, 2001, "Authorization for Use of Military Force" (AUMF) sanctions the use of United States Armed Forces against those responsible for the attacks on September 11, 2001, the document only distinguishes Al Qaeda by name and refers to other organizations not by name but only generically as associated groups/forces. On September 11, 2014, President Obama publicly announced to Congress that he wants an AUMF against the Islamic State. The Islamic State (also known as ISIL [Islamic State of Iraq and the Levant] and ISIS [Islamic State of Iraq and Syria]) is one of those groups that have been recently identified as posing a significant threat as well. Like Al Qaeda, "ISIL poses a threat to the people of Iraq and Syria, and the broader Middle East—including American citizens, personnel, and facilities." Obama, "Statement by the President on ISIL." However, Congress has not yet approved such an AUMF against ISIL so the Obama administration uses the 2001 AUMF as its authorization to target ISIL, citing that ISIL is similar in nature to Al Qaeda and must be disrupted, degraded, and ultimately destroyed in order to protect American lives and interests. Although there might be legal issues surrounding this (using a 2001 AUMF as the approval document and authority to engage an enemy that materialized in 2014), I prefer to bracket this topic for now.

3. Barack Obama, "Statement by the President on ISIL," September 10, 2014, Office of the Press Secretary.

4. "Lawfulness of a Lethal Operation Directed against a US Citizen who Is a Senior Operational Leader of Al Qa'ida or an Associated Force," aka "white paper." Although not an official legal memo, the white paper was represented by administration officials as a policy document that closely mirrors the arguments of classified memos on targeted killings by the Justice Department's Office of Legal Counsel, which provides authoritative legal advice to the President and all executive branch agencies.

5. In addition to the categories of state or nonstate actor, there could also be a substate actor, which has no intent or capacity to influence outside of the state. That is, its influence is contained within a specific state's boundaries and does not bleed over to the subregional, regional, or international domain. However, a substate actor can greatly harm the people of the state it influences or coerces.

6. St. Augustine, *De Civitate Dei (The City of God)*, Book XV, Section 4, 481, and Book XIX, Section 12, 687.

7. "Targeted killings are premeditated acts of lethal force employed by states in times of peace or during armed conflict to eliminate specific individuals

outside their custody." Jonathan Masters, "Targeted Killings," Council on Foreign Relations; http://www.cfr.org/counterterrorism/targeted-killings/p9627.

8. http://investigations.nbcnews.com/_news/2013/02/04/16843014-justice-department-memo-reveals-legal-case-for-drone-strikes-on-americans.

9. Ibid.

10. "White Paper," 7.

11. Ibid.

12. "Seriousness and closeness" is Michael Walzer's rendition of the components of imminent threat.

13. "The Responsibility to Protect," International Commission on Intervention and State Sovereignty (ICISS), December 2001, xi.

14. Charter Nuremberg Trial 1945 (Article 6); http://www.icrc.org/ihl.nsf/WebSearch?SearchView&Query=war+crimes&SearchFuzzy=TRUE&SearchOrder=4.

15. Allen Buchanan, *Justice, Legitimacy, and Self-Determination: Moral Foundations for International Law* (Oxford: Oxford University Press, 2004), 5.

16. Ibid., 261–63.

17. ICISS, 8.

18. Andrew Altman and Christopher Wellman, *A Liberal Theory of International Justice* (Oxford: Oxford University Press, 2009), 3.

19. David Reidy, "Political Authority and Human Rights," in *Rawls's Law of Peoples: A Realist Utopia?*, ed. Rex Martin and David Reidy (Oxford: Blackwell Publishing, 2006), 175.

20. Daniel Brunstetter and Megan Braun, "From *Jus ad Bellum* to *Jus ad Vim*: Recalibrating Our Understanding of the Moral Use of Force," *Ethics & International Affairs* 2, no. 1 (2013): 87.

21. Audrey Cronin, "Why Drones Fail: When Tactics Drive Strategy," *Foreign Affairs*, July/August 2013; http://www.foreignaffairs.com/print/136673.

22. Daniel Byman, "Why Drones Work: The Case for Washington's Weapon of Choice," *Foreign Affairs*, July/August 2013; http://www.foreignaffairs.com/print/136672.

23. Ibid.

24. United Nations, *A More Secure World: Our Shared Responsibility* (report of the High-Level Panel on Threat, Challenges and Change) (United Nations Foundation, 2004), 64.

25. Ibid.

26. Below is a further elaboration of the UNSC's five basic criteria of legitimacy for the use of force:

   1. *Seriousness of Threat*: Is the threatened harm to State or human security of a kind, and sufficiently clear and serious, to justify *prima facie* the use of military force? In the case of internal threats, does it involve genocide and other large-scale killing,

ethnic cleansing, or serious violations of international humanitarian law, actual or imminently apprehended?
2. *Proper Purpose*: Is it clear that the primary purpose of the proposed military action is to halt or avert the threat in question, whatever other purposes or motives may be involved?
3. *Last Resort*: Has every non-military option for meeting the threat in question been explored, with reasonable grounds for believing that other measures will not succeed?
4. *Proportional Means*: Are the scale, duration, and intensity of the proposed military action the minimum necessary to meet the threat in question?
5. *Balance of Consequences*: Is there a reasonable chance of the military action being successful in meeting the threat in question, with the consequences of action not likely to be worse than the consequences of inaction?

A More Secure World: Our Shared Responsibility, 67. The UNSC's five basic criteria of legitimacy for the use of force mirror current just war philosophy regarding *jus ad bellum* (justice of war) criteria of when a state can resort to war. Those *jus ad bellum* principles are *just cause, right intention, last resort, proportionality,* and *reasonable chance of success.*

27. Ibid., 3.
28. Ibid., 67.
29. U.S. Genocide and Atrocities Prevention Act of 2016; https://www.foreign.senate.gov/press/ranking/release/us-senators-introduce-bipartisan-genocide-and-atrocities-prevention-act-of-2016.
30. Shue, *Basic Rights*, 19.
31. Walzer, *Just and Unjust Wars*, xvi.
32. James Pattison, *Humanitarian Intervention and the Responsibility to Protect* (Oxford: Oxford University Press, 2010), 70.
33. Ibid.
34. Ibid., 72.
35. I am not suggesting that those adults actually believe that a drone will strike their child if he or she is out past 9 p.m. I am suggesting that drones are part of their family's environment. This is similar to my mom telling me (when I was a child) to come in when the street lights "come on," but with a twenty-first-century (and drone warfare) adaptation.
36. Audrey Cronin, "Why Drones Fail: When Tactics Drive Strategy," *Foreign Affairs*, July/August 2013; http://www.foreignaffairs.com/print/136673.
37. Ibid.
38. John Bennett "Is That Your Drone?" *Defense News*, May 18, 2015, 14.
39. John Bennett "Drone Wars Redux?" *Defense News*, May 4, 2015, 14.

40. Both the United States and the UK use the armed, U.S.-manufactured MQ-9 Reaper. France and Italy currently only have unarmed versions of the Reaper. The Netherlands will soon be authorized to buy the unarmed version of the Reaper from the United States as well.

41. Ed Royce, "Exporting U.S. Drones," *Defense News*, March 2, 2015, 21.

42. Andrew Chuter, "Swatting the Mini-Drone," *Defense News*, June 22, 2015, 9.

43. Pierre Tran, Andrew Chuter, and Tom Kington, "NATO's Reaper Users Cooperate to Cut Costs," *Defense News*, January 26, 2015, 6.

44. Tom Kington and Pierre Tran, "New European UAV Effort Raises Hope," *Defense News*, May 25, 2015, 1.

45. Ibid. 11.

46. Ibid.

CHAPTER 6. UPDATING THE FOURTH GENEVA CONVENTION

1. W. Michael Reisman, and Chris Antoniou, eds., *The Laws of War: A Comprehensive Collection of Primary Documents Governing Armed Conflict* (Art 27, Part III: Status and Treatment of Protected Persons, GCIV) (New York: Vintage Books, 1994), 240.

2. Ibid.

3. "Transitional justice concerns situations where a State, or a people, tries to move from a conflict situation to a post-conflict situation." Larry May, *After War Ends: A Philosophical Perspective* (Cambridge: Cambridge University Press. 2012), 44.

4. Elements of justice are required by right intention and so required in the period of transitional justice as well as the *post bellum* phase. Transitional justice and *jus post bellum* overlap and "both concern how to regard just practices and institutions after war" (May, 6). Although both transitional justice and *jus post bellum* are focused toward a just and lasting peace, "transitional justice often concerns the way to move from an authoritarian regime that did not respect the rights of the people to a regime that does respect rights, and *jus post bellum* normally concerns how to move to a situation of stability after war" (ibid).

5. Kristen Boon, "Obligations of the New Occupier: the Contours of a Jus Post Bellum," *Loyola of Los Angeles International and Comparative Law Review* 31, no. 57 (2009): 63.

6. This treaty is commonly known and referred to as the Fourth Geneva Convention or the GCIV.

7. *The Laws of War*, 231.

8. Boon, "Obligations," 66.

9. 1966 International Covenant on Economic, Social, and Cultural Rights (ICESCR) and the 1966 the International Covenant on Civil and Political Rights (ICCPR).

10. Carsten Stahn, "Jus Post Bellum: Mapping the Discipline(s)," *American University International Law Review* 23, no. 2 (2007): 325.

11. Allen Buchanan, "Human Rights and the Legitimacy of the International Order," *Legal Theory* 14, no. 1 (2008): 56.

12. Ibid., 58.

13. Ibid., 60.

14. Ibid., 48.

15. Ibid.

16. Ibid., 64.

17. Ibid.

18. It is permissible for basic liberty to be somewhat restricted in an occupied territory. Displaced persons may be temporarily placed in a refugee camp or restricted from travel for their own safety until essential infrastructure services are restored.

19. *The Laws of War*, 233. Even if there had been treaties prior to World War II that required more stringent accountability and responsibilities by the occupying powers, it is hard to imagine that Nazi Germany would have actually abided by them during the war.

20. *The Laws of War* (Hague Convention IV), 233.

21. Ibid., Articles 47–78, 245–54.

22. Ibid., 232.

23. Ibid., 247.

24. Ibid., 248.

25. Ibid., 250.

26. Protocol I provides additional protections such as Article 54, which states, "Starvation of civilians as a method of warfare is prohibited; it is prohibited to attack, destroy, remove or render useless objects indispensable to the survival of the civilian population, such as foodstuffs, agricultural areas for the production of foodstuffs, crops, livestock, drinking water installations, and irrigation works." Adam Roberts and Richard Guelff, eds., *Documents on the Laws of War* (Protocol I) (Oxford: Clarendon Press, 1982), 417. In addition, Article 55 states, "Care shall be taken in warfare to protect the natural environment against widespread, long-term and severe damage" (ibid., 418). On a side note, in 1991 Iraq violated Article 55 of Protocol I by dumping oil into the Persian Gulf and igniting hundreds of oil wells in Kuwait. Although Iraq claimed military necessity for these two actions (producing an oil slick to impede a possible Coalition amphibious landing operation and producing a smoke screen in order to hamper Coalition bomber attacks), its actions were not proportionate to the environmental damage that was caused.

27. *Documents on the Laws of War* (Protocol I), 428.
28. Stahn, 316.
29. International Committee of the Red Cross, "International Humanitarian Law and International Human Rights Law," 2003, 1–2.
30. Boon, "Obligations," 59.
31. Ibid., 57.
32. May states that "reconciliation as a *just post bellum* concept involves a process of returning previously warring parties to a point not only where they do not engage in violence toward each other but also where there is sufficient trust so that a robust and just peace can be attained—and where a just peace means that human rights are protected" (86). I believe that clearly defined and updated rules (legal embodiment of relevant moral norms) governing the obligations and restrictions of the parties to the conflict are essential to the reconciliation process. Having an updated preestablished legal framework facilitates a working relationship in which each party not only understands its own obligations ahead of time but is also aware of the other party's responsibilities and obligations.
33. Stahn, 317.
34. Ibid.
35. Ibid., 318.
36. Karen Boon, "Legislative Reform in Post-Conflict Zones," *McGill Law Journal* 50 (2005): 297.
37. Ibid.
38. Ibid., 298.
39. United Nations Charter; http://www.un.org/en/documents/charter/chapter1.shtml.
40. "Indigenous Affairs: Self-determination," International Work Group for Indigenous Affairs, 2002; http://www.iwgia.org/human-rights/self-determination.
41. United Nations Security Council, 2012; http://www.un.org/en/sc/documents/resolutions/ index.shtml.
42. Ibid.
43. *Laws of War* (GCIV), 247.
44. "ICCPR" and "ICESCR"; http://www.unhcr.org/refworld/docid/3ae6b36c0.html. There is no recognized international legal definition of "peoples," but the term refers to a group of persons that "enjoy some or all of the following common features: a common historical tradition, ethnic identity, cultural homogeneity; linguistic unity, religious or ideological affinity, territorial connection, and common economic life." "Indigenous Affairs: Self-determination," 8. In the context of an occupied territory the term *peoples* applies to the entire population within the occupied territory. The entire population has the moral and legal right to freely choose the type of government they want without coercion or interference. Because the state exists to serve and to protect the

peoples of a given territory, those peoples should be permitted to reform their own government in their own way.

45. "The Security Council and the General Assembly can appoint fact-finding missions to investigate and report on alleged violations of international law." "Summary of the Report of the Secretary-General on 'Implementing the Responsibility to Protect,'" International Coalition for the Responsibility to Protect (ICRtoP), 2009; http://www. responsibility toprotect.org/files/ICRtoP%20 Summary%20of%20SG%20report.pdf.

46. Article 39 (Chapter VII, UN Charter) stipulates, "The Security Council shall determine the existence of any threat to the peace, breach of the peace, or act of aggression and shall make recommendations, or decide what measures shall be taken in accordance with Articles 41 and 42, to maintain or restore international peace and security," United Nations Charter; http://www.un.org/en/documents/charter/.

47. "The Responsibility to Protect," International Commission on Intervention and State Sovereignty (ICISS) (Ottawa: International Development Research Centre, 2001), 39.

48. Ibid.

49. In chapter 3 on R2P, I focused almost entirely on the second tenet of the R2P doctrine (the responsibility to react using peaceful and/or coercive measures) and briefly mentioned the first tenet (the responsibility to prevent using subregional and regional education, awareness, and early warning signs). However, there is a third tenet, which is the responsibility to rebuild, which addresses the securing of institutions necessary for peace with justice, and I think that this R2P doctrine is a good fit to explain that there is also a need for the Geneva Convention to address some of these essential postwar issues that the R2P doctrine has already recognized as essential in postwar rebuilding.

50. "The Responsibility to Protect," 39.

51. Ibid.

52. "The Rule of Law and Transitional Justice in Conflict and Post-conflict Societies," United Nations Rule of Law, 2004; http://www.unrol.org/files/2004%20 report.pdf.

53. The Peacebuilding Commission (PBC) is an intergovernmental advisory body that supports peace efforts in countries emerging from conflict, and is a key addition to the capacity of the international community in the broad peace agenda. The Peacebuilding Commission plays a unique role (1) in bringing together all of the relevant actors, including international donors, the international financial institutions, national governments, and troop-contributing countries; (2) marshaling resources; and (3) advising on and proposing integrated strategies for postconflict peacebuilding and recovery and, where appropriate,

highlighting any gaps that threaten to undermine peace. UN Peacebuilding Commission, 2012; http://www.un.org/en/peacebuilding/.

54. Boon, "Obligations," 84.

55. Osterdahl and Zadel, 197.

CONCLUSION

1. Rawls, *The Law of Peoples*, 79.

2. Ibid., 94.

Bibliography

Altman, Andrew, and Christopher Wellman. *A liberal Theory of International Justice*. Oxford: Oxford University Press, 2009.

Anan, Kofi. "'In Larger Freedom': Decision Time for the UN." *Foreign Affairs*, May/June 2005, 1–6.

Anscombe, Elizabeth. "War and Murder." In *Nuclear Weapons: A Catholic Response*, edited by Walter Stein, 45–62. New York: Sheed and Ward, 1961.

Aquinas, Thomas. *Summa Theologica* II-II, Q. 40: Of War (circa 1270). http://www.op.org /summa/.

———. *Summa Theologica* II-II, Q. 64: On Murder, Art 8: Whether One Is Guilty of Murder Through Killing Someone by Chance (circa 1210). http://www.op.org/summa/.

Augustine. *The City of God (De Civitate Dei)* (circa 413). Translated by John Healey. New York: E.P. Dutton, 1957.

———. *The City of God (De Civitate Dei)* (circa 413). Translated by Marcus Dods. New York: Random House, 1950.

Bass, Gary. "Jus Post Bellum." *Philosophy and Public Affairs* 32, no. 4 (Autumn 2004): 384–412.

Beitz, Charles. *The Idea of Human Rights*, Oxford: Oxford University Press, 2009.

Boon, Kristen. "Legislative Reform in Post-Conflict Zones." *McGill Law Journal* 50 (2005): 285–326.

———. "Obligations of the New Occupier: the Contours of a *Jus Post Bellum*," *Loyola of Los Angeles International and Comparative Law Review* 31, no. 57 (2009): 57–84.

Brabandere, Eric De. "The Responsibility for Post-Conflict Reforms: A Critical Assessment of *Jus Post Bellum* as a Legal Concept." *Vanderbilt Journal of Transnational Law* 43 (2010): 119–49.

Bennett, John. "Is That Your Drone?" *Defense News*, May 18, 2015, 14.

Boyle, Joseph. "Just War Thinking in Natural law." In *The Ethics of War and Peace: Religious and Secular Perspectives*, edited by Terry Nardin, 40–59. Princeton: Princeton University Press, 1996.

Brunstetter, Daniel, and Megan Braun. "From *Jus ad Bellum* to *Jus ad Vim*: Recalibrating Our Understanding of the Moral Use of Force." *Ethics & International Affairs*. 2, no. 1 (2013): 87–106.
Buchanan, Allen. "Human Rights and the Legitimacy of the International Order." *Legal Theory* 14, no. 1 (March 2008): 39–70.
———. "Institutionalizing the Just War." *Philosophy and Public Affairs* 34, no. 1 (Winter 2006): 2–38.
———. *Justice, Legitimacy, and Self-Determination*, Oxford: Oxford University Press, 2004.
———. "Democracy and Secession." In *National Self-Determination and Secession*, edited by Margret Moore, 14–34. Oxford: Oxford University Press, 1998.
———, and Robert Keohane. "The Preventive Use of Force: A Cosmopolitan Institutional Proposal." *Ethics and International Affairs* 18, no. 1 (2004): 1–22.
Bush, George W. "West Point 2002 Graduation Speech." In *United States Military Academy PY201 Just War Reader*, edited by Louie Schwartz, 69–75. Mason, OH: Thomson Custom Publishing, 2004.
Byman, Daniel. "Why Drones Work: The Case for Washington's Weapon of Choice." *Foreign Affairs*, July/August 2013, 1–9. http://www.foreignaffairs.com/print/136672.
Carter, Stephen. *The Violence of Peace: America's Wars in the Age of Obama*, New York: Beast Books, 2010.
Charter Nuremberg Trial 1945 (Article 6). http://www.icrc.org/ihl.nsf/WebSearch?Search View&Query=war+crimes&SearchFuzzy=TRUE&SearchOrder=4.
Chesterman, Simon. "Leading from Behind: The Responsibility to Protect, The Obama Doctrine, and Humanitarian Intervention after Libya." *NYU School of Law, NELLCO Legal Scholarship Repository* (June 2011): 1–10.
Christopher, Paul. *The Ethics of War and Peace*. Englewood Cliffs, NJ: Prentice-Hall, 1994.
Chuter, Andrew. "Swatting the Mini-Drone." *Defense News*, June 22, 2015, 9.
Clausewitz, Carl Von. *On War (Volume I)* (1832). Translated by J. J. Graham. London: Routledge and Kegan Paul, 1968.
Coates, A. J. *The Ethics of War*, New York: Manchester University Press, 1997.
Cohen, Michael. "The Powell Doctrine's Enduring Relevance." *World Politics Review*, 2009. http://www.worldpoliticsreview.com/articles/4100/the-powell-doctrines-enduring-relevance.
Cole, Darrell. "War and Intention." *Journal of Military Ethics* 10, no. 3 (2011): 174–91.
The Convention on the Prevention and Punishment of the Crime of Genocide (1948), Article 2. http://www.un.org/en/preventgenocide/adviser/genocide_prevention.shtml.
Cronin, Audrey. "Why Drones Fail: When Tactics Drive Strategy." *Foreign Affairs*, July/August 2013, 1–9. http://www.foreignaffairs.com/print/136673.

Dean, Herbert. *The Political and Social Ideas of St. Augustine.* New York: Columbia University Press, 1963.
DiMeglio, Richard. "Evolution of the Just War Tradition: Defining Jus Post Bellum." *Military Law Review* 186 (2005): 116–63.
Dinstein, Yoram. *War, Aggression, and Self-Defence.* Cambridge: Cambridge University Press, 1994.
Elshtain, Jean. *Just War against Terror,* New York: Basic Books, 2003.
Farer, Tom. "The Ethics of Intervention in Self-determination Struggles." In *Ethics and Foreign Intervention,* edited by Deen Chatterjee and Don Scheid, 143–67. Cambridge: Cambridge University Press, 2003.
Finnis, John. "The Ethics of War and Peace in the Catholic Natural Law Tradition." In *The Ethics of War and Peace: Religious and Secular Perspectives,* edited by Terry Nardin, 15–39. Princeton: Princeton University Press, 1996.
Genocide Prevention Project. http://www.preventorprotect.org/overview/definitions.html, 2009.
Grotius, Hugo. On the Rights of *War and Peace* (1625). Translated by F. Barberrac. London: 1738.
Griffin, James. *On Human Rights,* Oxford: Oxford University Press, 2010.
Hague Conventions and Declarations of 1899 and 1907. Edited by James Brown Scott. Oxford: Oxford University Press, 1915.
Hart, Liddell. *History of the Second World War.* New York: Da Capo, 1970.
Hass, Richard. *War of Necessity, War of Choice,* New York: Simon and Schuster, 2009.
Hill, Thomas. "Kant and Humanitarian Intervention." *Philosophical Perspectives* 23, Ethics (2009): 222–40.
Hinde, Robert. *The Institution of War.* New York: St. Martin's, 1992.
Hobbes, Thomas. *Leviathan* (1651). Edited by J. C. A. Gaskin, Oxford: Oxford University Press, 1998.
Holder, Cindy. "Responding to Humanitarian Crises." In *War: Essays in Political Philosophy,* edited by Larry May, 85–104. Cambridge: Cambridge University Press, 2008.
Huntington, Samuel. *The Soldier and the State: The Theory and Politics of Civil-Military Relations.* Cambridge: Cambridge University Press, 1957.
Ignatieff, Michael. *Human Rights as Politics and Idolatry.* Oxford: Oxford University Press, 2001.
International Coalition for the Responsibility to Protect. 2013. http://www.responsibilitytoprotect.org/.
International Commission on Intervention and State Sovereignty (ICISS). "The Responsibility To Protect." Ottawa: International Development Research Centre, 2001.
International Committee of the Red Cross, "International Humanitarian Law and International Human Rights Law." 2003.

"International Covenant on Civil and Political Rights" 2013. http://treaties.un.org/doc/Publication/UNTS/Volume%20999/volume-999-I-14668-English.pdf.

"International Covenant on Economic, Social, and Cultural Rights." 2013. http://www.unhcr.org/refworld/docid/3ae6b36c0.html.

International Work Group for Indigenous Affairs. "Indigenous Affairs: Self-determination." 2002; http://www.iwgia.org/human-rights/self-determination.

Johnson, James Turner. *Can Modern War Be Just?* New Haven: Yale University Press, 1984.

———. *The War to Oust Saddam Hussein: Just War and the New Face of Conflict*, New York: Rowman and Littlefield, 2005.

Johnson, Rebecca. "*Jus Post Bellum* and Counterinsurgency." *Journal of Military Ethics* 7, no. 3 (2008): 215–30.

"Justice Department Memo reveals Legal Case for Drone Strikes on Americans." 2013. http://investigations.nbcnews.com/_news/2013/02/04/16843014-justice-department-memo-reveals-legal-case-for-drone-strikes-on-americans.

Kant, Immanuel. *Metaphysical Elements of Justice* (1797). Translated by John Ladd. Cambridge: Hackett, 1999.

———. *Perpetual Peace and Other Essays* (1784–95). Translated by Ted Humphrey. Cambridge: Hackett, 1983.

———. *The Metaphysics of Morals: The Doctrine of the Right* (1797). Edited by Mary Gregor. Cambridge: Cambridge University Press, 1996.

Kaufman, Whitley. "What Is the Scope of Civilian Immunity in Wartime?" *Journal of Military Ethics* 2, no. 3 (2003): 186–94.

Kington, Tom, and Tran. "New European UAV Effort Raises Hope." *Defense News*, May 25, 2015, 11.

Koeman, Annalisa. "A Realistic and Effective Constraint on the Resort to Force." *Journal of Military Ethics* 6, no. 3 (2007): 198–220.

Lee, John. "Iraq Auditor Questions $636m in Costs." *Iraq-Business News*. 2012. http://www.iraq-businessnews.com/tag/corruption/.

Lee, Steven. *Ethics and War: An Introduction*, Cambridge: Cambridge University Press, 2012.

Lichtenberg, Judith. "How to Judge Soldiers Whose Cause is Unjust." In *Just and Unjust Warriors: The Moral and Legal Status of Soldiers*, edited by David Rodin and Henry Shue, 112–30. Oxford: Oxford University Press, 2008.

Locke, John. *Second Treatise of Government* (1690). Edited by C. B. Macpherson, Cambridge: Hackett, 1980.

Lopez, George. "Iraq and Just War Thinking: The Presumption against the Use of Force." *Common Wealth Magazine* 129, no. 16 (2002): 12–21.

Luban, David. "Just War and Human Rights." *Philosophy and Public Affairs* 9, no. 2 (Winter 1980): 160–81.

Martin, Rex. "Just War and Human Rights." *Professional Ethics: A Multidisciplinary Journal* 10, no. 2–3–4 (Summer 2002): 159–79.

———. "Just Wars and Humanitarian Interventions." *Journal of Social Philosophy* 36, no. 4 (Winter 2005): 439–56.

———. "The Just War Theory of Walzer and Rawls." *Southwest Philosophy Review* 19, no. 1 (January 2003): 135–46.

Masters, Jonathan. "Targeted Killings." Council on Foreign Relations; http://www.cfr.org/counterterrorism/targeted-killings/p9627.

May, Larry. *After War Ends: A Philosophical Perspective*. Cambridge: Cambridge University Press. 2012.

———. *Aggression and Crimes against Peace*. Cambridge: Cambridge University Press, 2008.

———. "Conflicting Responsibilities to Protect Human Rights," in *Human Rights: The Hard Questions*, edited by David Reidy and Cindy Holder, 347–61. Cambridge: Cambridge University Press, 2013.

———. *Genocide: A Normative Account*. Cambridge: Cambridge University Press, 2010.

———. *Global Justice and Due Process*. Cambridge: Cambridge University Press, 2011.

———. "Reparations, Restitution, and Transitional Justice." In *Morality Jus Post Bellum, and International Law*, edited by Larry May, 32–48. Oxford: Oxford University Press, 2012.

———. *War Crimes and Just War*. Cambridge: Cambridge University Press, 2007.

McCready, Doug. "Ending the War Right: Jus Post Bellum and the Just War Tradition." *Journal of Military Ethics* 8, no. 1 (2009): 660–78.

McMahan, Jeff. "Debate: Justification and Liability in War." *The Journal of Political Philosophy* 16, no. 2 (2008): 227–44.

———. *Killing in War*. Oxford: Oxford University Press, 2009.

———. "The Ethics of Killing in War." *Philosophia* 34 (2006): 23–41.

———. "The Just Distribution of Harm between Combatants and Noncombatants." *Philosophy & Public Affairs* 38, no. 4 (2010): 342–79.

———. "The Morality of War and the Law of War." In *Just and Unjust Warriors: The Moral and Legal Status of Soldiers*, edited by David Rodin and Henry Shue, 19–43. Oxford: Oxford University Press, 2008.

Miller, Richard. "Legitimation, Justification, and the Politics of Rescue." In *Just War Reader*, edited by Louis Schwartz, 116–131. Mason, OH: Thomson, 2004.

Mollendorf, Darrel. "Jus ex Bello." *The Journal of Political Philosophy* 16, no. 2 (2008): 123–36.

Nagel, Thomas. "War and Massacre." *Philosophy and Public Affairs* 1, no. 2 (Winter 1972): 123–44.

Nickel, James. "Are Human Rights Mainly Implemented by Intervention?" In *Rawls's Law of Peoples: A Realist Utopia?*, edited by Rex Martin and David Reidy, 263–77. Oxford: Blackwell, 2006.

———. "Human Rights." *Stanford Encyclopedia of Philosophy.* 2010; http://plato.stanford.edu/entries/rights-human/#RefCit.
Norman, Richard. *Ethics, Killing and War.* Cambridge: Cambridge University Press, 1995.
Nozick, Robert. *Anarchy, State, and Utopia.* Englewood Cliffs, NJ: Prentice-Hall, 1968.
Obama, Barack. *Nobel Peace Prize Speech.* 2009; http://www.huffingtonpost.com/2009/12/10/obama-nobel-peace-prize-a_n_386837.html.
O'Brien, William. *The Conduct of Just and Limited War.* New York: Praeger, 1981.
Osterdahl, Inger, and Esther van Zadel. "What Will *Jus Post Bellum* Mean? Of New Wine and Old Bottles." *Journal of Conflict and Security Law* 14, no. 2 (2009): 175–207.
Orend, Brian. "Jus Post Bellum." *Journal of Social Philosophy* 31, no. 1 (2000): 117–37.
———. "Justice after War." *Ethics and International Affairs* 16, no. 1 (2002): 43–56.
———. *Morality of War.* Ontario: Broadview Press, 2006.
———. *On War: A Dialogue.* New York: Rowman and Littlefield, 2009.
———. "Right Intention." *The Stanford Encyclopedia of Philosophy.* 2005; http://plato.stanford.edu/entries/war/#2.1.
———. "War." *The Stanford Encyclopedia of Philosophy* (Fall 2008 Edition), edited by Edward N. Zalta; http://plato.stanford.edu/archives/fall2008/entries/war/.
Pattison, James. *Humanitarian Intervention and the Responsibility to Protect.* Oxford: Oxford University Press, 2010.
Pejic, Jelena. "Non-Discrimination and Armed Conflict." *International Review of the Red Cross* 2001; http://www.icrc.org/eng/resources/documents/misc/57jqzq.htm.
"Potsdam Declaration." http://www.ibiblio.org/pha/policy/1945 /450729a.html#1.
Rawls, John. *A Theory of Justice.* Cambridge: Harvard University Press, 1971.
———. *The Law of Peoples.* Cambridge: Harvard University Press. 2002.
Regan, Richard. *Just War: Principles and Cases,* Washington, DC: Catholic University of America Press, 1996.
Reidy, David. "Human Rights: Institutions and Agendas." *Public Affairs Quarterly* 22, no. 4 (2008): 409–32.
———. "Political Authority and Human Rights." In *Rawls's Law of Peoples: A Realist Utopia?,* edited by Rex Martin and David Reidy, 169–88. Oxford: Blackwell, 2006.
———. "An Internationalist Conception of Human Rights." *The Philosophical Forum* XXXVI, no. 4 (2005): 367–97.
———. "On the Human Right to Democracy: Searching for Sense without Stilts." *Journal of Social Philosophy* 43, no. 2 (2012): 177–203.
———, and Walter Riker. "Introduction." In *Coercion and the State,* edited by David Reidy and Walter Riker, 1–14. Netherlands: Springer Science+Business Media, 2008.

Reisman, W. Michael, and Chris Antoniou, eds. *The Laws of War: A Comprehensive Collection of Primary Documents Governing Armed Conflict.* New York: Vintage Books, 1994.

Rengger, Nicholas. "The Jus in Bello in Historical and Philosophical Perspectives." In *War: Essays in Political Philosophy*, edited by Larry May, 30–46. Cambridge: Cambridge University Press, 2008.

Riker, Walter. "Democratic Legitimacy and the Reasoned Will of the People." In *Coercion and the State*, edited by David Reidy and Walter Riker, 77–94. Netherlands: Springer Science+Business Media, 2008.

———. "The Democratic Peace Is Not Democratic: On Behalf of Rawls's Decent Societies." *Political Studies* 57 (October 2009): 617–38.

Roberts, Adam. "The Principle of Equal Application of the Laws of War." In *Just and Unjust Warriors: The Moral and Legal Status of Soldiers*, edited by David Rodin and Henry Shue, 226–54. Oxford: Oxford University Press, 2008.

———, and Richard Guelff, eds. *Documents on the Laws of War.* Oxford: Clarendon Press, 1982.

Roberts, Peri. "The Supreme Emergency Exemption: Rawls and the Use of Force." *European Journal of Political Theory* 11, no. 2 (December 2001): 155–71.

Rocheleau, Jordy. "From Aggression to Just Occupation? The Temporal Application of Jus Ad Bellum Principles and Case of Iraq." *Journal of Military Ethics* 9, no. 2 (2010): 123–38.

Rodin, David, and Henry Shue. "Introduction." In *Just and Unjust Warriors: The Moral and Legal Status of Soldiers*, edited by David Rodin and Henry Shue, 1–18. Oxford: Oxford University Press, 2008.

Rousseau, Jean-Jacques. *The Social Contract and Other Later Political Writings* (1762). Translated and edited by Victor Gourevitch. Cambridge: University Press, 1997.

Royce, Ed. "Exporting U.S. Drones." *Defense News*, March 2, 2015, 21.

"The Rule of Law and Transitional Justice in Conflict and Post-conflict Societies." United Nations Rule of Law. 2004; http://www.unrol.org/files/2004%20report.pdf.

Santayana, George. "Tipperary." *Soliloquies in England and Later Soliloquies.* 1922; http://plato-dialogues.org/faq/faq008.htm; accessed May 2012.

Scanlon, Thomas. *Moral Dimensions.* Cambridge: Harvard University Press, 2008.

Schmitt, Eric. "NATO Sees Flaws in Air Campaign against Qaddafi." *The New York Times*, April 14, 2012; http://www.nytimes.com /2012/04/15/world/africa/nato-sees-flaws-in-air-campaign-against-qaddafi.html?pagewanted=all&_r=0.

Scott, James Brown. *The Spanish Origin of International Law: Francisco De Vitoria and His Law of Nations.* Oxford: Clarendon Press, 1934.

Shue, Henry. *Basic Rights: Subsistence, Affluence, and U.S. Foreign Policy.* Princeton: Princeton University Press, 1980.

———. "Targeting Civilian Infrastructure with Smart Bombs: The New Permissiveness." *Philosophy & Public Policy Quarterly* 30, no. 3/4 (Summer/Fall 2010): 2–20.

———, and David Wippman. "Limiting Attacks on Dual-Use Facilities Performing Indispensable Civilian Functions." *Cornell International Law Journal* 35 (2002): 559–73.

Stacy, Helen. "Humanitarian Intervention and Relational Sovereignty." In *Intervention, Terrorism, and Torture: Contemporary Challenges to Just War Theory*, edited by Steven Lee, 89–104. Dordrecht: Springer, 2007.

Stahn, Carsten. "Jus Post Bellum: Mapping the Discipline(s)." in *American University International Law Review* 23, no. 2 (2007): 311–47.

Stein, Rob. "100,000 Civilian Deaths Estimated in Iraq." *Washington Post*, October 29, 2004; http://www.washingtonpost.com/wp-dyn/articles/A7967-2004Oct28.html.

"Summary of the Report of the Secretary-General on 'Implementing the Responsibility to Protect.'" International Coalition for the Responsibility to Protect (ICRtoP). 2009; http://www.responsibilitytoprotect.org/files/ICRtoP%20Summary%20of%20SG%20report.pdf.

"Summary of the Report of the Secretary-General on 'The Role of Regional and Sub-regional Arrangements in Implementing the Responsibility to Protect.'" International Coalition for the Responsibility to Protect (ICRtoP). 2011; http://www.responsibilitytoprotect.org/7%20July%20Summary%20of%20the%20SG%20report.pdf.

Swift, Louis. *The Earthly Fathers on War and Military Service*. Wilmington, DE: Michael Glazier, 1983.

Talbot, William. *Which Rights Should Be Universal?* Oxford: Oxford University Press, 2005.

Tan, Kok-Chor. "Military Intervention as a Moral Duty" *Public Affairs Quarterly* 9, no. 1 (January 1995): 29–46.

"Terms of Surrender." http://www.pbs.org/behindcloseddoors/pdfs/TermsOfGermanSurrender.pdf.

"The Universal Declaration of Human Rights." United Nations. http://www.un.org.rights.html.

United Nations. *A More Secure World: Our Shared Responsibility* (report of the High-Level Panel on Threat, Challenges, and Change, United Nations Foundation, 2004; http://www.un.org/en/events/pastevents/a_more_secure_world.shtml.

United Nations Charter. http://www.un.org/en/documents/charter/.

United Nations General Assembly 2005 World Summit, para 139. http://www.un.org/summit2005/documents.html.

United Nations Peacebuilding Commission. http://www.un.org/en/peacebuilding/.

UN Security Council. *Security Council Holds Iraq in "Material Breach" of Disarmament Obligations, Offers Final Chance to Comply, Unanimously Adopting Resolution 1441*, 2002. http://www.un.org/News/Press/docs/2002/SC7564.doc.htm.
UNSCR 1483 (Iraq). 2003; http://www.uncc.ch/resolutio/res1483.pdf.
UNSCR 1885 (Liberia). 2009. http://www.unhcr.org/refworld/country,,,RESOLUTION,LBR,4ab34abd0,0.html.
UN Security Council. http://www.un.org/News/Press/docs/2002/SC7564.doc.htm.
U.S. Catholic Bishops. "The Harvest of Justice Is Sown in Peace." 1993; http://www.usccb.org/beliefs-and-teachings/what-we-believe/catholic-social-teaching/the-harvest-of-justice-is-sown-in-peace.cfm.
U.S. Department of the Army. *The Law of Land Warfare*. FM 27-10. July 1976.
U.S. Department of Defense. *Joint Operation Planning*. JP 5-0. December 2006.
U.S. Department of Defense. *Joint Targeting*, JP 3-60. April 2007.
U.S. Department of Defense. *Law of War Manual*. June 2015.
U.S. Department of Justice White Paper (020413). "Lawfulness of a Lethal Operation Directed against a U.S. Citizen who is a Senior Operational Leader of Al Qa'ida or An Associated Force."
U.S. Foreign Policy. http://www.whitehouse.gov/issues/foreign-policy.
U.S. Senate Commission, *U.S. Genocide and Atrocities Prevention Act of 2016* https://www.foreign.senate.gov/press/ranking/release/us-senators-introduce-bipartisan-genocide-and-atrocities-prevention-act-of-2016.
"U.S.: Insurgents Using Teens in Iraq Attacks." NBC News. 2009; http://www.msnbc.msn.com/id/31142126/ns/world_news-mideast_n_africa/t/us-insurgents-using-teens-iraq-attacks.
Vattel, Emmerich de. *The Law of Nations* (1758). Translated and edited by C. G. and J. Robison Paternoster-Row. London: 1797.
Vitoria, Francisco de. *Political Writings* (1532). Edited by Anthony Pagden and Jeremy Lawrance. Cambridge: University Press, 1991.
Walzer, Michael. *Arguing About War*. London: Yale University Press, 2004.
———. "Judging War." Speech given at Heinrich Boll Foundation, Berlin, July 2, 2003.
———. "Just and Unjust Occupations." *Dissent Magazine*. 2004; http://207.97.238.133/article/?article=400.
———. *Just and Unjust Wars*, New York: Basic Book Press, 1977.
———. *Obligations: Citizenship, War, and Disobedience*. Harvard: Harvard University Press, 1970.
Wells, Donald, ed. *An Encyclopedia of War and Ethics*. Westport, CT: Greenwood Press, 1996.
Welsh, Jennifer. "A Normative Case for Pluralism: Reassessing Vincent's View on Humanitarian Intervention." *International Affairs* 87, no. 5 (2011): 1193–1204.

———. "The Security Council and Intervention." In *The United Nations Security Council and War*. Oxford: Oxford University Press, 2008.

———, and Alexandra Gheciu. "The Imperative to Rebuild: Assessing the Normative Case for Postconflict Reconstruction." *Ethics and International Affairs* 23, no. 2 (2009): 121–46.

Williams, Robert, and Dan Caldwell. "*Jus Post Bellum*: Just War Theory and the Principles of Just Peace." *International Studies Perspectives* 7 (2006): 309–20.

Zupan, Dan. "A Presumption of the Moral Equality of Combatants: A Citizen-Soldier's Perspective." In *Just and Unjust Warriors: The Moral and Legal Status of Soldiers*, edited by David Rodin and Henry Shue, 214–25. Oxford: Oxford University Press, 2008.

Index

Altman, Andrew, 50, 173, 175, 184, 188
Augustine, St., 1, 10–18, 40, 53, 128, 170, 174, 187

Backup obligor, 5, 76, 81, 100–01, 105, 136, 143
Basic liberty rights, 73, 94, 96–98, 167
Beitz, Charles, 111–12, 121, 185, 186
Bennett, John, 189
Boon, Kristen, 149, 190–94
Braun, Megan, 188
Brunstetter, Daniel, 188
Buchanan, Allen, 72, 79, 149–50, 171, 173, 179, 181, 183, 188, 191
Bush, George, 47, 186
Byman, Daniel, 188

Coercive measures, 89, 98, 104–05, 108–09, 111, 135, 137, 193
Cronin, Audrey, 188–89

Drones/UAVs
  Drone strikes, 127, 129, 186
Dual purpose/dual use, 24–25, 27, 65–66, 69–73, 85, 107, 178

Ethnic cleansing, 88–89, 97–98, 182
Ex post, 24, 39, 44, 61, 72, 78

Genocide prevention project, 182
Griffin, James, 63

Hill, Thomas, 112, 185
Hobbes, Thomas, 92, 183
Human rights, 2–6, 18, 22–25, 31, 63–65, 73–74, 81–82, 89, 94, 136–38, 149–53, 154, 157, 165–67

International Coalition for the Responsibility to Protect, 183, 193
International Commission on Intervention and State Sovereignty (ICISS), 86, 160, 176, 181, 188, 193
International Committee of the Red Cross, 192
International Covenant on Civil and Political Rights (ICCPR), 154, 157, 166, 191, 192
International Covenant on Economic, Social, and Cultural Rights (ICESCR), 154, 166, 191
International Humanitarian Law (IHL), 154, 161, 188, 192
International Work Group for Indigenous Affairs, 192

Iraq, 45, 47–55, 61, 67, 127, 151, 155–57, 174–75, 191
ISIL, 133–34, 142, 187

Just cause, 1, 9–14, 22, 25, 28, 59, 128, 158, 189
Justice after war (*jus post bellum*), 4, 38, 41–44, 59–61, 147, 162
Justice of war (*jus ad bellum*), 3–6, 10–12, 37–38, 41, 117, 176, 189

Kant, Immanuel, 17–18, 51, 63, 171, 175, 176
Kuwait, 45, 60, 151, 191

Last resort, 5, 12, 39, 87, 105, 128, 135, 189
Law of armed conflict, 37, 55, 66, 77–79, 129
Locke, John, 92–94, 106, 124, 174
Luban, David, 94, 184

McMahan, Jeff, 69–71, 112–16, 122, 177, 178, 186
Military necessity, 36, 46, 66–72, 135, 182, 191
Miller, Richard, 174, 178

NATO, 27, 85, 141, 184
Nazi Germany, 13, 19–20, 29–30, 36, 45, 113, 180, 191
Nickel, James, 105, 185
Noncombatant immunity, 4, 25, 61–65, 81–82, 146, 177
Nonintervention, 5, 23, 31, 86–95, 132–33
Nonliberal society, 32–35, 178
Nonstate Actor (NSA), x, 104, 112, 128, 131, 148, 187

Obama, Barack, 56, 134, 176, 187
Occupying power, 150–53, 157, 191

Operation Desert Storm, 45, 50, 67
Orend, Brian, 37, 42–43, 55, 169, 170, 174, 176

Pattison, James, 129, 137, 189
Peace, 1, 14–21, 51–54, 147–53, 159–62, 173, 174, 190, 192, 193
Preventive (Preventative), 32
Proportionality, 25–27, 43, 46, 49, 67–74, 78–80, 107, 138, 189
Proportionate response, 39, 129, 133, 177
Protocol I, 153–54, 191

Rawls, John, 2, 18–19, 23, 28–30, 34–38, 63, 169, 171, 172–73, 174, 176, 184, 194
Reidy, David, v, 2, 184, 186, 188
Responsibility to Protect (R2P), 5–6, 86–92, 129–32, 159, 167, 182
Right Intention, 3, 6–7, 9–12, 14–18, 24–25, 38–39, 51, 60–61, 86, 128–33, 146, 149, 166–68, 173, 189, 190
Riker, Walter, 30–31, 172

Self-determination, 28, 156, 173
Shue, Henry, 78–79, 96–98, 119, 177, 179–80, 184, 185, 186, 189
Stahn, Carsten, 156, 191

Tactical bomber pilot, 26, 69–71, 74–75, 178

United Nations
    A More Secure World: Our Shared Responsibility, 184, 186, 188, 189
    United Nations Charter, 192

United Nations General Assembly 2005 World Summit, 87–91, 182
United Nations Peacebuilding Commission, 161, 163, 193–94
United Nations Security Council (UNSC), 39, 85, 88, 156, 189–90
Universal Declaration of Human Rights (UDHR), 149, 166
US Department of Justice White Paper (020413), 130, 187
US Genocide and Atrocities Prevention Act of 2016, 136, 176, 189

Vattel, Emmerich de, 1, 50–51, 120, 125, 186
Vitoria, Francisco de, 1, 82, 181

Walzer, Michael, 2, 11, 25, 37, 42, 53, 61–62, 116, 137, 169, 170, 171, 172, 174, 176, 177, 178, 186, 188
War crimes, 5, 88–90, 97, 108–11, 131–34, 182–83, 185
Wellman, Christopher, 50, 173, 174, 175, 184, 188
Welsh, Jennifer, 91, 183, 186
Wippman, David, 78–79, 179

Vita

Todd Burkhardt is a Lieutenant Colonel in the U.S. Army. Over the last twenty-five years he has served in variety of positions as an enlisted tank crewman and infantry officer, including deployments to Saudi Arabia and Afghanistan. He has also spent more than five years at the United States Military Academy as an assistant professor in philosophy teaching the ethics of war to future Army officers. As of the summer of 2016, Todd is the Professor of Military Science of Indiana University's Army ROTC program. He graduated from Moravian College with a BA in Sociology in 1994, from the University of South Carolina with an MA in Philosophy in 2004, and from the University of Tennessee in 2013 with a PhD in Philosophy. His research interests include both political and just war theory.

Made in the USA
Lexington, KY
16 July 2018